A Child's Heart Speaks

Surviving Sexual Abuse

by
Claire Silva

Bloomington, IN Milton Keynes, UK

authorHOUSE™

AuthorHouse™
1663 Liberty Drive, Suite 200
Bloomington, IN 47403
www.authorhouse.com
Phone: 1-800-839-8640

AuthorHouse™ UK Ltd.
500 Avebury Boulevard
Central Milton Keynes, MK9 2BE
www.authorhouse.co.uk
Phone: 08001974150

First published by AuthorHouse 1/14/2008

ISBN: 978-1-4259-7540-1 (sc)
ISBN: 978-1-4343-6220-9 (hc)

Printed in the United States of America
Bloomington, Indiana

This book is printed on acid-free paper.

Cover Designer:
Joanna Gazzola

For more information, visit:
http://www.clairesilva.com

Dedication

This book is dedicated to my sons who have been my brave soldiers trudging through life.

My eldest son helped me write our story through his memories and own words. His brave disclosure was what forced me to intervene and protect my children. My middle son often listened to lengthy discussions, shared his understanding, and ultimately gave me the title for this book as a four-year-old boy. My youngest son gave me the motivation and energy to write while he was in the womb. During those many sleepless nights as an infant, he provided company for me while I wrote.

Boys, you have shown me the potential for love, kindness, compassion and resiliency found in the human spirit. There are no words to express my love for you and my feelings of pride that you are my children. You have survived the unthinkable and despite the trauma, have grown into kind, sensitive, and conscientious people. Through your story, your lives are brilliant stars that illuminate a path to heal others.

"The mind confuses us, rationalizes and makes
us second-guess ourselves.
The heart speaks the truth." ~ Claire Silva

Table of Contents

Introduction

Sexual abuse against children is a prevalent and silent crime, which creates hundreds of victims everyday. Estimates of the number of children that will be victimized during their lifetimes fluctuate depending on the source. The total number of kids that are sexually abused each year is not certain, since most reports concentrate on a few states or restrict analysis to cases where the child was twelve or older. Usually young victims, who are under twelve years of age, are not included in most calculations.

I believe millions of children being stripped of their self-identity, personal value, and individual power is worthy of alarm. Yet, sexual abuse is an epidemic that our society keeps as a dark hidden secret. We do not openly discuss sexual abuse because it is such an overwhelming subject. Resources and support for survivors and families are not provided. Proactive research, preventative programming, and effective perpetrator tracking methods are not implemented. Thus, the crime of sexual abuse against children is allowed to pervade throughout every community in our nation.

Children who are sexually abused endure horrible crimes against their bodies, minds and spirits. During the abuse, the children need to mentally escape from their horrendous realities in order to survive. As juveniles and adults, these survivors have constant memories of their abuse and seek a different form of reality. Some seek professional counseling, but many turn to drugs and alcohol and other self-destructive behaviors. Some victims, who do not seek treatment, may even become abusers themselves.

Legal, social service, mental health, education and faith-based systems often ignore complaints of sexual abuse by victims, refuse to acknowledge the needs of survivors and their families, and ultimately lend support and resources to the perpetrators. Institutions seldom rectify portions of the organization that need to be changed to enforce sexual abuse laws and the protection of children. This book serves as a personal call to individuals within those departments, agencies, institutions and systems who can make it a personal mission to speak about the need for more resources and effective programming.

This book is written from personal family trauma and incorporates knowledge gained through hindsight, other families' tragedies, family members' and friends' reactions, and interviews with adult survivors from across the country. The interviews I conducted with adult survivors served as an invaluable source of information for understanding perpetrators, sexual abuse and survivors. All of the stories are true. Pseudonyms were used for all of the children and most of the adult survivors to protect each individual's identity, privacy and confidentiality. However, several survivors wanted their true names to be used when telling their stories.

Throughout this work, I do not refer to the victim as "victim". I refer to the child who has been forced to endure sexual abuse, as a "survivor". The crime of sexual abuse against a child is extremely damaging. If the child lives through the experience without being killed or later completing a suicide attempt, then he or she is a "survivor". No matter how dysfunctional a survivor's life can be for years after the abuse, survivors are trying to live through the experience, and are struggling to re-claim their lives. They are survivors trying to emerge victorious over almost insurmountable mental, physical, emotional and spiritual obstacles.

I love my children more than words can explain. If I had the power to reverse time to protect them from what happened, I would. But, I don't have that power. If telling our tragedy can help an individual or a family, then our effort to share our story is worthwhile. My goal in writing this book is to educate parents on: true prevention, what to do if sexual abuse has occurred, and how to survive. The most important ideals are to protect children from becoming sexually abused, and help young survivors—who are living in silence and terror, to feel safe again.

If this book serves either of those two purposes, then our suffering has not been in vain.

My challenge to you as the reader is to learn about: sexual abuse, perpetrators, and survivors—and then become active in your community. Start conversations with neighbors, colleagues and legislators. The chains of sexual abuse silence must be broken for our society to understand this crime, provide effective services to survivors and their families, and develop true education and prevention measures that work.

Acknowledgements

I would like to thank several people who have helped my family during an extremely painful time, and who have given me inspiration and direction. First and foremost, I would like to thank my friend Julia, who trusted her instincts and saved my children's lives. There is no possible way to thank her enough. Her strength of spirit, and immense understanding of people and life, has helped me learn several life-changing lessons. She has taught me about Ego, personalities, dynamics between people, good versus evil, and most importantly to trust intuition and a Higher Power. Her personal trust in her senses, and following through with gut-level feelings, is what saved my children's lives. I would also like to thank Robert, who trusted and verbalized his reaction. Without him paying attention to his instincts, I would have never openly communicated with my children about sexual abuse—which ultimately helped them to disclose their worst fears and experiences.

I acknowledge Beth for helping me get out of my "workaholic" state and focus on my children and my family. I am grateful to my husband for being a pillar of strength, and for his support in writing our story. It has been a difficult path, but I am proud to say that we have walked it together. I appreciate the unending support my parents have given us throughout this ordeal. They have been a shoulder to cry on throughout my life, and have always found solutions to every situation. They edited, re-edited, and re-read different sections of this book numerous times. Their patience and constant support were invaluable to me. I salute my friends and spiritual teachers: Tony Santos and Barbara Ann Colangelo who encouraged me to develop my own spiritual abilities and trust my instincts, messages and visions. Without their support, I don't think I would have made it through as strong as I have.

I would like to thank several close friends who have read through this book several times and provided invaluable feedback and edits: Danene, Leigh Ann, Sakinah, Augusta, Pam, Julia, Joe, Barbara Absi, and Joanna. They have been endless supports to me while pursuing my personal spiritual growth and writing this book. Their unconditional love and support has helped me find the internal motivation to take a tragic period in time, and turn it into a message for others. I especially would like to thank Danene for being a wonderful "mom" to my children during my working hours, and by giving them the love and support they needed after we learned of the trauma they had suffered.

Thanks to several other close friends who have been supportive of our family to the end and who have served as that sympathetic ear during a difficult time: Charlene, Ania, Ronni, Barbara B, Jean, Kathy and Rich, Linda and John, Miladys, Ken, Patti, Cynthia, Maria and Luis, Mike and Anna, Maria and Mark, Bonnie, Tunin, Elvira, Sue, Mary Beth, Boupha, Luz, Linda B., Janene, Louise, Janice, Dawn, Christine, Patty and Ronnie, Brian, Sis, Nicky, Jayne, Channavy, JoEllen, and Lorraine. I also appreciate the support from many other family members and friends.

I thank my aunt, Joanna Gazzola, who designed the amazing cover for this book, and a special person - Stephen Wolf, who designed my website. I value the input Lisa Tener gave me as a Writing Coach and I am thankful that she believed in the vision of this work. I appreciate all of the help SNAP, Survivors Network of those Abused by Priests was able to provide. SNAP graciously found people I could interview—survivors who could tell me their stories, which will now help educate others.

I would like to send a special individual thank you to each of the fourteen adult survivors of childhood sexual abuse who allowed me to interview them for this book. I was fortunate to find such spiritually advanced people who have learned through personal introspection and by studying people's behaviors and motives. I am grateful that they willingly shared personal stories of torture and fear, in order to help me write a well-rounded view of survivors and perpetrators. It was very humbling for me to have the opportunity to see the strength that exists in each of them personally—as they struggle and strive for peace and clarity in their own lives. They survived, despite their bodies, minds and souls being horribly violated and tortured. It was an incredible honor to hear their stories of survival. They are true heroes!

Since our society's institutions continue to use systems that protect and empower perpetrators, I felt it only fair to share viewpoints of survivors, which are normally not heard. Unfortunately, children do not have the verbal skills or the life experience to inform people how sexual abuse will grip their lives on every level for many years to come. But, the survivors I interviewed are now adults who have the verbal skills and the life experience to educate others. Their openness in telling their stories was admirable and phenomenal. Their courage, honesty, and commitment to expose the evils of sexual abuse, serve as an example of the strength of the human spirit. I pray the knowledge they have shared in this book serves to: help parents and guardians to keep their children safe, help current survivors progress through their personal journeys of healing, and force institutions, agencies and the various systems to empower survivors of sexual abuse.

Above all, I would like to thank God, my personal Spirit Guides, my Angels, and loved ones who have passed for guiding us through this difficult time. I know they have all worked collaboratively to place specific people in our lives at precise moments. I thank God for the awareness to piece everything together from several different realms—allowing me a clear understanding of this traumatic event and sexual abuse in general. I begged for answers and God responded, giving me a clear path for our story.

Chapter 1
The Journey Beyond

I hear the tires come to a screeching halt. I run to the window to see what is happening outside. A brown four door Chevrolet has stopped in the middle of the street and two young men have jumped out. As they race to the trunk, and pop it open, they reach inside—grabbing a rolled up carpet. They throw it in the road and hop back into the car. They speed off down the street, leaving the carpet where it lay.

I stare at the roll in total confusion. As my gaze fixes, I notice the mass is moving. As I stand in shock, I see a young man slowly climb out and stand up. It is my stepson, Adam! He has a bewildered face—not understanding how he arrived or where he is. He collects himself and walks towards the house. Before I can stop him, he barges his way inside and walks through the kitchen. I run to him and declare, "This is not your home! You cannot stay here! You are not supposed to be here!" He makes faces, rolls his eyes sarcastically and laughs at me. My words mean nothing to him. I repeat that he is not welcome, and he briskly passes by me—walking down the hall towards my bedroom. I am furious and begin to scream at him. How has he become so obnoxious and disrespectful? As I yell, I lose control of my emotions and begin to swing wildly at his face. I slug him in the jawbone and slap him on the other side of his face. He is outraged and starts to shout at me. His arms flail everywhere—hitting my face and upper body. His attacks are filled with an uncontrollable rage. I know he will seriously hurt me because my punches cannot measure up to his strength. I screech for help and beg my husband Bob, to come quickly. Within seconds, Bob runs in the room, and immediately jumps in to protect me. I slip over to the other side

1

of the room and watch as the two men throw punches back and forth. I back myself close to a wall. I am so afraid I can't breath! I gasp for air and open my eyes to see that I am alone in my room and half under the covers. As I catch my breath and feel the anxiety leave my body, I breathe a sigh of relief to know it is only another nightmare. As I lay back down in bed, I think about the dream and realize—the bedroom that Adam was invading was actually my bedroom from my childhood!

I had been having dreams like this for quite some time and could not understand where they were coming from. Why was I filled with such hate towards my stepson in my dreams? The rage I felt towards him as I slept was indescribable. I swore at him with a vengeance and physically assaulted him. How could I have so much anger towards a child?

Adam had only lived with us for a short time when I started having the nightmares. A few months earlier, we had traveled to his native country, Cape Verde, to get him and bring him home to America. Adam was only five years old, when Bob first left Cape Verde in June 1995. Bob intended to visit America for one month and return home. But, once in America, Bob met a young man who encouraged him to stay—informing him that he would have a better life, and be able to send money home to his family. At that point, Bob decided to stay in the States since he would finally be able to help his family rise out of their poverty stricken lives.

During his second month in America, Bob and I met. Each of us went to a local club to see a famous Cape Verdean musician. I went with some friends and Bob arrived with some people he knew. I worked with one of the women from Bob's group who decided to match Bob and me together to dance to a few songs. At the end of each dance, I said "thank you", and Bob looked at me—not knowing how to respond. He could not speak one word of English. A few days later, my colleague said she was going to visit the house where Bob was staying and invited me to go with her. When we arrived, he was shocked to see me again and was happy we could try to communicate with each other. As the weeks passed, and my visits continued, Bob and I realized we could understand each other if he spoke slowly in Portuguese and I spoke slowly in Spanish. After a couple of months, we found we were able to communicate clearly, and soon our friendship blossomed into a close loving relationship.

Before Bob and I got married, he had explained that he had a son named Adam who lived in Cape Verde. As we discussed his child's condition, we agreed we would eventually bring him home to America to live with us. Knowing the hunger and poverty he suffered from in Cape Verde, we knew we could give him a better life. A few months after we were married, we heard that Adam, who was six-years-old at the time, was left alone for a few days on top of the mountain where he lived in Cape Verde. The neighbors were horrified to witness Adam and another boy throwing rocks at a villager's cow—an animal necessary for a family's survival. At that point, Bob and I no longer felt comfortable with him being raised by his maternal grandmother. We sent word through family that we wanted Adam to live with Bob's parents until we were able to bring him to America. But Adam's maternal grandmother objected, stating we only wanted him to live with Bob's parents, "Now because he is a strong boy who can help with chores." Since she had raised him from the time when he was an infant, she stated he was staying with her until we personally came to bring him to America.

Adam's maternal grandmother had always been more of a mother for him than his own biological mother. His biological mother had five children after Adam, and I was told she was not an appropriate parent figure. Apparently, she was mentally challenged and did not know how to raise children since she was emotionally and mentally a child herself.

Despite Adam's maternal grandmother's explanation of why Adam had been left alone on top of the mountain, we still did not feel comfortable with him living there. But we had no power over the situation. At the time, I was pregnant with our son Joey, and I was only able to find temporary work. We mutually decided to work hard and save money—knowing it would take us several years to be able to save the thousands of dollars necessary for an eventual trip to get Adam. After three years of hard work, we had saved enough money. Since Bob was not yet an American citizen, I submitted the papers to Immigration for me to be the sponsor for my stepson, Adam.

From the beginning, the process of filling out the papers was difficult. After filing numerous forms and documents for INS, and paying registration and filing fees, we did not hear from the visa office for several months. We did not know when the appointment was scheduled or who could bring Adam for the interview with the American Embassy in Cape Verde. No one from Adam's mother's family could read or write, so they would not be able to file any of the paperwork necessary during the Embassy interview. Bob's family would also not be able to read the English paperwork. It was obvious that the only way to get Adam through the interview was for Bob and me to bring him to the Embassy in Cape Verde ourselves.

After weeks of trying to call the Embassy in Cape Verde with no response, I contacted our state Senator and asked if his office could intervene. Immediately we were contacted and informed of the scheduled interview date, but no known location or time. When I tried to contact the Embassy directly, I was told that the American Embassy would only accept phone calls from relatives within Cape Verde, not from America. This meant that we had to wait until we made our journey to Cape Verde to get all of the answers.

The trip would involve flying from America to the first island, Sal, and then to another island, São Vicente. We would then need to take a boat from São Vicente to Bob's home island of Santo Antão. Bob warned me that we were probably going to experience a violent, stormy boat ride. Then, after we met up with Adam, we would need to return to São Vicente and then take a plane over to Praia, Santiago—the capitol of Cape Verde where the American Embassy is located.

The plane ride took about seven hours. For our son Joey, it was a new adventure. He was two years old at the time, and had never been in an airplane. He was excited to see so many new things and understood that we were taking the big trip to eventually bring his brother back home with us. He also understood that he would get to meet his grandparents, aunts and uncles and many cousins who were anxiously waiting for him.

When the plane landed, we had to climb down many steep stairs directly onto the airport runway. There was no hallway to walk down to eventually enter directly into the airport, like in America. I was shocked to look out and see that the airport building was a tiny facility. I found it odd to see our huge plane and only a few small planes scattered around the building. As we went down the stairs, the blustery winds instantly hit us with the hot humid air of Cape Verde.

Since our prior efforts to send clothes, food, and cooking equipment to Bob's family were unsuccessful, we traveled with several extra, fully-packed suitcases. We paid dearly for packing too heavily, but were finally going to get the much-needed supplies to our relatives. Previous attempts to send things never worked. The export company, with which we tried to send things to Cape Verde, stole the two full barrels we were trying to ship. When we tried to send money through the mail, the money orders were always stolen. At the time, we were desperate to get the supplies to my mother-in-law since we knew her health was deteriorating, due to the difficult life in the mountains. Eventually we were successful in getting money to Bob's parents through a different mail system and with our support, they were able to relocate to the more developed area of the island.

Now, the extra bags and suitcases we carried were filled with the things we had only wished we could get to them previously—clothes, pots and pans, shoes, and food. We were proud of ourselves that we were finally going to be able to help family. As we dragged the numerous suitcases and bags, I saw many faces staring at our belongings. My husband had warned me that there were many people, usually around the airport—who would swipe the baggage in one second. We had to pay close attention and watch everything carefully.

Joey was exhausted from the trip and begged us to carry him. It seemed impossible to protect everything and carry an almost 40 pound baby! I felt an enormous sense of relief when the taxi driver began hoisting everything into the trunk of his car. Before we left the airport, we checked when the next available flight would go to São Vicente.

We were extremely disappointed to learn that it would be a three day wait for the next flight. The travel agency staff tried to console us by explaining that they were putting our names on a waiting list. In case there were any cancellations, we would be able to take those available seats. Once our spot on the waiting list was secured, we asked the taxi driver to bring us to a comfortable hotel in the section of the island that we had heard was incredibly beautiful.

Each day, as we walked through the streets, people held their hands out and asked for money. Bob knew he had come from nothing and always gave to each person he passed. A few cents for us meant a whole meal for them. During one of the morning walks one day, a child, who couldn't have been any more than three, followed us into a travel agency and hid under the chair. Her clothes were dirty and ripped. Her hair looked like it had not been brushed for a long time. She entertained Joey by calling his name and giggling. I asked Bob where her parents were and was shocked when he said they were probably at work and left her home alone. He explained that it was common for parents to go to work all day, leaving their young children home—fending for themselves.

As the days passed in Sal, we grew more anxious, knowing it was less time we would have with Bob's family. We knew much of our vacation would be lost when traveling to Santiago for the Embassy interview. We figured I would only have about one week to get to know Bob's parents, eight brothers and sisters, over thirty nieces and nephews, and numerous aunts, uncles and cousins, plus my stepson. Our emotions ranged from excitement to aggravation that we were stuck on this foreign island.

The day we were able to leave the island, we felt elated. Again, we had to load up all of our heavy baggage into the tiny passenger plane. The flight lasted about an hour to São Vicente where we found Bob's brother and sister waiting for us. Bob's sister had traveled over from Bob's island, Santo Antão, just to greet us as we landed. Both siblings planned on bringing us back to Bob's parents' house the next morning. At first, I was nervous speaking to them with my broken Portuguese mixed with some Cape Verdean Creole, but soon I realized—I could understand them and they could understand me. Their warmth and excitement was contagious. I instantly felt close to them, as if I had known them forever.

My brother-in-law's apartment in São Vicente was one bedroom and was too small for all of us, so we had to find a hotel room. Since we did not have a reservation and all of the rooms were taken, we got a tiny hotel room on the third floor. There was a bathroom, but it was at the far end of the hall. We enjoyed looking out over the city from our high story window. I was so happy to finally arrive and meet some of Bob's family.

The next morning, I wanted to take a shower. I gathered everything together and raced to the bathroom hoping no one else was using it. Excited the space was free—I quickly jumped into the shower. The ice-cold water sent my body into instant shock! I did not know that most showers in Cape Verde do not have hot water, and most people do not have the luxury of a shower in their home. I tried to adopt a new affirmation. I convinced myself that I was lucky to take a shower, as my body felt total pain from the ice-cold water.

When I returned to our room, Bob explained that his brother was very concerned about us going to my in-law's home. I asked Bob, "Why is he nervous?" Bob told me there were no chairs in his parents' house, and his brother had been feverishly looking for some chairs. He was mortified to have me enter into their home and not see a single piece of furniture inside. Bob also explained that his brother was worried about me because there was no bathroom or running water in his parents' apartment. But, Bob finally told his brother, "Claire does not care. She is not concerned about how poor our family is, she is happy to finally meet everyone." His words put my brother-in-law at ease and we set out for our boat ride.

When it was time to board the boat, Bob and his brother decided to stay on the deck in the open air. I did not want to stand and grabbed a seat inside with Joey, on the lower deck. Bob and his brother carried all the heavy suitcases and plopped them down next to Joey and me. Before we left, I saw all of the other passengers begin to lie down on the benches as if they were preparing themselves to avoid getting sick. I thought, "How ridiculous! This will be a piece of cake!" After all, I had been on boats all my life. As the boat started to move out into the harbor, I looked around with sympathy at all of the people who were preparing, and thought, "How difficult it must be for people who get sea sickness."

After a few minutes of travel, I looked out through the tiny porthole, and saw the scene shift dramatically. At first when I looked out, I saw a blue sky. But once we were moving for a while, I suddenly saw ocean water, then the sky, then ocean, and then the sky—alternating as quickly as lightening. The ride inside got awfully bumpy as the wind and waves rocked the boat relentlessly. We literally had to fight to stay in our seats.

After a few minutes I felt desperate! As nausea enveloped me, I wished I had a way to head upstairs and get Bob's help. Miraculously I saw a white woman whom I assumed must speak English. I ran to her as I clutched Joey close to me, and asked if she could speak English. When she said "yes", I begged her to go find my husband upstairs and quickly spit out the words to describe his appearance. As she left, I ran to the side of the boat because I knew I was going to throw up. I ran so fast to the railing, I nearly hurled Joey and myself off the boat. Thankfully, a man standing by the side grabbed my arm to stabilize us. Right away Bob came and held Joey. As he saw me throwing up, he followed suit! Poor Joey watched calmly after being passed into the arms of an old man who worked on the ship. As the two of us sat heaving over the side of the boat, I finally understood what Bob had warned me about!

When we pulled into the port, I saw a sea of men yelling to the boat passengers. As they yelled, some broke out into arguments and fighting amongst themselves. They desperately competed over who got the business as a taxi driver or who could help load baggage into the trucks. Luckily, family who had been waiting for us at the dock had already made arrangements with a friend. We were quickly able to escape the volatile scene and pile into his truck.

When we arrived at my in-laws' home, my mother-in-law stood smiling with tears in her eyes. She placed her hand on our heads to bless my husband and me as we entered through the door. Bob's father also had tears in his eyes, as did everyone in the room. Immediately Bob's sisters lined up one by one, took turns lifting us as high as they could, and proceeded to hug us tightly. Everyone in the room began laughing and smiling. They had waited an eternity to see Bob and meet his new family. Within a few seconds, the music went on and everyone began to dance. The celebration continued throughout the evening until we were all exhausted.

My in-laws gave us the best bedroom in the house saying they preferred to sleep on the cement floor. When I told Bob I would rather sleep on the floor since I did not feel comfortable taking their bed, he told me I had to accept their bed. I explained if I refused, they would be horribly offended. We were guests and it was the norm that we should have everything that was the best in the house. I suddenly understood the Cape Verdean saying—"Small house, but a big heart."

We could not meet Adam for the first few days, since his uncle had brought him to São Vicente. They were hoping to catch us in the middle of our journey to Santo Antão. But, since they missed us, we had to wait until they made the trip back over to Santo Antão.

For the first few days, we traveled to several different towns, visiting relatives and friends. Bob's father and brother usually came with us on these day trips. As we drove on the bumpy cobblestone roads, the truck or van usually bounced uncontrollably. The drivers traversed up the steep mountains back and forth to get from one town to another. As the twisty path crept up the mountainside, I could see that there was only enough space for one car in several spots. The various drivers were adept at negotiating the mountain roads. When another car was approaching, they would beep to signal their location as they neared each other. I glanced over the terrifying edge to see how high we were and became instantly dizzy and disoriented. I learned quickly not to do that again.

I found myself emotionally overloaded as we passed through the twisty mountain ridges. I thought of all the men and women who had built these roads by hand. I knew that the Cape Verdean history was filled with times where people were used for slave labor. I thought of the desperate people who worked long, hot days carrying heavy rocks and bricks on their heads, only to be paid with a few morsels of food for the day. In my mind, I could see the men occasionally fall to their death, as they tried to place the rocks on the treacherous cliffs.

When we reached level ground, rocks and dirt surrounded us. On the open lands there were no trees, bushes or plants. The only vegetation was in the village centers or high up in the mountains. There were no trees because the people had stripped away all forms of wood to use for fires—their only manner to cook their food.

On several of these day trips, we passed areas where the earth was dug out in huge deep gaps. Bob explained that those wide crevices were once rivers that ran through Cape Verde. At one time, Cape Verde was covered in green, hence the name Verde which means green. People had better lives back then. They were able to grow food, and had plenty of water to drink. As the droughts became more frequent and several years would pass with a single day of rainfall, all of the rivers dried up.

As we drove through these areas, I imagined myself going to the river each morning. I thought about what it must have been like for people to realize each day there was less and less water. As the rivers turned into muddy brooks and finally disappeared, the families had to search for other sources of water. Bob explained that most people normally walk two or three hours one-way to reach a place where they can fill two plastic containers with water.

Bob explained that Cape Verde had no food for several years. In the 1940s, people were dying everywhere. The government paid men in food, rather than cash, to bury the bodies. Since the number of bodies buried determined how much food each worker was given, the men often buried people who were not yet deceased. Bob knew a man whose face was crushed in from the heavy earth, yet he lived and climbed out of his grave. Bob's father told us a story from his childhood when he witnessed the men burying a woman—who he knew, was still alive.

Each time we arrived back at Bob's parents' house, I took a deep breath of relief. The days were excruciatingly hot, with few places to find any shade. The cement apartment was over-crowded, had no running water, no bathroom, no kitchen and electricity in only two rooms. Yet, escape from the sun into the tiny cement home was wonderful.

One evening we heard loud noises escalating in the street. We ran outside to see women dancing, as men drummed in unison to a particular rhythm. My mother-in-law explained this was the customary dance, and usually the women performed in competition with each other. As I watched, I saw the women back up from each other, waddle forward, like a drunken duck, and then hit their groin areas together as their arms went in the air. They repeated this movement and often changed partners. As we watched, my mother-in-law turned to me and said, "The dance is beautiful isn't it?" I told her, "No one dances like this in America. People would think it was very strange." She laughed and could not believe I had never seen anything similar.

A couple of months before the Saint John festival, men, women and children already begin preparing. Everyone sets aside their best clothes without using them during the year, to save them for this special day. People cook special foods like cachupa - a stew made of cracked corn and beans and pastel - fried dough with tuna or chicken inside. The drumming and dancing were all a part of the preparations.

That evening, as we watched the performance in the street, the electricity went out in the neighborhood. This was a weekly occurrence. Most people didn't mind, since only a few homes had electricity. When we returned to the house, we entered in total darkness. As we made our way through the doorway and past many people inside, someone with strong arms grabbed me and lifted me high in the air. I did not know who this person was and I could not see if it was a man or a woman. I felt very uncomfortable.

When I was let back down, Bob's mother introduced the woman who had lifted me, as Adam's grandmother. She said she was happy to meet me and happy we had finally come to Cape Verde. She talked non-stop. Although I spoke a little Portuguese and Creole, I couldn't follow her conversation. She spoke like a speeding train and didn't seem to take a breath in between her sentences. Finally, Bob's mother jumped into the conversation, asking if I understood any of it. I was able to say "a little."

When the lights finally came on, I could see Adam's grandmother. I instantly noticed her light blue eyes and pale weathered face. I remember finding her appearance odd since everyone around me had dark skin and dark eyes. Bob later explained to me that Adam's grandmother was a woman whom people avoided, because she talked incessantly about subjects of no importance. People often found it difficult to escape her conversations. Bob said many times people would duck behind things when they saw her coming, or would stop her in mid sentence to get away from her never-ending words. Somewhere in the confusing conversation, she said that we would meet Adam the next day. I felt happy that we were finally going to meet him. I had waited a long time for the moment to gaze upon him, knowing he would soon be coming home with us.

The next morning as we walked down the street, we saw a young boy walking toward us. Bob leaned over and told me it was Adam. As the two spoke, I had a chance to study this child who was my stepson. I could see that the family must have taken great care to make sure he was presentable. They dressed him in a long sleeved, button-down shirt and pants, which were clearly for a grown man. He had a tiny frame for a boy his age, so the clothes draped over him as if he was wearing a tent.

As Bob spoke with him, Adam hardly answered the questions and several times glanced up at Bob and immediately looked down at the ground. When I spoke with him, he would look at me, but not respond. I remember wondering if he was somewhat mentally challenged because his behavior seemed odd.

Bob asked him if he was hungry as we walked to the center of the town. Adam explained to Bob that he had gone over to São Vicente to wait for us. When he and his uncle realized they missed us, Adam came back on the boat alone. I was shocked to hear that his family had let him travel totally alone at a mere nine years of age!

When we reached the center of town, Bob asked Adam what he wanted to eat. His first response was ice cream. He had never had one before and always wanted to try it. Since he had never eaten any food that was cold, it was uncomfortable for him. He managed about two bites and said he couldn't eat anymore. We walked through the town to the local shops, buying Adam sneakers, socks, t-shirts and shorts.

When we returned to the house, Bob helped him get dressed. Since Adam had never owned any shoes, he had no idea how to tie them. Bob later told me that Adam was so happy to have so many new pairs of underwear. He said that the one pair Adam was wearing had so many holes—it looked like Swiss cheese. Adam had lived his whole life up in the mountains. His job in the family was to take care of the animals—often traveling for hours with the family donkey to fill jugs with water and then bring them back to the house. There was no electricity and no running water. Adam was not accustomed to any of the luxuries we took for granted everyday.

As the days passed, we ran around trying to get the last minute work done in preparation for the Embassy interview. The first thing we had to do was get Adam's immunization record. We rented a car and climbed the huge mountain. On the top of the mountain was a church with a line of people out to the street. Since Bob knew the people in charge of the facility, he passed everyone in the line to find the head person. As we got to the front of the line, Bob explained what we needed. The gentleman was happy to see Bob, handed him the documentation and we were quickly on our way back.

We had to hire a lawyer to obtain an identification card and passport for Adam. Since most people do not have computers or typewriters, the lawyer had to help us prepare the documents for Adam's mother. Her permission for us to take Adam home with us needed to be documented. Since she could not read or write, Bob had to find three people who would go to the town hall and act as witnesses as she put her fingerprint on the document. They would authenticate her identity and the fact that she willfully wanted her signature on the document.

The day we went to meet Adam's mother, she was lying in bed. She had recently been hospitalized while giving birth to her sixth child—and she almost died in the process. She needed several blood transfusions and her brothers all served as the donors. When she came out of the room I was struck by how light her skin was. Since she looked wobbly, we assured her that we could get a car to bring her to the town hall. But she insisted she could walk. As we walked down the street I was stunned to see there was no conversation between her and Bob. I tried to make conversation with her and couldn't understand why she seemed so bewildered. As she looked at me with a distant gaze, I got a clear feeling that she was not quite present mentally. I was not sure if it was due to her recent hospitalization, or if her mental fogginess was her normal condition.

I found myself thinking about the relationship between her and Bob. They had been together when they were very young. Bob was only seventeen when he heard the news that she was pregnant. Their relationship had only lasted about two months. Bob had told me, after their relationship, she was with many different men, each producing another child.

Upon hearing the news of her first pregnancy, her family immediately began searching throughout the village for the potential father—any man she had been with who had the most money. When the baby was born, the mother's family forcefully told Bob he was not allowed near the infant. They were still searching for the best father for the child, and would not consider Bob—who was poor and had nothing to offer. But, as the baby developed, the resemblance was clear and everyone agreed Bob was the true father. After that, the situation was always awkward. The maternal grandmother made a habit of humiliating Bob in front of other people—saying that he was so poor and unable to support his own son.

When Bob would take Adam to his parents' house for a visit, the toddler would cry uncontrollably and wanted to go home to his maternal grandmother. Bob would see Adam sometimes weekly and other times monthly, but due to the difficult circumstances, Bob was not a regular part of Adam's early years.

As we walked down the streets with Adam, I could see Bob's feelings of pride shine through—knowing he was finally able to help his child by bringing him home to America. The only thing left to do was for us to go to the Embassy interview and get the final acceptance for his visa. But, it was not an easy task. We soon found ourselves stranded once again on a strange island, with no available flights out for many days.

Now we were stuck in Santiago with no family or friends there. During the Immigration interview, the American Embassy refused the United States money order I had brought to cover the fee of over three hundred dollars. They would only accept cash, so we had to give them almost all of our remaining funds. We were counting on this cash to see us through to the end of our trip. I had brought plenty of credit cards and an ATM card to get cash at any agency if we needed it. But we quickly learned that no businesses on the entire island would accept a credit card or an ATM card.

We tried the bank—the same bank we had put money in while we stayed in Santo Antão. But, the bank personnel in Santiago informed us that it would take several days for the money to be available. We could not wait that long since we had to catch our flight back to São Vicente. For the next two days we stayed in the cheapest hotel we could find. It was absolutely disgusting! Every time we opened our door, we were overcome by the objectionable smells from the bathroom across the hall. The shower walls were coated in a thick layer of slime. Mosquitoes attacked us as we tried to shower or use the toilet. Luckily our flights were paid for, but with only a small amount of money left, we survived on oranges and mangoes for breakfast, popcorn for lunch, and a cookie and a few sips of milk for dinner. While Bob, Joey and I thought we were dying of starvation, Adam thought he had died and gone to Heaven with such a feast. I thought about all those people we had given money to who were begging in the street. I realized the irony that we could soon join their ranks and sit alongside them with our hands outstretched, begging for a few cents.

With only a few seconds left on the phone card to call America, I called my mother in desperation. I screamed the hotel telephone number into the phone, repeated it and heard the fateful dial tone. All of the calling units were used and I had no way to reach anyone in America! I went back to the hotel room, feeling that we were drowning in hopelessness. When I got back to the room, Bob and I laid down on the bed—totally defeated with no plan for action. Minutes later, we heard the phone ring in the hotel. Miraculously, a friend was calling for us from America! My mother was able to retain the numbers I yelled to her, called a friend of ours, and he had already made arrangements to bail us out. If we could quickly make it back to Santo Antão, his brother-in-law would lend us money for travel expenses to catch the two flights home. After that incredible phone call, my parents called saying they could not wait until we were home safe in America.

As we traveled back to Santo Antão, we realized we would literally have to run into Bob's parents' house, grab our belongings, and jump back onto the boat so we would not miss the ride back to São Vicente and our flight to Sal the next day. We raced to Bob's parents' house and quickly packed our things. As we said goodbye to everyone, they gave us quick hugs and wiped the tears from their eyes.

When we arrived back at the port to leave for our journey, we found Adam's grandmother and uncle there to send us off. Since we had to wait to board, his grandmother was able to speak with Adam. She bent down and explained, "Clara (Claire) is now your new mother. You must respect her and listen to everything she says. You must study hard in school and be a good boy." As she finished talking with him, she stood up at his side. I took a few quick pictures of the three of them standing together and suddenly saw their faces change in front of me.

The grandmother began to sob uncontrollably. She turned, kissed Adam on his face, placed her hands on his shoulders, and dropped to the ground crying. As she grabbed Adam's feet, I saw Adam start to cry and the uncle's eyes became filled with tears. The grandmother lifted herself up and waved to us as we quickly climbed aboard the ship. I remember believing Adam's family had so much love for each other and this separation was going to be very difficult for them. Once on board, I looked out to find the grandmother, but she had disappeared.

We had to sit on the boat for a while as all the people entered and their belongings were stowed. Then suddenly, the horns blared through the air as we slowly began to move through the water. Adam said he was tired and fell asleep on my lap. As we slowly made our way through the water, I turned around to see how far we had traveled from the small island. As I glanced back, I noticed someone had climbed up on top of a large cement wall and was waving a white sheet back and forth through the wind. I told Bob to look and we both used the zoom lens on the camera to get a clearer view. It was Adam's grandmother saying her last goodbye to us and to her grandson!

As we traveled on the return journey, staying in various hotels, we got to know Adam a little more. He was fascinated with electricity and running water, since these were things he had never experienced before. He had lived his entire life on top of a mountain with no luxuries. In the hotels, he usually closed himself in the bathroom and played with the sink, toilet and light switches for long periods of time. I began to think maybe he had some sort of autism since he seemed overly fascinated with the repetition of sounds. At first, we allowed these peculiarities, but then it started to get annoying. What was upsetting for us to see was that Joey, who was two at the time, could pay attention, follow directions and understand how to behave. Adam was nine and everything seemed totally foreign to him. Bob and I would speak Cape Verdean Creole, Adam's native language, yet he still could not understand or completely ignored our conversations and directions. As parents it was difficult to see such marked differences in the development of both boys. We were frustrated that we had to explain and re-explain everything and still Adam did not understand.

We also quickly realized that Adam had no concept of personal hygiene. He had never owned a toothbrush, taken a shower or used a toilet in his life. As his father, Bob patiently taught Adam the basics and stayed with Adam until he understood. Everyday tasks to us were new lessons in this child's life. Some things he understood quickly and others took more time to grasp. His world was exploding with new sensations and experiences.

Once we arrived in America, Adam was shocked to see so many cars. He could not believe that food was ready in a few seconds at drive-thru windows, and he found the huge American stores to be from another world. The first day we arrived home, he instantly ran into his and Joey's bedroom and started playing with the toys. He was fascinated with anything that had buttons or made noises.

Late one evening during the first week home, I heard fireworks outside. I excitedly yelled to the boys to follow me as I ran to the apartment balcony. Joey and I were excited to see the colors and Adam quickly ran to see what all the commotion was about. But as soon as Adam saw the display, he screamed and ran back inside. I followed him, and found him shaking and hiding under his bed. I asked what was wrong, explaining that the fireworks could not hurt him. He responded that he had heard adults talking about the world possibly ending in the future, so when he saw all the light, he thought the end was really happening.

Unfortunately, Adam's sweet innocence quickly disappeared within that first week. When we traveled to Cape Verde, I learned that kids usually obey their parents unequivocally. If they don't, they will be physically reprimanded. Yet during our first week home, Adam started testing the lines. One day I took Adam and Joey to the beach. After swimming and playing for several hours, I wanted to leave. I told Adam it was time to go. He looked straight at me and then ran down to the water—totally ignoring me. I had to yell at him again before he came. Once in the car, Adam ate a bag of chips and blew it up to pop it. I told him, "Give me the bag." I was shocked when he immediately responded with a clear, "No!" When we arrived home, I asked him to go take a shower and again he ignored me. I couldn't understand his defiance. I spoke with Bob and together we confronted Adam.

The next day I took the boys to the park. Adam climbed on top of a huge slide and said he was going to jump down. As I yelled for him not to jump, and instructed him to go down the slide normally—he looked right at me and took a huge leap off the top of the slide. I was furious and declared that it was time to leave. Adam then defiantly ran over to the swings to purposely show me that he did not have to listen to me.

On both defiance occasions, Bob spoke with Adam—informing him that I was his new mother figure and he had to listen to me. After reiterating this for the second incident, Bob ran into the bedroom and got his belt. He showed Adam the belt and said, "We've talked to you twice now. The next time there will be no conversation."

When I had walked down the streets in Cape Verde, I often heard fighting in the various homes. I quickly learned that belts were a familiar tool for parents who wanted to reprimand their children. When Bob brought out the belt, Adam, Bob and I instantly understood what the belt meant. From that point forward, I never had a problem with Adam ignoring or disrespecting me.

As the weeks passed, we noticed that Adam was obsessed with taking apart toys. If it made a rattle or beeping sound, he would destroy the object just to see what was inside. Most of the time, he could not figure out how to put the toys back together, so he would just leave them on the floor. Bob and I felt frustrated since many of the toys were expensive and needed to be shared between Adam and Joey. Numerous times we asked Adam why he took apart and broke the toys—and with complete conviction, each time he stated he did not do it. But, we knew it was Adam every time, since Joey was two-years-old at the time, and did not have the motor skills to operate a screwdriver. Each time, we clearly told Adam that we knew he did it and we expected him to tell the truth. But he never apologized or admitted his guilt.

Something that was extremely frustrating was that Adam constantly urinated all over the entire toilet—regardless of the numerous times we reiterated exactly how to go to the bathroom. It became a daily problem of him peeing all over the seat, the sides and the floor surrounding the base. Despite Bob and I constantly bringing Adam into the room to show where he had an accident, he still said with conviction that it was not him. After months of frustration, Bob lost control one day and screamed at Adam. He pushed Adam's shoulders a few times and demanded that he pay closer attention to what he is doing. From that point forward, Adam suddenly stopped peeing all over the toilet.

No matter what evidence we showed Adam, in his mind he was never at fault. All boys will pee on a toilet, but once you explain and show them where they had the accident, they can make the connection between the mess and their own actions. Likewise, no matter how young the child, he knows when he has broken something. Usually when a child turns two or three years of age, he or she will confess any messes or broken objects. Adam never admitted that he broke something or made a mess. He could not make the connection between his actions and the consequences. He created masterful lies declaring his innocence. It was as if he truly believed his own fabrications.

As the time for school approached, I decided to help Adam prepare. Since he could not speak any English, I tried to assess how much he knew in Portuguese—the language he would have learned in school in Cape Verde. I soon discovered that he did not attend Cape Verdean school for any measurable length of time, and really did not know anything in Portuguese. His only language was Cape Verdean Creole. All he had learned in school was to count to one hundred, and he could barely write his first name.

I started to teach him his A, B, C's in English. Since Joey was two-years-old at the time, it worked out well for both boys. Adam and Joey were of different ages, but were at similar learning stages for the English language. The three of us would sing little songs as we drove to different places and tell each other made-up stories—practicing putting words and phrases together.

For years, I had worried that Adam would fall behind in school since he was not raised speaking English. I spent many hours working with him to improve his limited English and mathematical abilities. A few months after coming home from Cape Verde, I became pregnant with my son David. I felt very sick those first few months. During that time, I paid so much attention to helping Adam with his schoolwork, manners and cultural etiquette—I often felt that Joey was not getting the attention he needed. Adam was extremely needy and overly demanding. He expected every ounce of energy that I had to be dedicated to him. If I was diverted from giving Adam my total concentration, he quickly made sure to gain my attention within minutes.

A year later, we moved out of our apartment and into our first home. I was ecstatic to learn that Adam had been assigned to Robert, a very special teacher at the Middle School. When we first met Robert, I could instantly see that he was a warm and sincere person who was dedicated to seeing all of his students excel. I told him my concerns about Adam falling behind the other kids, and he immediately assured me that I could relax. Robert explained his teaching style and that he would be able to spend a lot of individual time with Adam—making sure he was learning and understanding his schoolwork. Knowing that Adam was going to get the individual attention he needed, I finally stopped worrying about him.

Chapter 2
Box of Shame – Secrets Revealed

After six months in the new school, I could see marked differences in Adam's academic abilities. He was beginning to read and write with ease and was getting good grades. As my worries about him subsided, I also felt my uncomfortable feelings about him disappearing. I began to truly accept Adam as my son. Many times we would sit together, talk, laugh, play, and really enjoy the time together. I had the same emotions for him as I did my other children—positive hopes for his future, worry for his safety, pride for his daily accomplishments, and love for him. I could now see that Adam was a bright boy who had many good qualities. He was becoming a young man and I was proud that he was my son. But, soon all of those positive emotions came to a crashing halt.

Two years after moving into our home, Bob and I began hearing Adam's name mentioned in relation to items that were missing or stolen from other families' homes. Friends and family members listed several items that had disappeared, while Adam was visiting. But with all the commotion of the 2002 holiday season, we could not see what was happening.

We did not pick up on these "hints" to Adam's stealing behavior until something happened that I could not ignore. One day, while doing laundry, I unexpectedly found my father's college ring in Adam's jeans. I instantly came out of my mental fog and could see there was a definite problem. Upon calling my father to let him know that Adam had his college ring, he informed me that he had been looking for the ring for several weeks. He had suspected Adam may have taken it, but as

Adam's grandfather, he did not want to admit or discuss his suspicions. It was then that my father also informed me that his Walkman headset was missing, as well as one of his favorite music tapes.

When I confronted Adam, he said he found the ring on top of our dryer and knew nothing of a Walkman headset. According to Adam, "Someone left the ring on top of the dryer. I found it and did not realize it was valuable." He rationalized in his mind—since the ring was left lying around, it must not be of great value and would not be a big deal if he used it. As a parent, I desperately wanted to believe him and tried to rationalize how this ring could have magically appeared on top of a dryer. I envisioned my father's last visit to our home. I imagined him taking off his ring, putting it in his coat pocket, piling his coat on top of the dryer, and the ring silently falling out of the pocket. Then I thought, "Maybe my father dropped his ring in the living room when he was sitting watching TV and the next day someone innocently picked it up and placed it on top of the dryer." None of the possible explanations seemed realistic. When I spoke with my father again, he told me about the last time the boys visited him at my parents' house. He said, "Adam came out of my bedroom one day as I was going in. I got a distinct feeling that he had taken something. I wasn't sure if he had, and I didn't want to say anything."

After speaking with my father, I explained to Adam the value of the ring and the distress he had caused my father. Yet Adam showed no signs of guilt or embarrassment at not reporting the "found" ring. He convincingly stated his version of reality numerous times and with such determination it seemed almost believable. I kept thinking about how he remained unaffected and indifferent towards my father's apprehension. He did not feel any empathy for my father who had been frantically searching for his ring for the past few weeks. Again I stressed the importance and sentimental value of the ring. And still, Adam showed no feelings of guilt or sadness.

Immediately after learning about the ring, we began to understand the other incidents. As I told a friend about the ring episode, she reminded me that during our family's last visit to her home—her husband's hand-held voice recorder was missing. Another day, Joey, went to his elementary school and returned home furious with Adam. Joey's friend had accused Adam of stealing one of his belongings. During

Joey's friend's recent birthday party at his home, an expensive Yu-Gi-Oh card disappeared from his collection. The boy had watched Adam who was studying his cards intensely. The next day, the boy noticed his special card was missing.

Right before Christmas, my mother and father came to take the boys for the weekend to visit relatives in New York. We had already told Adam he could not go because his name was coming up too many times regarding missing items. We did not want to give him any more opportunities to swipe things from other homes. Bob and I suddenly could see Adam for who he was—a true kleptomaniac. After the weekend, my parents returned with Joey and David, and my father went up to Adam's room to confront him about the stolen ring. After a few minutes, my father came down from Adam's bedroom very upset. He said, "Adam's face was cold as stone and he made no attempt to apologize." Adam adamantly stood by his lie that he had found the ring on top of the dryer and had no idea how it got there. My father, who had volunteered for years in the local prison, teaching decision-making skills—saw a familiar tactic used by the prisoners. They always had an explanation for their crimes and never would consider themselves guilty. My father then said to me, "Good luck, Claire, that kid has a lot of problems."

From the day we brought Adam into our family, my parents always treated him as their grandson. Now, to have Adam lie to my father's face was painful for my father and unbearable for Bob and me. I found myself consumed with anger towards Adam. Every time I looked at him, I hated him. For years I had denied my emotions and feelings. I ignored dreams I had of him where I would fight him with horrible words that would escalate into physical fights. Now I did not hold back my emotions and feelings. I felt my rage and did not subdue my emotions. I wanted to say the words I had felt guilty for saying to him in my dreams. I found myself screaming those words in my mind every time I saw him or thought about him. I did not try to psychologically analyze my feelings of disgust towards Adam. I allowed myself to feel the hate I had towards him. I had hidden those feelings and felt shame for years, but now I did not feel guilty.

After hearing how coldly Adam behaved with my father about his ring, and knowing of two other homes where things were missing—Bob and I realized we had to go through Adam's bedroom to see what else was in there. Bob spent Christmas Eve searching Adam's room while I took Adam out of the house "to find some last minute Christmas gifts."

Every store was closed because of the holiday and the only place to go "shopping" was a local 24-hour pharmacy. I knew my husband needed enough time to look through everything in the room, so I walked aisle by aisle in the store stopping to study every product. When enough time had passed for Bob to search through the contents of Adam's room, he called me on my cell phone to say we could return.

When Adam and I came home from "shopping", Bob took me upstairs and dumped out all of the gadgets he had found. In disbelief, we did not say a word as our eyes scanned over the items. There were scientific calculators, electronic word spellers, calculators, a palm pilot, binoculars, after-shave lotion, and checks from people purchasing magazines during a recent school fundraiser. As we looked through the objects, we realized he had been stealing from different people for a long time. Bob and I never saw the problem before, and now we felt a sinking feeling of failure. Where had we messed up with raising this child? Why did we not see something was wrong?

Bob and I felt every emotion possible—anger, confusion, guilt, sadness and fear. We traced back in time to try to see when Adam began his stealing spree. We recalled when we first moved to our house in 2000, and Adam began some strange behavior. That fall, ten-year-old Adam often stepped off the school bus eager to show us things he had "found" during the day. Usually he found a quarter, a nickel, and sometimes a dollar. When he found a scientific calculator I told him he needed to find the owner and return it immediately. His explanation was, "Mom, I found it on the side of the road when I was walking home. How would I figure out who it belongs to? We'll never find out whose it is."

From that point forward, Adam always had a reasonable explanation for everything. Objects he brought home were always, "borrowed from a friend" or "found on the street." I never suspected anything since several times I witnessed Adam letting friends borrow his toys and gadgets. After a while this "trading" back and forth seemed to be the norm.

When we confronted Adam with the stolen items, he was completely indifferent. As we questioned him and expressed our disappointment and anger, his only concern was for the presents he would receive the next morning for Christmas. As disbelief and rage began to take hold, Bob decided to discipline Adam. Normally we did not use physical discipline, but at that point, I agreed a good spanking was in order. Since our children were raised with very little physical reprimands, and we did not want them to know about Adam's stealing behavior, we decided I should take the boys out of the house while Bob spanked Adam. At 10:30 pm, I gathered five-year-old Joey and two-year-old David, to take them out to the car to go see, "Christmas lights on all of the houses in the neighborhood."

As I drove around with the boys, showing them the lights on each of the houses, I waited for Bob to call. The plan was that he would call me when he was done disciplining Adam to let me know it was time to bring the boys back. As I drove, I remembered thinking about the children in Cape Verde. They are raised with fear and respect for their parents from an early age. Bob had explained to me how Cape Verdean parents who had little education normally used physical punishment to discipline their children. They often used belts, branches from bushes, their hands or anything else that was close by to cause pain and show physical consequences for poor behavior. I thought, "The physical punishment that is done in Cape Verde is the only thing that Adam will understand at this point. Since our words don't have any affect on him, getting hit is the only thing that will get through to him."

When Bob called me to say it was time for us to return home, he told me that he did not have to hit Adam at all. As soon as Adam saw me leave with the two boys and knew he would be alone with his father who was furious about something big, he was very open to confession. Just the fear of physical discipline motivated Adam to suddenly remember where all of the items came from. Adam told Bob from whom he stole each object. He then explained to Bob that he would see something at school or at someone's home "and just take it." He did not know why he was doing it. After their lengthy discussion, Bob naively told me, "Everything is going to be fine now. We discussed everything and Adam will never do this again."

Before this time, we could see a few minor "problems" with Adam, which seemed normal for a typical pre-teen. He occasionally had selective hearing and managed to escape from responsibility. Sometimes he

24

would "forget" to do his share of chores or not finish his homework. Bob and I sporadically noticed that Adam had too much energy if he did not have structured tasks to do, and would play too rough with the boys. But overall, Adam had matured into a polite, kind young man. He no longer took toys apart with screwdrivers and was finally able to get himself up in enough time to catch the bus each morning.

When Adam was in seventh grade he had a horrible time waking himself up in time to get ready for school. He constantly missed the bus. For a while it seemed like I was fighting with him every morning. I often had to wake him up, and I would see that he was in a deep sleep. I could not understand how he would go to bed early each evening and still need so many more hours of rest. When Bob and I told him he needed to get up for school on time and get himself ready, our words had little effect on him. I finally found that losing opportunities such as a school field trips or school dances became big incentives for him to get up in the morning. Soon he was getting up on his own without a problem.

By eighth grade Adam showed everyone that he had grown into a responsible person. To see him mature into a respectful and responsible young man, and then learn of the secret stealing behavior was devastating. It was a crushing blow to Bob and me. When we told family and friends of Adam's kleptomaniac behavior, people showed mixed emotions. Family members who had raised teenagers tried to assure me that it was common for kids to try stealing—they usually grew out of the behavior as they got older. Other family members and friends were confused and could not understand how Adam, who seemed like such a good boy, could take things from other people.

After the origins of the objects were explained that Christmas Eve, there were still other things that needed clarification, such as money that Adam had mysteriously "found." Two months before finding my Dad's ring and other objects, my parents, Bob, the boys and I all went to see a Jack O' Lantern exhibit at night in a public park. As we walked in the darkness to the exhibit, Adam suddenly announced that he found money on the ground. At the time, my mother, father and I thought how lucky Adam was to find $40.00. But, Bob wasn't excited, he became suspicious. That night he told me he didn't believe Adam and stated, "I can't find money like that during the day, how is he finding money in the dark?" Bob told me he was afraid Adam was stealing. His suspicion surprised and upset me. I assured him that Adam was a good boy and was experiencing a lucky streak.

About three days after that event, I took the boys to Wal-Mart. As we were getting out of the car, Adam yelled, "What the!" He then bent down to pick up an envelope on the pavement. He said that the envelope had made his foot slip as he was trying to climb out of the car. In disgust, he handed the white envelope to me. I opened it and was shocked to see money inside. The envelope contained $142.00! I would have loved to keep the money, especially since I was really low on cash that week, but ethically I knew I had to return it to its owner. I told the boys, "We have to go inside the store and tell the store manager." Adam was very fidgety and strongly stated, "Mom, you don't have to tell, just keep it." I then adamantly stated that we had to tell the store manager since it was the right thing to do.

As we walked inside, Adam was visibly nervous. He seemed aggravated with me that I was not keeping the money for myself. Once inside the store, I spoke with the manager and gave him my name and telephone number. I told him in case anyone called the store regarding their lost envelope of money—I had it in my care. At the time, I did not tell the store personnel how much money was inside. I figured that would help identify who the rightful owner was. The store manager informed me that the store policy was—after 48 hours, if no one claims the money, it goes to the person who found it.

A few days passed and out of the blue I received a phone call from a woman. She was so happy and relieved stating, "It is so nice to know that there are still honest people in the world." After discussing how happy she was, I casually asked her how much money she had lost. She said she lost roughly $670.00. I told her the envelope I had, contained significantly less money. Then I asked her to describe her envelope. She said the envelope was a bank deposit envelope with the name "Richard" written on the outside. The envelope I found was a plain white envelope that was blank. When I told her that I thought it was a different envelope, she said, "No, the people at Wal-Mart gave me your name and told me you had the envelope with $670.00 inside." I told her that was impossible since I never told Wal-Mart staff how much money I found in the envelope. I informed her that she should call the store and ask if they had another envelope locked in a safe since we were clearly talking about two different envelopes.

From the day we found the money, I was extremely anxious. My mind was constantly racing and I felt uneasy. My insides were turning and I found myself relentlessly questioning if I had handled the situation in the right manner. After days of worrying, I was mortified when Adam said to me "Mom, why do you get so nervous about things? Why do you think everything is your responsibility?" I thought to myself, "How pathetic! My stepson can see my personal mental issues. They must be really out in the open if my children are noticing!" I thanked him for his input and told him, "You are right, I don't know why I feel so responsible for everything."

When the local police called the house that night, I was shocked and terrified. The officer interrogated me regarding the money found at Wal-Mart, and then instructed me to go immediately to the station to sign a statement. It was about 9:00 pm and I asked the officer if he could come to the house since I had three children I would have to bundle up. His words were very cold and he stated, "Mrs. Silva, you need to come into the station tonight." I then explained that the amounts of money were different and the envelopes were completely different. He said he was going to contact the woman again, to clarify the story, but he wanted me to get ready to come down to the station. As I started getting everyone ready, the phone rang again. The officer apologized and said that the elderly woman had just found the envelope of money in her dresser drawer. I did not have to go to the station. The officer then said I should return the money to the store manager to avoid this type of situation. I immediately called Wal-Mart, and spoke with a manager to find out what I needed to do with the money. He said he would call me back. Days and weeks passed and I never got a response. I kept the money separate from our finances in case someone called to claim it. I did not feel comfortable handing it in to the store and did not know why.

As Bob and I questioned Adam that Christmas Eve, Bob asked, "What about the money from Wal-Mart?" Adam responded, "We found it in the parking lot." Bob asked again and received the same response. Finally Bob said, "Adam, I know that is not true because I met with the store manager and he showed me the security video tapes from the parking lot. You can clearly see that you dropped the envelope and acted like you found it." Only after Bob invented this fib, did Adam finally confess he had stolen the money from his math teacher at school.

As we remembered different "found" objects and money, we began questioning Adam in a steady stream. I was struck with how emotionless Adam was. When we drilled him with questions, he had no expression. At one point I began crying said, "Adam, I've been your mother for three and a half years and I'm looking at you, realizing I don't know who you are. You've been living in my house and you're a stranger to me. I'm afraid of you!" He remained cold and indifferent. It was as if I was speaking a foreign language that he did not understand. He showed no remorse for what he had done or how upset Bob and I were.

I thought about the next morning, Christmas Day, and how could I possibly give presents to this kid—rewarding him for stealing? I told him, "Adam, you are not getting any presents tomorrow and by the way, there is no such thing as Santa Claus!" His eyes opened wide, and his mouth dropped open as he was in total disbelief. This thirteen-year-old boy still believed in Santa Claus! He was not upset that Bob and I were in total pain. The entire time we spoke, he showed no emotions yet when he found out there was no Santa Claus and he was not going to get any presents, it was the only thing that had any affect on him.

When we awoke that Christmas morning, I was disgusted. I knew I had to act as if everything was fine so I would not destroy the special time for Joey and David. But my anger was boiling inside. That morning, after all of the presents were opened, and the wrapping paper and open boxes were left on the floor—I began my creation of the Box of Shame. I picked up a box from my son David's Buzz Light Year toy, and decided it was the right size. After each present was opened and all of the wrapping paper was cleaned off the floor, I began to mentally plan the next few days. I went upstairs where Bob and I had hidden all of the stolen items, and began placing them inside the box. I braced myself for the next task at hand—returning all of the stolen objects to their rightful owners. As I placed all of the stolen objects into the Buzz Light Year box, I thought about how Bob, Adam and I would visit each of the families involved and tell them what happened. As a parent how do you do this? If your child feels no remorse, guilt or embarrassment, what do you do?

It was painful to watch the lack of response and emotion from Adam when we brought the objects to each of the owners. It was scary to see that Adam was not internally moved to apologize or explain his actions. I remember carrying the box to each household and realized the box was for Adam. I had placed all of the objects inside which would give any normal person a feeling of guilt, embarrassment, anger—a range of human emotions. Yet, Adam showed no response. I had created the Box of Shame—hoping it would teach him to feel the emotions he should have felt as we visited each home. But as we traveled from house to house, I realized the Box was not helping Adam feel shame or guilt. I could see that he was unable to feel those emotions. Adam was completely disconnected from his actions, and how they affected others.

As I carried the Box of Shame to each family's home, I acknowledged that most people have a Box of Shame, but it is an internal box buried deep within their subconscious. The Box is filled with each person's most personal private fears, thoughts, or actions that they are ashamed of. Pains, embarrassments, fears, feelings of guilt, unnecessary "obligations", and angers are tucked deep inside the Box. Each of us covers the Box so others will not see the personal items within, and we lie to ourselves that the Box does not exist. We bury the Box deep within our souls never to be opened and for each item never to be explored.

I could see that people who have acquired personal growth, spiritually and mentally, have discovered their internal Box of Shame and at some point in their lives, were brave enough to open the Box and analyze the contents. The items inside may have been prejudice towards other people, judgment of others, self-esteem issues, trauma from childhood or difficulties with intimacy. By analyzing the contents, they allow themselves the process of self-discovery and understanding. They are then able to conquer their fears and create their own personal freedom. They free themselves of the contents of their Box and avoid putting more items inside.

After carrying Adam's Box of Shame, I realized that I had created my own Box of Shame deep within myself for several years. I filled my Box with "shoulds" and negative messages to myself that I was not a good mother for Adam. I suffered mentally and emotionally from my

29

constant internal struggle of being Adam's stepmother. From when I first met Adam and brought him home to America, I believed there was something seriously wrong with him. I could not put my finger on what was wrong, so I began pointing the finger at myself. I convinced myself that there must be something wrong with me.

My Box of Shame contained the barrage of negative internal messages I gave myself, and the numerous dreams about Adam that haunted me. Since I could never explain the negative emotions, I experienced around Adam, I internalized them. I believed that I was the worst mother in the world for Adam, telling myself, "I'm not qualified to be Adam's mom." I fed myself this mental nonsense and convinced myself that someone else would be able to do a better job of raising Adam than me.

In my dreams I was filled with complete hatred towards Adam and screamed at him uncontrollably. As I followed him, taunting him with progressively cruel words, I prepared for the physical confrontation. In each dream, I was always the first person to start the physical altercation. I always punched him or slapped him in the face. Then Adam quickly returned the attacks against me and each time I had to yell for Bob to run in to help me. The dreams were terrible and I was too embarrassed to share them with anyone. I was horrified to have such intense emotions against my stepson. I hid the dreams within my Box of Shame and had no intention of ever talking about my night terrors. Instead, I hid my shame and guilt.

It did not matter how many people complimented my husband and me on what a great job we were doing with parenting Adam. In my mind, I always believed I was failing him and would forever fail him. I never felt comfortable hugging Adam and felt uncomfortable sitting close to him. No matter how much I tried to convince myself that the problem was with me, I always felt bizarre senses when I was near Adam.

One of the instincts Bob and I confessed to each other and felt horribly guilty about—was a feeling that Adam was dirty. It was as if he had a permanent condition. We could not understand where the feelings came from. Yet, neither one of us wanted Adam to drink from our cups. Everyday, Bob and I had to remind Adam to take a shower and once in the shower, he often did strange things. Regularly he would urinate in a cup and leave it for the next person. After each shower I had to fight with him to stop it—explaining that no one wanted to look at his urine. Even though we forced him to shower regularly, Bob and I confessed that we felt Adam was still not completely clean. We confided in each other and discussed how we felt horrible about our strange feelings and overcome with guilt. We could not understand why we looked at Adam in such a way.

During one of our many private conversations about Adam, Bob stated that when he studied Adam he noticed, "If you give Adam an inch, he will take an arm. If you joke around a tiny bit with him, he goes off the deep end." Both of us felt that we had to be very strict with Adam because if we were lenient at all, he would take advantage of the situation and misinterpret things. Then his misinterpreted understanding meant free reign to go wild. We both witnessed that if we joked around a little with Adam, he wouldn't be able to pick up on social cues to understand when enough was enough. Then he would act out so much we would have to yell at him to stop joking around. We quickly learned to be serious with him most of the time and keep joking to a minimum.

I found I felt anxious every time Adam came to talk to me. His incessant talking and always needing total attention, made me very uptight. I often felt my insides screaming, "Leave me alone," when I saw him coming towards me. I did not feel emotionally close to him. There was always something blocking us from each other. Similar to when you walk into a room where people have just been fighting, but you don't know they were fighting. You can feel the tension and negative energy in the room. Instinctually, you feel like you should leave the situation. That tension is what I felt with Adam. I could not understand why I had instincts to stay distant from him. I hated my feelings. In my mind, a mother should love and feel emotionally close to all of her children and welcome any chance to communicate with them. I fought my feelings of distance with Adam the best that I could and forced myself to try to bond with him. I tried to ignore my instincts and focused on accepting him as my son.

But after Adam had been living with us for a while, I noticed that Bob and I had become different parents. I witnessed Bob get physically tense and emotionally agitated when Adam was around him. Before

Adam lived with us, Bob was carefree and joyous. He and I used to hug Joey, play, and joke around constantly. As soon as we brought Adam home, Bob and I tightened up physically and felt mentally uneasy. We both showed less physical affection toward Joey and we monitored every action and every word from our mouths.

By the time our second son David was born, I was desperate to sit and hug my two little children. I still did not feel comfortable hugging Adam, but I did not want to treat him differently. I avoided hugging the boys when Adam was around, and usually snuck in my hugs for Joey and David when Adam was watching TV or occupied with something else.

I found I was so puzzled by my distant feelings with Adam, I often reflected on who I was before he entered into our family. I needed to understand if I had similar feelings before. But, I remembered being young and always loving all children. I was the girl who was constantly holding the newest baby. I babysat for local families every weekend and found children a joy to be around. I recalled being about six-years-old and getting lost in the grocery store. I was terrified and afraid that my mother was intentionally trying to leave me there. But, I comforted myself by thinking, "It is okay. If I'm left here, I will make it my home and take care of all the children whose parents don't want them anymore."

As a young adult, working in the human services field, I found myself surrounded by children. For a couple of years, I worked with tough street kids. Winning them over and getting beyond their "toughness" became a personal challenge for me to conquer. I enjoyed working with the toughest, most unreachable kids because I knew every child had a spirit that longed to be loved. I learned that giving respect and kindness to these youth often won over the coldest of hearts. It was a personal miracle for me each time an "unreachable" teen opened up and spoke on a personal level. I witnessed gang members break down crying and distant teens turn to me for help. After working with the gang members for many months, I had many tell me they were desperate for a "normal" job and begged me to help them escape from their fast lives of selling drugs. They quietly hinted that a minimum wage paying job was fine. They did not want to worry anymore about the police finding them. They wanted to feel like they were just like everyone else.

My work gave me valuable lessons in connecting with, and reaching, challenging kids. The experiences helped prepare me for when I was to become a mom. I often thought about what I had learned from working with the tough kids, and wanted to apply those life lessons in the future—when I would be raising my own children. I looked forward to having children and creating my own family. The idea of creating a life and helping that individual grow, learn and blossom into a beautiful human being was fascinating.

Before Adam entered into our lives, I loved being a mother to Joey. He was the center of my world. Everywhere we went, people felt instantly drawn to him. Older women in the grocery store used to come up to him and pinch his chubby cheeks or comment on his beautiful eyes. He was a popular hit everywhere we traveled. He had a wonderful ability of manipulating his facial expressions. When he was eight-months-old he was able to make a "serious face" or "happy face" and entertain anyone who passed by. Total strangers used to stand around him in the store, just to watch the show. He made strangers laugh and had a glow and humor about him that was contagious.

Before we brought Adam home, Joey was my only child. At times Joey seemed to be lonely. There were no other children where we lived, and he had no other siblings. He enjoyed hearing stories about one day meeting his older stepbrother, Adam. We planned for the day when Adam would come home and be a member of our family. Joey looked forward to that time and the chance to meet his older brother.

But those hopes of being one big happy family did not come true for us. After only a few days of Adam being with us in Cape Verde, Joey seemed annoyed and aggravated with Adam's peculiarities. I struggled with my own disturbing feelings as I watched him run from electrical switch to flushing the toilet to locking the doors and opening them. I originally intended for Adam to be totally integrated into our family. But after meeting him and bringing him home, I could see that he was very different. I soon became overwhelmed with alarming feelings and emotions. I tried to ride it out, but as the weeks and months passed, I still did not feel emotionally close to Adam. I did not feel a shared emotional feeling of warmth. My feelings were that he was not my son, and I needed to stay physically distant from him. I fought the thoughts as hard as I could and tried to think positively. But, the discomfort continued. I felt like a failure when I watched people hug Adam and sit close to him—things I could not do. It bothered me that I could not bring myself to act like everyone else. But, each time I tried to hug Adam, it felt false and I instantly wanted to back away.

At the time, it was unexplainable why I felt I had to show Adam physical boundaries between people. But, for some reason I believed his boundaries had in some way been compromised. I could not explain it, but I felt that Adam's broken boundaries were from something sexual. I felt that he needed to understand there was physical space around a person that needed to be respected. I taught him what boundaries were and how to respect them for himself and other people. I deeply believed that if I was physically close with Adam, such as hugging or cuddling, it would trigger something in him.

I didn't know why I had such disturbing feelings and I often felt guilty as I admitted them to friends and family, who could not understand my discomfort. I used to agonize over the fact that I did not want to get physically close to this nine-year-old boy, who I had welcomed into our family. The guilt was excruciating. I quickly realized I was the only one with the uncomfortable feelings. I then rationalized, "Since I am the only person with these uncomfortable feelings, then there must be a problem with me." I was afraid that people would misinterpret my feelings of distance with Adam—as my admittance of failure and regret at taking on the responsibility of raising a child that was not mine. But that was not the case.

I stopped talking to people about my discomfort and wrestled with my feelings on my own. I had a constant dreaded feeling that I would never be a good mother for Adam since I could not give him all the love he needed. I berated myself with insults. I was disgusted that I could think such horrible things about an innocent child.

The internal mental damnation I subjected myself to, made me more committed to prove myself wrong. I challenged myself to feel comfortable with Adam and to eventually accept that he was my child. I forced myself to disregard my instincts and stop the internal dialogue. I tried to trick myself into believing that Adam was my son and I was a good mother for him.

Adam, from early on, called me "Mom," which was a title I eventually became comfortable with. As the years progressed, I finally convinced myself to believe that Adam and I were bonding beginning to understand each other. After two years, I accepted that he was my son. When people asked me how many children I had, my immediate response automatically included Adam. I got to the point where I never had to explain Adam as my stepson and not my birth son, because he was my son. I treated all three boys the same. As we all grew closer, Adam often became confused, and asked me what he was like when he was a baby. Then he would remember I was not his biological mother and had no idea what he was like as an infant. When people asked Adam questions about his mother, he always answered the questions as they pertained to me.

In hindsight, I realize the cues and uncomfortable feelings Bob and I struggled with were our instincts yelling to us loudly. We were receiving messages, warning us of who Adam really was, but both of us felt guilty for our feelings and tried to hide them. As we discovered the stolen objects and witnessed Adam's indifference, I realized no human being could have given Adam the love he needed. I had not changed into a cold person who didn't like children. I was not supposed to mentally beat myself up over the uncomfortable and bizarre senses I experienced during those previous years. All of my uncomfortable feelings were serving as warnings of who this person really was—that I had willingly welcomed into my home and family.

To deal with the problem of Adam's stealing, we sought professional help. I scheduled a neurological assessment, thinking maybe there was something wrong with his memory or brain chemistry. Maybe he need-ed some sort of medication and then he would go back to "normal." I thought maybe he was split into two different personalities—the young, polite, kind young man we thought he was growing into, and the other personality as a kleptomaniac and a liar. As the neurological assess-ment indicated, there was nothing clearly wrong with him that would lead him to the steal. He tested extremely low on several IQ tests, but this was explained as possibly due to the language barrier. The doctor explained that his IQ may indeed be much higher, but it was difficult to determine without a language assessment.

As our family faced Adam's stealing behavior, the atmosphere in the home became unbelievably uncomfortable. Bob and I realized we re-ally didn't know Adam as we thought we did. Though some people felt his stealing behavior was a phase, Bob and I knew it was extreme. He didn't steal a candy bar or a pack of gum. He had stolen hundreds of dollars worth of valuable items from people who were close to him. He didn't need the goods or money to support a drug habit or to purchase alcohol. He was stealing, and he himself did not know why he was doing it. The worst part about it was that he felt nothing for the people he stole from—he expressed no remorse for their losses or anxiety he had caused them.

Shortly after returning all of the stolen objects, there was an evening late in January 2003, when Joey asked me if he could meditate with me. A few months earlier, I had taught the boys how to meditate—believing everyone should have a place in their mind, where they can visit anytime they need to feel peace and relaxation. No matter what was happening in their lives, I wanted the boys to understand they had a safe place in their mind where they could escape. I taught them how to breath, relax, and envision themselves on various journeys. Since the discovery of Adam's secret stealing episodes, I did not feel comfortable meditating with the boys anymore. I felt like Adam was now analyzing all of us in the family—studying us to discover each of our personal vulnerabilities. I told Joey, "No, I want to meditate by myself for a while." But, he continued to plead with me.

I suddenly remembered the meditation I had learned a few weeks before during my weekly class. The meditation helped you focus and release anything negative, so you could send all of your worries and problems away. When I first learned the meditation, I thought, "This would be great for kids to learn." Then I rationalized and argued with myself thinking, "Kids don't have any problems." My body and mind began an internal battle. Suddenly I felt my heart respond with, "Oh, yes, kids certainly do have problems." So when Joey persisted in wanting to meditate with me, I finally agreed.

I taught him how to breath, relax his body and picture a pink balloon above his head. I told him to put all of his fears, feelings of anger or loneliness, and any worries into the balloon. I instructed him to visualize the balloon getting bigger and bigger, as it filled with all of his negative emotions. I then told him to exhale and picture the balloon floating higher and higher away from him. With each breath out he imagined the balloon rising until he could no longer see it. As the balloon was out of sight, we both felt the comfort of being present with no mental anxieties. We experienced the peace and serenity that exists when all personal concerns and worries have been removed. Once the meditation was over, Joey slowly turned to me, and calmly said "Mom, Adam scares me a lot, and makes me do things I don't want to do."

I asked Joey, "What do you mean? How does Adam scare you?" He began to tell me very terrifying things. Joey said, "Adam told me there are bees the size of buildings that can come after me and kill me." Adam had also told him the mannequin "Chuckie" from the movie, "Is real and has a knife the size of a staircase railing that can chop me up." Adam told him about a vampire and a cat with rabies that would bite him and scratch him to death. When I asked Joey "What types of things does he make you do that you don't want to do?" Joey responded, "If I don't want to play on the Play Station with him, he scares me or if I don't want to talk to him, he makes me talk to him by scaring me." I went through each of the scary threats Adam had created with Joey and told him, "Joey, none of those things are real." I knew kids could sometimes be mean to each other and scare each other, but this seemed more than normal. I told Joey I did not understand why Adam was scaring him so terribly. I said, "If Adam scares you again tell him, 'I spoke with mom and she knows you have been scaring me' and then tell me immediately." I decided not to confront Adam about the scary tales. But, now I knew to pay very close attention to him. The stealing behavior and learning of him scaring Joey to such a high degree were excessive.

About two days after that episode, Bob took Adam for his first counseling appointment. We had set up the appointment immediately after learning of Adam's stealing behavior and witnessing his lack of emotion. We hoped a counselor would shed some light on Adam's bizarre behavior and hopefully help us learn some skills for parenting Adam.

During Adam's appointment, Joey, David and I stayed home. That morning, Joey told me he wanted to get something downstairs, and proceeded to go down the staircase closest to my bedroom. Our house had two staircases. One set was near my bedroom, and the other was on the opposite side of the house and led from the living room up to Adam's bedroom. As I was sitting in my room, I heard a loud tumbling sound, a loud bang, and then a piercing cry. I ran down the stairs to see that Joey had missed one of the last steps and fallen down the remaining few steps. I grabbed him and tried to comfort him. Joey was shaking and sobbing saying, "Mom, I just remembered I had to do this before". I asked what he was talking about. He said, "As I was rolling down the stairs, I hit my head. I remembered I had to roll down the stairs before, and I hit my head then too." As the memory quickly came to him, he began to tell me everything he could remember.

Joey explained that Adam often did dangerous things to Joey when he used to watch the boys for a couple of hours. For a brief time in the beginning of the 2002 school year, Adam watched the boys for a couple of hours each day when Bob went to work, and I was on my way home from work. Joey described what happened to him during a couple of those afternoons. On one of those days, Adam forced him to do a somersault down the stairs and caught him half way down. When Joey fell down the stairs (the set closest to my bedroom), he hit his head on one of the steps. As his body repeated the same falling motion, and he experienced the same blow to his head—Joey remembered everything Adam did to physically and emotionally abuse him.

I asked Joey, "Why on earth would you listen to Adam and do some-thing like that? You could have gotten really hurt!" He then told me, "If I didn't do it Adam said the bees would come and get me." I asked him what else Adam did, and Joey began to unfold his living nightmare of terror. He walked through the house and reenacted each event for me to understand everything that had taken place. He explained how one afternoon, while Bob and I were at work—Adam chased him around the house with a knife, telling Joey he was going to stick it in him many times. Joey was so terrified, he ran down the street to Danene's house—a neighbor we had recently met. Another day Adam told Joey the "bees" were coming to get him. Joey hid under a sheet on top of one of the beds, but Adam told him they could still smell him. Joey then desperately ran into the bathroom to escape, and again Adam said, "The bees can still smell you!" Adam then took Joey downstairs and reassured him that he had to pretend he was half dead so the bees could not smell him. Adam sat behind Joey and with one hand covered Joey's nose and mouth and with the other, he choked Joey by pressing into his neck. When tears streamed down Joey's face because he had no air left, Adam let him go.

On another day, Adam took the small skewers that hold turkey or chicken legs in place for cooking, and stuck one into the wall. He told Joey, "Oh! You are lucky! The bees were just here and they shot this at you!" I was sickened that Adam would do such things to Joey and shocked that Joey believed Adam's larger-than-life lies.

I tried to figure out when Adam first started scaring Joey and wondered why he was terrifying a little boy so horribly. I remembered when we first bought the house. Since Bob and I were both working, I brought the boys to the babysitters' house every day. I had a long commute and had to juggle bringing the boys back and forth. After about one year, Bob could see I was exhausted. As the work slowed down in his job and the company began to cut his hours, he volunteered for a lay-off. This allowed him to collect unemployment and he was able to stay home with the kids—alleviating a ton of stress from me. For almost a year, Bob was able to stay at home with the boys. But in July 2002, Bob got a job close to the house and we needed to find daycare.

Since we really did not know anyone in the neighborhood, I called a few places to see if there were any openings. The prices the businesses charged per hour and per child were outrageous. Each place I called did not have any slots open. I was very anxious and worried to find someone to watch the children so Bob and I could work. Adam saw that Bob and I were struggling to find someone and immediately explained that he was old enough and perfectly capable of taking care of them. We only needed someone to watch the boys for two hours in between the time Bob would leave for work and I would come home from work. Bob and I talked about it at length and could see that Adam had really matured during the past year and did act responsibly. After many rules and guidelines were set in place, Bob and I hesitantly allowed Adam to watch the boys.

I regularly called home every half hour to check on the boys and every time things seemed fine. Even though things seemed to be working, Bob stated several times that he did not feel comfortable with the situation. But, at the time we had no other alternative. After two incidents and through our friend Julia's intervention, Bob and I realized Adam watching the boys was not a safe situation. We did not know our neighbor Danene too well, but I arranged for her to watch the boys each afternoon.

As I desperately searched through time to discover when Adam had access to Joey to mentally and physically torture him so horribly, I realized it was during those afternoons when Adam was watching the boys. Poor David was an infant and witnessed Joey running through the house in complete terror. As Joey disclosed what happened during those days when Adam watched him, I was distraught, confused and disturbed. How could Adam torture Joey like this? I wished Joey was making up the stories, but I knew he was telling me the truth. I quickly called Danene, who by then had become a good friend. I asked her about the day Joey said he ran to her house to escape from Adam, who had chased him through the house with a knife. She told me Joey did run down to her house one day and was terrified. She explained that shortly after Joey arrived—running down the street in the rain, with no shoes on, Adam walked down carrying David. When Adam got there, he laughed saying "I was only joking. It was a play knife. It wasn't real." At that point, Danene and her mother told Adam he should never frighten someone like that and he had gone too far. Adam responded saying, "I really didn't know he was that scared. I won't do something like that again." Adam had never before misbehaved or shown any alarming behavior around Danene and her family. Despite him down playing the event and explaining everything as a joke, Danene and her mother yelled at him to never do something like that again. At the time, Danene and her mother didn't think to tell me about the incident since they had already scolded him.

Since Danene confirmed Joey's running to her house and she already knew of the stolen objects and the scary tales—I told her about the other things Adam had been doing to Joey. When she made the connection between Adam scaring Joey and the terrifying things he was doing to him, she felt horrible. She felt helpless that Joey had run to her house for protection and safety on that rainy day, yet she was not able to understand how terrified he truly was. She apologized for not telling me of the knife incident and was baffled how she and her mother did not think to tell me. I assured her that Adam had fooled us all and no one ever knew to question him. None of us really paid close attention to him since he acted like a responsible, good boy all the time.

When Bob came home, I told him about all of the scare tactics and physical things he had forced on Joey. I told Bob and Joey that I would confront Adam. I wanted Joey to hear what I said to Adam, but I did not want Joey directly in the room. When I confronted Adam, Joey was in the next room and could hear everything through the open doorway. I told Adam, "I know about all of the scary things you have been saying to Joey and I know about the times you forced him to do dangerous things." In detail I then explained each of the events and horror stories he had told. I asked him why he was doing the horrible things to hurt Joey and he had no answer. As Adam stood listening to me, he made the same strange face he made when we confronted him about all the stolen objects—a face of confusion, disbelief and no comprehension. Again, it was as if I was speaking another language to this person. He did not understand a word I said. I then told him, "I don't know why you are scaring Joey like this and doing these things to him. No one understands why you are acting this way. You'd better start sharing this with your counselor if you want any help. You are not a safe person. Your teachers, your father and I know what you have been doing and everyone is going to be watching you. I'm going to check with the boys every day to see if you say or do anything to scare them when you guys are at Danene's house. Adam, you have a lot of adults watching everything you do now. We know you are not the person you wanted all of us to believe. You better start acting right and talking to your counselor because I don't know how to help you."

About a week later, as I was getting Joey and David bathed and dressed to see Sesame Street Live—I remembered a comment Adam's teacher, Robert, had made a few days earlier. I had left a message for Robert asking him to call me since I wanted to tell him, "Some more things we have learned that Adam has been doing against the boys." He returned the call and asked if Adam had sexually abused Joey and David. I was shocked by his question and assured him it was not of that nature. But now remembering Robert's question, I casually said, "Joey, no one ever touches your peeper or your bum, right?" Joey turned to me and said, "Yeah Mom, all the time." I thought I didn't understand him, so I asked again. He said "Yeah Mom, all the time." He went on to explain "Adam makes his peeper hard, sticks it in my bum and then pees inside." My first reaction was that I laughed nervously out loud and thought, "He must have heard that from somewhere." But then Joey looked at me seriously and said, "Mom, why are you laughing?" I suddenly realized, this was not a joke and fearfully asked, "Wait a minute, Joey, please tell me again. What did you just say?"

As he repeated every word, my mind began to race. Joey said Adam did it to him everyday, early in the morning, while everyone in the house was still sleeping. As I heard the details a second time, I realized no five-year-old would know such detailed information. By instinct, I knew to act calm and not make a big deal out of the situation. I did not want to upset Joey and David so I casually told them, "OK, stay in this room, finish getting dressed, and I'll be back in a second." I told them I had to talk with their father.

I ran outside to tell Bob, who was doing yard work. He instantly became enraged and distraught. He told me he was too upset to listen anymore and could not believe that it was true. He said he could not discuss it any further. I told him that it was all right if he could not deal with it, but I was going to confront Adam immediately.

I went into Adam's room and told him that Joey had disclosed what he had been doing to him. He looked at me with that same confused expression and responded sincerely, "Mom, I really can't remember." I asked him if he knew what the truth was and for him to give me a definition. As he answered me, I told him, "You better look deep within your brain for the truth. If you can find it, then we can try to get you some help for you. If you can't find the truth then you become my enemy! Do you understand?" He stated he understood and I explained to him that he was never to be in a room alone with the boys again. I told him he could never go in the bathroom with the boys and they could never sleep in the same room.

Suddenly Bob came upstairs and angrily asked, "Is it true what Claire told me?" Adam said it was true. In disbelief, Bob yelled "What? What did you do?" Adam responded, "I did what mom said." He then added more details to what he did to Joey. He tried to minimize the acts by making the comment, "I only did it once or twice and it was a long time ago." Bob and I were horrified. There are no words to explain what we felt! Bob immediately began to scream. Not knowing what to do with his anger, he began to smash the entertainment center that was close to him. As he shattered the wood into pieces, he yelled, "That is it!

You are going back to Cape Verde! You have caused enough problems for this family!" As he stormed out of the room, Adam nervously began to cry and stated, "I just remembered my uncle used to do it to me."

Not knowing what to do, who to call or where to turn for help, we did not know how to deal with the situation. We did not know how to separate everyone and ensure the safety of our children. Joey and David witnessed Bob destroying the furniture and screaming loudly. They were scared and needed to feel safe immediately. I quickly called Danene, who knew about everything Adam had done up until that point, and asked if he could stay at her house for a few hours. I told her there was much more to the story and we just needed to get away from him for a while. I told her he should sit on the couch and not move from the living room the whole time. She said it was fine to leave him there and assured me a few adults were going to be at the house and would watch every move he made.

I quickly packed up the boys and got all of us out of the house. I dropped off Adam telling him he was to stay there until we returned later that evening. He was confused and could not understand why we were all upset. He did not know why he was not able to go with us. As we drove away, Bob and I quietly discussed that we had no idea what to do. We went to the Sesame Street Live performance, to give the boys some peace and for Bob and me to get away from the situation and try to make some sense of our emotions.

That night when we picked up Adam, we had no words left to say. I told him to stay in his room the entire night and the next day we would discuss everything. He was completely indifferent to the whole situation—totally clueless to how upset we were. He was so unaffected—we became very frightened of him. We did not know what he was capable of. We were afraid he might try to hurt all of us, or try to attack Joey and David during the night. Bob and I were terrified for our family's safety. We locked Joey and David in our bedroom with us. Bob and I nervously tossed and turned in bed the entire night—afraid that Adam might sneak outside and set the house on fire to kill us all.

The next day I told Adam he had to stay in his room and I brought food up to him during each mealtime. I told him he was only able to leave the room to go to the bathroom across the hall and back into his bedroom. I called the pediatrician for the boys, and explained the story.

43

I asked how I could get them both physically examined. Normally he would report the incident, but since we were colleagues on a board together, he advised me to contact the police and the state child protection agency myself and he would follow up to make sure I had called. He explained that there was no order to the calls, but both needed to be contacted. He also told me whom to call to get an examination, since his office did not have the magnifying equipment necessary.

I called the police first and they assured me an officer would be over to the house quickly. When the officer arrived, he filed his reports and then left saying he would bring back a state worker from the child protection agency. A few hours later, he came back with the state worker. She interviewed Joey and David to get their story. Then she went up to Adam's room and interviewed him. He had refused to speak to the police officer, but openly admitted to the state worker that he had sexually abused Joey. When all of her reports were complete, the police officer and caseworker walked outside of the house with Adam and the three of them climbed into the police car. They did not need to use force or hand cuffs on Adam. He did not scream or object to be taken out of the house. He peacefully walked behind them with no demonstration of any type of emotions. The officer brought him to the station for finger printing, and that evening brought him to the juvenile detention facility for the night.

When Joey first disclosed the torture he had experienced, he was upset and worried that Adam was going to be sent back to Cape Verde. I assured him we really didn't know what was going to happen, and we would take it step by step. Before I called the police that morning, I told Joey I had to call. Regrettably, I never explained to David what was happening prior to the police coming into the house. As the police officer took Adam outside, David started asking why the policeman was taking Adam and where were they going. I explained to him that Adam had done some bad things to Joey and now had to go to a school for boys where they would help him.

Two months after Joey disclosed the sexual abuse, David who had just turned three, began to bombard me with questions. He constantly asked where Adam was, why was he not in the house and when was he coming home. I told him, "Adam did some bad things to Joey and scared him a lot. He did some bad things at school too—so he has to go to a school where they will teach him how to be nice to people." David remained upset that Adam was not coming home.

Even after the explanations, David could not understand why the policeman took his brother. Then David started a routine each morning of asking me, "Mom, is Adam a bad boy?" I would respond with, "Yes, he did a lot of bad things to a lot of people." Then he would ask, "Am I a bad boy?" I would then assure him that he was a good boy and he would always stay home with us forever. This routine happened for weeks until I finally let him answer his own questions. When he asked if Adam was a bad boy, I asked him, "What do you think?" Then he would answer with the response I had previously given. Then he would ask, "Am I a bad boy?" I would again ask him, "What do you think?" He would then respond stating he was a good boy._

One evening, Joey, David and I were sitting at the kitchen table as David played with some Play Dough. Joey and I were talking about Adam and we casually asked David if he remembered anytime when Adam hurt him. David then took the ball of play dough and made it into a long piece. As he rolled the piece in between his hands making it longer he said, "Adam make his peeper bigger, bigger, bigger. He hurt my peeper." He then demonstrated by digging his nail into the skin on his forearm with force. He explained that Adam dug his finger nail into David's penis. For months I had wondered what Adam had done to David, but had no way to know. David's disclosure proved that Adam had already begun to use his demonic tactics against him too. I thanked David and told him that he was very brave to tell us what had happened to him. I let him know that Adam was wrong and should have never done that to him.

To realize Adam had sexually abused both of our children was now our family's reality. Our shock and despair followed us like a shadow— never leaving our side. Joey had great verbal skills and I found myself wondering why he had never told us what Adam was doing. I needed to know how Adam had silenced both of my children so thoroughly. Through many questions and discussions, Joey explained how Adam used his fear against him. Adam had convinced Joey that all of the beings: the bees the size of buildings, Chuckie with his knife the size of a staircase railing, the vampires and a white cat with rabies—all of them would simultaneously know if Joey ever told anyone and would instantly come to kill him. Adam told Joey that he himself had powers to call on these beings. By using his mental powers, Adam could summon the beings to come and instantly attack Joey. Joey could never cry when Adam was hurting him, because the beings would hear him and immediately strike.

When eleven-year-old Adam started the tales of terror, Joey was four-years-old and trusted everything his older brother said as true. Joey loved Adam and did not have the capacity to question such extreme tales of horror. After Joey disclosed the past year and a half of torture, he was able to remember more of Adam's tactics. It became clear to me that Adam had taken every opportunity to remind Joey of the beings and expand on the horrifying details. I began to get an understanding of how twisted Adam was and how he forced Joey into inescapable silence.

Adam had already started "grooming" David, making him his next victim. I could never understand why David had an extreme fear of Adam's room. He was so terrified—he would not set foot inside. Once Adam was removed from the home, David's fear of monsters swelled to the point that he could not eat a meal in the kitchen without being right next to me. He trembled and cried in terror and I could not understand where it was coming from. He told me several times that there was a monster in Adam's room. I constantly had to reassure him that monsters were not real and there were no monsters in Adam's room. I remembered Joey had a fear of monsters at around the same age, but it was never excessive like this. Joey suddenly made the connection one afternoon when he remembered hearing Adam tell David, "There are monsters in my closet and if you don't stay in my room, they will come out and eat your hand off!" As I heard these words, I suddenly believed David. There really was a monster in the bedroom. The monster lived inside of our home—and his name was Adam.

Chapter 3
Effects on Parents, Guardians
& Other Care Takers

Since our situation involved one child against another, it was difficult to handle our anger. If an outside adult had committed these acts against our children, we would be able to completely feel our rage. But our son had committed heinous acts against our sons. What complicated the matter was to learn that Adam had been a victim of sexual abuse himself. We also learned that Adam had a below average IQ according to various psychological evaluations. We were left wondering—if the person is not of the highest intelligence and was a victim of sexual abuse himself, how angry are you allowed to feel?

As I told other family members and close friends, about Joey's and David's disclosures, each person became very distraught. Everyone had to process his or her emotions in their own way. I think the most common emotion was total shock. Most people told me that for about three days, they could not stop thinking about what had happened. Many friends and family that had supported Adam and felt proud of his accomplishments, now felt personally betrayed. They were disgusted to learn what he had done to the boys. Before the disclosures, people all around us were astonished that Adam had only been in America for a few short years, and was already mastering the English language. He was so polite and respectful to everyone. Friends later said, they would have easily let Adam baby-sit their own children and would have never suspected anything.

Each person innocently trusted and believed they knew who Adam was. We all became bombarded with disturbing images and questions of how and why this could have happened. Several close friends stated they were so traumatized by the thought of the abuse Joey and David had suffered—they found it difficult to have sexual relations with their partner for a few days. They had connected their own sexual relationship with the image of the sexual abuse Joey had suffered. Others stated they just could not stop thinking about the whole situation and felt mentally and physically drained. Many were angry and most felt stricken with sadness and despair.

Friends and family members explained their reactions as shock, disbelief, and total devastation. Each of them had to now begin the process of examining their own trauma. Usually the first concern was if Adam had perpetrated against the boys or any other children in their own home. Then the concern shifted to worrying about their children and if they had been victimized by Adam. Since sexual abuse is not a subject people know that much about, a common reaction was, where did this come from? Is it a biological thing passed down through generations? Will Joey and David be perpetrators since they are siblings of a perpetrator?

People felt sorry for Bob and I that we had to deal with such a tragic situation. They especially felt sad for Bob and how torn he must feel. They were sad and angered by the terror the boys had experienced. Upon learning that Adam himself had been a victim, some felt sorry for him, thinking he probably acted out what happened to him as a child. They also wondered why Joey and David never told anyone earlier. They did not understand that the boys' behavior was telling everyone that they were not safe—but no one knew the signs. We all could not comprehend the terror tactics Adam had so meticulously structured within Joey and David's minds.

Friends and family became confused and nervous of how they should talk to Joey and David. Should they act as if nothing happened and, hopefully, everything would go back to normal? Should they purposely bring it up to discuss what had happened? Should they tell the boys that they knew what happened, or do they wait until Joey and David start the conversation?

Knowing how to act regarding such an awful situation is impossible. We are not taught how to respond to the perpetrator and most importantly—how to respond to the survivor and the survivor's family. The most common sentiment expressed by the adults who were close to our family, was that they were shocked they did not experience a sense or feeling—telling them something was wrong. They wondered why they didn't see a sign, feel something, or know something was unbalanced. They wondered how Adam had fooled everyone into thinking he was a wonderful person. Why were they unable to see who Adam really was? Why were they not able to see that Joey and David were suffering? All of the adults around us now did the same thing my husband and I did as parents—retrace through the past, to desperately find any sign, any indication that something was wrong. As they found the clues, they began to blame themselves. They felt guilty they didn't know something was wrong earlier, and they didn't intervene. They blamed themselves that their intuition never kicked in to alert them or warn them. They blamed themselves that they did not protect Joey and David.

As a mother, my reaction was very intense. As soon as we learned what happened to the boys, I was devastated. I was filled with shock and disbelief for the first few days. I could not sleep for about three days. I would catch a few minutes of rest and then jolt awake in fear and grief. I saw persistent images of the sexual abuse as if I was now the victim. Reliving my sons' trauma, I began to see penises as evil. In my mind it was a penis that caused all of this pain. For me, the idea of sex became more like rape. I could not even think of sex as something enjoyable. It was a disgusting, vile act where someone took power and control over another human being. I shared my feelings with my husband, who luckily was very sympathetic and understanding.

After three days of mental hell, I analyzed how I felt and the only words to explain it were "road kill". That is what I had become. I had no bones left to support my structure and no flesh intact. My mind and spirit had been shredded. I did not know how I could continue in life. One of those first nights, I drove on the highway and screamed to God. "Why, why, why! Not my Joey! Not David! Not Adam! What about my poor Joey and David? God, why did this happen? Why? Why!" I remember demanding God to give me an explanation. I told Him that I would not be able to make it through this, unless He gave me insight and understanding. If I could not go back in the past and stop this from happening, then God had to help me understand why it happened. I had to know how it happened and why Joey and David had to endure this. I had to know why God would allow such horrible things in our family.

In the beginning, I blamed myself—as I cried for weeks. I kept thinking I should have known something was wrong. I should have seen a sign that would alert me to the fact that my children were not safe. I believed it was my fault for bringing Adam to America—for letting the boys spend any time together, and for letting Joey and David out of my sight for 30 seconds. I thought of all the times the boys used to go upstairs to play or watch a movie. I thought of all the opportunities Adam had taken to feed terror into my children's minds—tales of monsters, killer bees, Chuckie, vampires, and rabid cats. I was Joey's and David's mother and I should have known something was wrong. I should have been able to protect them. I was not able to keep my children safe. In my mind, I had failed as a parent.

I felt angry for many things. Why had I sponsored Adam to help him come to America? I was angry about all the time I had dedicated to him, making sure he learned English, did well in school, and adjusted to life in America. I thought of all the support, guidance, and opportunities our family, friends, and his teachers had given him since he came to this country. He had everything he could have ever dreamed of. He went places many American born children do not get to see. He had so many people around him who cared about him and were proud of him. We all had such high hopes for him—and he betrayed us all.

I felt guilty that I had helped Adam fit into society. I taught him how to sit properly at the table when eating food. I taught him how to say "please" and "thank you." I taught him to hold the door open for people and to assist others whenever possible. He was able to trick his family, friends and everyone around him. Now he had learned how to blend into society and be viewed as a respectful, considerate young man. He would now be able to trick anyone who did not know his history. He would be able to create many more victims. I had helped him to disguise who he was. I believed it would be my fault if he harmed anyone else. If I had never taught him personal hygiene, manners, and how to act respectfully— other people would see him as the strange child he was when he came to us. People would have known to stay away from him. But, now it was too late. He had already become a chameleon that could use his camouflage to get close to other people, and ultimately hurt them as he did our family. I was afraid he would eventually commit worse crimes than those he had perpetrated against my children.

Adam had stolen both of my children's childhoods and innocence. Joey now knew of things no child should ever know of, or endure. The amount of abuse he and David had suffered was just starting to unfold and it was terrifying. David had been helpless and witnessed Adam using fear and force to terrorize his brother. Joey had experienced mind and body torture. He had been drowning in a world of fear and terror with no way out.

I was angry that Adam purposefully put himself between my sons and me—using himself as a barrier. I used to complain to family members and friends that Adam constantly talked my ear off every day. He literally followed me from room to room throughout the whole house. The only time he would leave me alone was when I would escape and lock myself in the bathroom. But he was usually standing right outside the door—waiting for me. On a daily basis, I had to ask him to stop talking for a while to give my ears a rest. I knew Adam was too demanding on my attention and manipulated every situation so he could be the center of focus. I used to explain to him that it was poor manners to talk so incessantly and to demand that everyone listen to every word he said. His stories or ideas usually did not make sense—yet he expected everyone to listen intently to every detail.

Adam rambled incessantly, just to hear himself talk. He could speak about a kid at school who did something wrong, and immediately switch to explaining how small his sneakers were becoming. His maternal grandmother had the same problem. She talked people to death. In Cape Verde, people would see her coming and purposely go the other way to avoid any contact with her. People who were around Adam, stated they noticed the same thing. He was extremely needy and could not stop talking. We all believed he just liked to talk a lot. And we tried to understand that he probably did not get much nurturance and positive reinforcement as a child. We tried to understand that maybe Adam was trying to make up for years of neglect.

The reality for family and friends was to now realize that Adam purposely barraged everyone with his words—so no one could suspect or see what he was doing in secret. Through his incessant talking, he confused people. By bombarding everyone with words, he made them less attentive to the details in their surroundings. By confusing people's senses he was able to walk into people's homes, steal valuable objects, and act as if nothing had happened. Of course, no one suspected him—they blamed themselves for losing their valuables. Everyone thought Adam was a wonderful, young, polite, respectful and curious child who was fascinated with learning about new things.

I felt total anger to now see how Adam had purposely confused everyone around him. He had built a cement wall between all adults and Joey and David. People couldn't see Joey and David through the thick wall of incessant talking built by Adam. The attention that would have gone to the boys was shifted to Adam's incomplete sentences and fragmented stories. Adam craftily told each tale with dramatic energy as if it was an emergency—begging for our attention. He was out of breath each time he spoke and often stuttered because he was so "excited" to get the words out. Everything about Adam was a lie.

As I thought about all of the opportunities Adam had to terrorize my children in our home, others worried if the abuse had happened in their homes. The boys had slept at my parents' house many times. Now my parents were disturbed by the idea that Adam possibly violated Joey and David in their own home. The memories of hearing the boys whispering late at night in their house—now became distressing images of Adam mentally and physically terrorizing the boys.

As a parent, realizing your child has committed such heinous acts—is inconceivable. I was lucky Adam was my stepson because eventually I was able to recognize that I stopped being his mother the day he decided to terrify and rape my children. It took me several months before I had this clarity.

When Adam was taken out of the home, I did not immediately stop being his mother. I packed up his clothes and took special care folding each article neatly. I felt obligated to worry about him, especially since we learned that he was also a victim of sexual abuse when he was younger. I felt sorry for him that he was so lost. From all of the incidents leading up to that point, and witnessing his emotional coldness, I knew he would never be able to see how his actions affected all of us.

The next day after Adam was taken out of the home, we had to go to court. They escorted him into the room with handcuffs on his wrists. He looked confused and bewildered. After the court session, he asked us in the hallway, "Am I coming home tonight?" Bob had to explain to him that he was never coming home and that he would be in a locked facility until he was a man.

Two months later, my anger started to build. We had to go to court for Adam's pre-trial, which had been rescheduled several times. In the hallway, my eyes scanned for the Chief of Police, or the Patrolman or the Caseworker. I suddenly saw Adam—and for a moment my heart was happy to see him. At the same time, his face was happy to see me too. This was my son for almost four years, and I had not seen him in a long time. Then suddenly my brain remembered why we were actually there, and I was overcome with feelings of anger and pain. I withdrew into myself and stepped far away from him.

Court was cancelled for that day, so Bob and I headed home. As we drove, I could not stop crying. I realized the bizarre situation I was in. I had finally accepted Adam as my son—only to have him ripped away from me. I had raised, nurtured, supported and loved him. I was proud of him. But, he could no longer be my child. The child I thought I knew had disappeared. I sobbed uncontrollably and the tears streamed down my face. As I cried out in pain, I reminded myself that I did not make him into the monster I now knew him to be. I still cared for him, but in reality he was a dangerous stranger.

I had been raising Adam for three and a half years, yet I did not know who he truly was and what he was capable of. The emotions I felt were somewhat similar to mourning the death of one of my children. The Adam I had imagined I knew, was gone. All of the dreams I had for his future of doing well in school, going to college, eventually obtaining employment, getting married, and starting a family of his own—had now vanished. I used to imagine the future with Adam bringing his family to our home for holidays, and watching his children grow. Everything came to an abrupt end. Adam could never be a part of our lives again. My children would never have to face their abuser as long as I was able to protect them. All connection to Adam had to end for us to feel safe.

Around this time, the anger and desperation were overwhelming. I found myself constantly wishing the whole situation was not real. On a daily basis, I had to face the harsh reality and admit to myself that this did actually happen. This was not a bad dream that I could somehow snap out of, and it would be all over. This was our reality. My instincts were to overprotect my children and smother them. I constantly reflected on the trauma they had experienced. I wanted to be with them every second and protect them from everyone. But I knew I had to deal with my own trauma and allow my children to still be kids. I could not hand them my own monsters of fear and anger. I had to hold back my adult emotions of being so serious with everything, and allow them to be children again. Joey and David needed to play, laugh and have fun. They were relieved Adam was no longer in the home. They were finally able to live free from any fear.

During that time, Bob and I were lucky to have Danene and her husband Brian in our lives. They knew our kids very well since Danene watched them everyday. Well before we knew who Adam really was, Danene had made her house into a second home for my children while Bob and I worked. Upon hearing about the sexual abuse, Danene was devastated. There were many times we sat and cried together—trying to process what Joey and David had been through. She was a true friend throughout our family's ordeal. She patiently listened to every detail as the story unfolded regarding court, social service, medical and mental health situations. She was always there supporting me emotionally. She never hinted to the boys how much she knew and tried to make things as normal as possible. She made them feel safe, respected and valued—and helped Joey and David re-gain their childhoods. I know her entering into our lives was a definite gift from God.

As the months continued and the boys experienced peace in their lives, complete fear began to take hold of me. Suddenly I realized, my children were "victims" and could potentially carry out that role throughout their lives. The fear of other children hearing about the abuse and then teasing them became a true possibility. I was paralyzed with terror that other perpetrators would see my children's broken boundaries, and now be able to commit more crimes against them. I was terrified that now my children could potentially become perpetrators. My children had been force-fed a firsthand education on sexual abuse. They learned the art of manipulating, hurting, and torturing another human being. What if they decided to give that education to another person?

I found myself re-traumatized constantly during the first few months. Initially, Joey was copying the same behaviors and mannerisms that Adam exhibited. He suddenly liked the same foods, music, and clothes that Adam liked. He started the same conversations and said the same jokes. I was frightened and could not understand why he was copying someone who had violated him so horribly. When Joey was copying these behaviors, I got the sense from him that he was seeking my approval. He would proudly say, "Mom! Look what I can do." Several times I sat him down and talked to him. I said, "Adam was a bad boy. I don't want you to act like Adam and copy him. You are a wonderful person and I love you for you. You are Joey and that is who I want you to act like. You are your own person and you don't have to act like anyone else. Be yourself." After several months and constant reassurance, Joey stopped copying Adam's behaviors and started to form his own ideas and thought processes.

The quality of my children's future became a constant source of apprehension. I worried if the sexual abuse would affect their sexual orientation. Would they ever be able to maintain a healthy intimate relationship with another person? Would their boundaries be destroyed forever? Would they self-medicate with drugs and alcohol to deal with the memories? Would they take any internal anger out against our family and friends? The questions seemed endless with no answers.

I was lucky to have my parents and many close friends whom I was able to speak with in a very candid and open manner. The many conversations were what helped me to analyze, process, and eventually understand how such trauma happened to my children. Through openness and sincerity, we were able to discuss a painful situation, and help each other process our emotions together. I knew I was extremely lucky to find such a huge source of support through many kind and compassionate people.

As many families experience, we did have some friends and family members who were too uncomfortable with our ordeal to offer their support. They had no words of encouragement, since they themselves had no idea how to cope with such trauma. They could not lend a supportive ear, since specific details made them feel too uncomfortable.

When I spoke with other parents in similar situations, most were not lucky to find a strong support system like I had found. Often times, extended family and friends were in such denial—they sided with the perpetrator, and turned against the survivor and his/her family. It is too disturbing for most people to truly face sexual abuse for what it really is. Sexual abuse is a crime where a dominant person takes total control over a more vulnerable person through force, manipulation or fear. When I spoke with other families, I found that many people around them minimized the effects the sexual abuse had on the survivor saying things like, "Well, it is over. You don't have to think about it now." These people discussed the situation in a superficial and removed manner, which left the survivor and/or the survivor's family feeling more isolated and hopeless.

I have talked to a few families where the sexual abuse ripped apart the entire family. With the support going to the perpetrator and his/her immediate family, the survivor and his/her family were left re-traumatized. Not only did they have to face the actual sexual abuse crimes committed against their children or child, now they also had to face losing most of their family members and friends. The people who should have served as support and strength to them suddenly became constant sources of blame, mistrust, isolation and despair.

When a child has been sexually abused, the child and the parents need the support of family and friends. They can be a valuable source of strength and support for a family during such a difficult time. I believe the best thing people can do to be supportive of the individual survivor and the entire family, is to talk, listen and be mentally present. They should not encourage the family to forget about it—as if the incident will miraculously disappear. They should help the family face the sexual abuse boldly and not be afraid to hear and discuss the details.

Support a child who has been sexually abused by the following steps: 1) Tell the child you know what happened to him/her and explain that you are happy he/she was brave and told someone. 2) Tell the child you are upset that the abuse happened and it should have never taken place. 3) Tell the child it is not his/her fault and it will never be his/her fault. The perpetrator is always the person who should be blamed. The perpetrator knew what he or she was doing and it was wrong. 4) Tell the child you are always available to him/her if he/she ever wants to discuss any emotions, feelings or memories.

Support the family members of a child who has been sexually abused by the following steps: 1) Tell the parents/guardians/caretaker that you are there for them—and then truly be there. When they need to discuss things they are remembering, be that quiet sympathetic ear that listens. 2) Tell the traumatized family members and friends that they are not at fault. The perpetrator always needs to carry the blame. Sexual abuse is something we are not educated about. It is natural that we can't see and understand any signs that sexual abuse may be occurring. 3) If the family member is ready to hear it, give any input you can—to aid the parent in retracing when this could have started and how long it lasted. 4) Support the parent in the emotional roller coaster he/she will be going on. Realize the high times and the low times are all valuable to his/her processing the trauma. 5) Your openness, honesty and sincerity are crucial to the parent since you may be their sole support. 6) Most importantly, never say things that could potentially be construed as blaming the parents/guardians/caretakers.

My husband's mechanisms for coping, were very different from mine. I spoke to several friends and family members and tried to process the trauma from beginning to end. My husband spoke to one or two friends and a few select family members. He discussed the situation minimally with me, stating, "I don't talk about things that upset me." For him, it was more difficult since he felt advocating for Joey and David was choosing sides over another child. For him, it was better not discussing the situation at all. He knew Adam was dangerous and had to be removed from our lives. We had already discussed our fear of Adam burning down the house while we slept, or sneaking back in the home to harm us. Yet his love for his children kept him confused and angry. He ideally wanted his entire family together.

Talking about emotions and expressing feelings was not part of Bob's culture. He had learned not to discuss personal pain and emotions. Since most people in Cape Verde did not have jobs or television to occupy their time, gossip and talking negatively about others, was the only source of entertainment. Anyone who had pride and a respect for their own private life, quickly learned to never share personal feelings. This was the only way to make sure your personal life did not become public gossip.

Bob was raised to be a man that didn't cry, so he bottled up all his emotions inside. He barely shared his feelings with anyone. As the weeks passed, Bob withdrew into isolation. He gave quick one-word answers and hardly made any eye contact. Occasionally he would say a few sentences about how he felt, but it was obvious he was quickly sliding into a major depression. I saw his emotional state deteriorating as he became more and more despondent. He didn't want to discuss anything. The only thing he was interested in discussing, was his need for a truck. He was driving an old Chevy that kept breaking down every time he went out. We knew eventually we had to buy a new vehicle. So one day we decided to tour all the local dealers until we found a good deal. When the salesman and Bob came bounding out of a snow bank with a huge four by four, it was the first time I saw Bob smile in months. We decided to buy it, and Bob's expression took new life. Now he had something else to think about. He spent all of his energy thinking about new things for the truck or finding new gadgets inside. Every week he would vacuum the inside, wash the outside, buy accessories, and plan what else the truck needed. By having something to pour all of his concentration into—he didn't have to spend as much time thinking about all of his personal pain.

After several months, Bob was finally able to discuss his first reactions upon hearing what had happened to the boys. He explained that for a man, the first thing you want to do is attack the person who hurt your child. However in our situation, he could not attack Adam since this was also his child. He felt angry, confused, and upset and did not know how to process his emotions. He felt totally responsible since Adam was his son. He blamed himself for having Adam at such a young age. He blamed himself for leaving Cape Verde and having such a horrible family raise his child. I reminded him several times that Adam's mother's family did not want to claim Bob as the father, since they wanted to search out a father with more money. I reminded him of the times we told his parents in Cape Verde to get Adam and raise him, since we did not want him living with his mother's family. I assured him that he was not to blame. We had done the best we could and brought Adam into our family with the best intentions.

Bob eventually admitted to me that all he really wanted to do when everything first happened was escape. He just wanted to take off and forget about everything. But, he was hit with the constant realization that Joey and David now needed him more than ever. Escaping would only make him an absent father and leave the boys more traumatized than before. At that realization, he then committed himself to being the strongest support he possibly could be for his children. He knew Adam was probably beyond help, but insisted on visiting him monthly. Bob also made sure he was supportive of Joey and David, giving them the best chance for survival from the horror they had experienced.

As time went on and the initial shock wore off, Bob felt torn between two different worlds. He had his family, Joey, David, Paul and me, that he loved and wanted to be with—and he had his son Adam, that he wanted to support to hopefully turn his life around. When we shared any quality family time, Bob enjoyed the time together, but then instantly became saddened because he would think of Adam and realize—part of the family was missing. Adam was Bob's biological child and he could not fake or forget that tie to his child.

In the beginning I felt torn just like Bob. Adam never had any respect for his biological mother. I was the only "mother" he ever had. I struggled in the beginning to accept him, but eventually believed Adam was my child. After knowing everything that happened, I wanted to support Adam—who obviously had extreme emotional and mental issues. But being torn between two worlds became too confusing and upsetting for me. I finally decided that I was only a mother to my own biological children.

Chapter 4
Instincts and Dreams

As I reflected on past events leading to my sons' ordeal, I realized instincts and dreams were being sent to me for many years as gifts. At the time, I could not understand the messages. I was being warned and did not realize other Forces were trying to protect us. I have since learned that God, our Angels, Spirit Guides, and Loves Ones who have passed on communicate with us through visions, feelings, thoughts, whispers and emotions. For years I ignored that small inner voice that would say things like, "Don't put that there because it will fall". Then when the object fell, I was too stubborn to acknowledge that someone was warning me and trying to help me. Throughout the years of having Adam in our home, and even before he entered into our lives, I was receiving messages. Other forces were actively trying to help me protect my children, but I ignored them completely.

I have learned that the small inner voice we hear is one way our Guides work with us. If we listen and respect those messages we receive, we can gain great insight and wisdom. Feelings and emotions are other means our Guides use to communicate with us. When we pay attention to our feelings, we are utilizing the tools God has given us. Sometimes when we do not pay attention, our Guides will give us huge experiences or gut level feelings that we cannot ignore.

I believe feelings of discomfort with no explanation are usually warnings, serving to keep us safe and protect us from harm. A painful or really upset stomach for no apparent reason can also signify something is wrong. In hindsight, if I had paid closer attention to my children's fears, my own instincts, and the many dreams I had throughout the years—my children would not have had to endure as much as they have. If I trusted my feelings and emotions, instead of doubting and mentally turning against myself, I would have seen that spiritual forces were actively warning and protecting us.

In our culture, we are not taught to trust our sixth sense. We are not taught to look behind the scenes and look for clues, trust our senses and suspect the unthinkable from people we love. We do not question or analyze family members and friends that we care about. We are taught to trust people at face value and accept the image they portray.

The thought of a child being sexually abused is probably one of the top fears of all parents. It is similar to the fear of having your child kidnapped or murdered. It is a fear all parents have—yet we do not discuss it openly. Since we don't discuss it, we cannot be taught how to prevent it from becoming a reality in our families. Consequently, the general public does not get accurate information about perpetrators and survivors, how to protect children, and the crime is allowed to continue.

Sexual abuse is something so evil—most people cannot believe there are individuals that operate on such a low level. We are not taught that predators like that exist in every area of our lives. I found that my previous thinking was always "those" perpetrators or "those families". There was a huge gap between them and my family. I would have never believed that my stepson was a predator. I could not have imagined that my children would one day be sexually abused.

I see each day how our society finds comfort in denying sexual abuse. We don't acknowledge that perpetrators are everywhere and we blame victims for the perpetrators' crimes. We run away from the families where sexual abuse has happened—to avoid any conversations and keep our family safe from "those people". I believe an adult who has been forced to face the issue of sexual abuse, either through personal pain or vicariously through family or friends—has a moral responsibility. The responsibility is to educate other parents and help them to see sexual abuse as a huge risk for all children. We need to help prepare all families for the unthinkable, and give them every tool possible for keeping their children safe.

In hindsight, I can see that I had instincts and dreams warning me about Adam from the beginning. I questioned everything about him because something just did not feel right. I knew there was something seriously wrong with him, but I could not put my finger on it. I believed he was slightly slow or mentally challenged. At one point I thought he might be Autistic since he was fascinated by repetitious noises from toys or other objects. Bob and I confided in each other that we both were witnessing the same things. We joked on the flight home to America from Cape Verde, that Bob should stay awake the entire flight. He had envisioned all of us sleeping, and suddenly Adam's head appearing in the pilot's cockpit. The pilots would not notice the small boy who had sneaked in. Like a comical movie, we envisioned his fingers slowly reaching over the chairs to then start clicking every button possible.

Once home in America, I could see that Adam had learning disabilities. I often taught him something each day, and by the next day, he would totally forget what he had mastered the previous afternoon. I asked several family members, friends, and professionals about Adam's behavior. All of his behaviors were easily explained as "pre-pubescent" and "normal for his age".

As Adam became accustomed to American life, I experienced increasing mental confusion and felt I was in a continual dilemma. I knew at a gut level that there was something wrong with Adam. But I was willing to take any explanation that normalized his peculiar behavior and mannerisms. I purposely ignored my instincts—because by doing so, I could quiet the uncomfortable thoughts I was experiencing. I could comfortably live in denial. By quieting the feelings that there was something wrong with Adam, I did not have to live with my constant internal conflict—knowing there was something wrong with Adam, but trying to accept him as my son.

As the uncomfortable instincts and feelings persisted, I turned against myself. I took all warnings, which were given to me to protect my children, and reinterpreted them into negative self-talk. For each negative instinct I had about Adam, I wiped the thought out and replaced it with, "I'm a terrible mother. God made a huge mistake giving me this child to raise. I'm not capable of being a good mother to him." I drowned my instincts about Adam in a sea of personal mental damnation and psychological self-torture.

During the clouded years of Adam living with us, I forgot about two dreams I had several years before I ever met my husband, Bob. In one dream, *my baby boy is sound asleep on one of the beds in my parents' house. No one is paying attention to the baby and where he is sleeping. As people visit during the afternoon, everyone blindly piles their coats on top of the bed where he is sleeping—leaving the baby under a suffocating heavy pile. When I recognize I don't have the baby with me, I race into the bedroom to find him. I'm horrified to see a mountain of clothes on top of him. Desperately, I comb through the coats and jackets to find my poor forgotten baby. I blame myself—"what a horrible mother I am for not paying closer attention. I did not protect him. I could have lost my child."*

A few weeks later I had another dream in which, *I have a young boy, who is sitting on the couch. I'm confused whether the boy is really mine or not. Part of me knows he is my son, but the other part of me knows he really is not my child. I stare at the boy and before my eyes he begins to turn into a teenager. As his metamorphosis completes, he looks at me and starts saying sexual things to me. I am so upset at his behavior—I slap his face and yell at him. "I am your mother! You cannot talk to me like that!" He begins to wail like a toddler in pain. Even though he has the body frame of a young man, I suddenly understand—he is still a small child. I feel horrible and apologize for hitting him. I explain that he has to treat me with respect. I state that people don't talk to each other that way. Then the dream suddenly ends.*

Many years later, I met Bob. After one year together, we decided to get married. I became pregnant immediately and went into shock. I had not planned on getting pregnant so quickly. I was very nervous about the whole process. I didn't feel I had enough time to prepare. I thought, "I don't think I'm ready to be a mom. I need more time." But, everywhere I went, I was bombarded with the reminder that in a few months I was really going to be a mom. Everywhere I went, I saw a pregnant woman in front of me. If I went into a public restroom, there was always a pregnant woman leaving the stall I was entering. If I went down an aisle in a store, there was always a pregnant mom facing me. Bob laughed hysterically at me because he could see that I was very nervous and didn't feel ready. He was entertained by how anxious I was.

He knew I was going to be a great mom, and he felt very comfortable being a father, so my anxiety was entertainment for him.

During the first few months of pregnancy, I had extreme emotions and serious thoughts. One day I stood in the baby's future bedroom and sensed I was carrying a petite daughter. As I thought about this vulnerable child, I was suddenly crippled with fear that she was going to be raped. I was panicked and became determined that I would do everything possible to protect her once she was born.

When the baby was being born, everyone was shocked at how big the head was. Since the shoulders were too wide, the baby became stuck. As the baby's head turned a deep purple color, the mid-wife screamed for help. Four people instantly ran in, pushing Bob and my mother out of the way. They climbed on top of me and with full force pushed down on my stomach. Finally a limp, lifeless purple body came out and was instantly raced out of the room. As we stood motionless, stunned and speechless, the silence enveloped the room. We then waited for what seemed to be an eternity. Miraculously, after several minutes, we heard the baby scream. The medical staff quickly showed Joey to me and then rushed him off to the intensive care portion of the pediatric area.

To our surprise, Joey was a gigantic baby boy, who was born the size of a three month old. He was above every height and weight chart and fit into clothes meant for children twice his age. I had believed I was going to have a small vulnerable daughter, and now gave birth to a huge strong son. Yet I still had that persistent feeling that I needed to educate him about people who may try to harm him. I continued to have an overwhelming fear that someone was going to steal him or rape him.

As soon as Joey was able to speak and understand words, I taught him his name, his parents' names, where he lived, and eventually added in our home phone number. From very early on, I spoke to him about his body. I explained that there were specific circumstances such as medical reasons or for hygiene that people might have to touch him or see his private areas. He knew Mom, Dad, Grandma, Grandpa, and Tee Tee Linda, a close friend who was like a second mom to me—were the only people allowed to help him in the bathroom. He knew the appropriate words for all of his body parts, and he knew no one should touch those areas.

I also taught him tricks a stranger might use to lure him away from his family, so he could be taken. He knew no adult should ever ask him for help to find a puppy or find a bike. He understood that adults would only ask other adults for help—not kids. We discussed if anyone ever touched him in his private areas and told him, "If you tell anyone I'll hurt you", or "I'll kill you" or "I'll kill your mother." He knew he should immediately tell Bob and I, and we would make sure he would be kept safe. I explained how "bad people" will scare kids so they don't tell anyone when something bad is happening.

All of that preparation seemed to be enough. I felt that Joey knew no one should ever touch him in his private areas and no one would be able to trick him into submission. I also believed if anyone ever did touch him or threaten him, that he would come to Bob and me immediately. However, through all the preparation, I did not teach Joey how to protect himself from his own fears. I did not know that a perpetrator had the ability to study a person to see what were his/her most fundamental fears. I did not know that a perpetrator would take those fears and craftily make them larger than life to then use against the child—forcing him/her into total submission and silence.

From a very early age, Joey had a strong sense of instinct and intuition. He was extremely perceptive, and could always sense if something was wrong. One night when he was about four months old, he was sound asleep in his bedroom. Bob and I had a small argument, but made sure not to raise our voices to wake the baby. Suddenly, Joey awoke startled and screaming. I believe he could feel the tension in the home.

The day Joey turned five-months-old, he got his first tooth and spoke his first word. He looked right at me from across the room and yelled, "Mom!" By the age of two, he was speaking in complete sentences. From when he was young, he had amazing verbal skills, with no problem expressing himself or his emotions. His intuitive senses were advanced too.

One day while I was driving, I thought to myself, "We have way too many peanut butter jars in the house! What am I going to do with all that peanut butter?" I thought about giving some jars to my parents and suddenly I thought, "I could just make peanut butter cookies." At the time, Joey was about two-years-old. He was sitting in the seat behind me and out of the clear blue stated, "Mom, I don't like peanut butter cookies". I asked him why he was thinking about peanut butter cookies—had I said anything out loud. He said he didn't know where the thought came from, and I had not said anything while I was driving. All he knew was he did not like peanut butter cookies. There were several instances when he was young that it seemed he could read our thoughts.

Those early years, newly married with Joey as a baby, limited money, and living in various apartments—were difficult times. But, as our family grew, we had many times of peace and happiness. Joey was a wonderful child and Bob and I thoroughly enjoyed him. We were proud to be his parents.

Once Adam came into our lives, the peace Bob and I experienced as parents was destroyed. As soon as we brought Adam home, the mental discomfort began. I suffered with my "distant" and guilt feelings of not wanting to be close to Adam—with no justification for those feelings, until one particular incident. One evening, when I sat on the floor so Joey and Adam could sit behind me and "braid" my hair, my feelings were justified. Each boy took half of my hair and pretended they knew how to braid. As they were working intensely, I suddenly felt that Adam was coming closer to me. I got an intense feeling that he was going to reach from behind, move his hand over my shoulder and put it down my shirt to grab my breasts. I was so distressed by this thought—I quickly jumped to my feet saying the braiding session had finished. Later, I tortured myself for having the feeling. I was disgusted with myself that I could think such a horrible thought about a child. Why was I thinking such terrible things? But soon, I learned the answer to why I experienced such a disturbing instinct.

Since his maternal grandmother raised Adam from birth, I often wondered how he could come to America and not miss her. According to him, he loved her and felt very close to her. Yet months after coming to America, Adam still never showed any signs of sadness at leaving her or his grandfather. They had raised him from birth—up until we brought him to America as a nine-year-old boy. I often asked him if he missed them and if he was sad to be without them. He would say he missed them a little, and would immediately change his focus to a toy or gadget in the house.

About two days after I had the disturbing instinct, Adam and I went to the local grocery store to pick up some things for dinner. We discussed his maternal grandparents and Adam explained how much his grandmother loved him. He stated that the family was too poor to have toys in the house, so for entertainment, "Every night, me and my brother used to compete for my grandmother's breast. Whoever won, got to suck on it all night. It was kind of like a toy. She really loved us." Adam explained that he would just walk over to his grandmother, reach into her blouse and pull out one of her breasts. The nightly competition between the two boys consisted of them running to the grandmother—whoever reached her and pulled out one of her breast first won the race. Adam explained how the grandmother was very happy to allow them this "treat."

I was horrified, and immediately told Adam that his grandmother was wrong for allowing and encouraging that type of behavior. I explained that in America, she would be put in jail for abusing children. I strongly stated that what she did was wrong, and that type of activity was only for a man and woman or for a mother providing breast milk to a nursing baby. I explained to Adam that behavior like that should never happen between an old woman and a young boy. But he was adamant and argued with me saying, "No, it was love! There was nothing wrong with it!" I then asked him, "Adam, if there was nothing wrong with it, then your grandmother who never stopped talking must have bragged to everyone in the neighborhood about how she would let her nine-year-old grandson suck on her breasts. Did she brag to the neighbors?" He hesitated in confusion and then answered, "No." I tried to rationalize with him. I explained to him that if this truly was something wonderful and something to be proud of—then his grandmother, who talked non-stop, would have told everyone. I explained, she would have bragged to neighbors about it. I said, "Since she never told anyone, she knew what she was doing was wrong. She kept it a secret because she knew that type of behavior was unacceptable and should never happen between an adult and a child."

As I continued to explain what sexual abuse was, I could see he did not understand. He truly believed that his grandmother had shown him love. He was so adamant that there was nothing wrong with what his grandmother did—that I became confused, thinking maybe there was a cultural tradition in Cape Verde that I did not understand. Maybe it was common practice for grandmothers to offer their breasts as toys. I immediately asked Bob who was extremely aggravated with my questions and said, "I don't know. The family was innocent." He was angry and did not want to discuss it any further. I then asked a friend of ours who is Cape Verdean. She was horrified and immediately said, "No Claire, that should not happen—what the grandmother did is child sexual abuse."_

In hindsight, I now realize I should have found a counselor for Adam immediately. But, at the time, he could only speak Cape Verdean Creole. Finding a therapist for Joey after the abuse was extremely difficult. To find a sexual abuse specialist who spoke Cape Verdean Creole for Adam—would have been impossible.

After hearing what Adam's grandmother allowed and encouraged in her home, I finally understood why I had feelings of Adam's personal boundaries being broken. Now I knew why I was so uncomfortable with the idea of hugging him or being too close to him. His grandmother had destroyed Adam's personal boundaries. She had perpetrated against him and he was left confused and still seeking that "love." Now I knew my instincts were correct the day when I jumped up from the boys who were "braiding" my hair. Adam was trying to grab my breasts. His intention was to replicate the relationship that he had with his grandmother, and experience the same "love" with me.

Shortly after Adam disclosed his grandmother's abuse, we had an incident happen in our home. I was talking with Adam one day, and when I started to walk past him into another room, he grabbed me. He purposely grabbed one of my breasts as I passed by. I was very upset and firmly explained to him that he is never to touch anyone's personal areas on their body. I explained what the private body parts were and said, "Each person has their physical space that no one can enter. You cannot touch someone's private body parts. It is violating another person's body is very wrong. Also, no one should ever make you touch their private areas." When I asked if he understood what I was saying, he said he understood.

I then recalled the dream I had seven years prior to our family trag-edy, and understood the warning I had received. The dream that I had of a boy on a couch who suddenly became a teenager—was a warning about Adam. In the dream, the teenager began to talk about sexual relations between him and me. When I slapped him in the dream and he cried, I realized he was only a child. The child in that dream was Adam at nine-years-old. The child in the dream said inappropriate sexual things to me just as Adam was now showing inappropriate sexual behavior toward me.

Several times I spoke with Adam about the situation with his grand-mother. On numerous occasions, I explained about people's personal body space and privacy. I often felt like a military sergeant demanding proper behavior from this child who had no understanding of what was expected.

At the time, Adam was also inappropriately going into my bedroom and taking anything he wanted. One day I saw him playing with my grandmother's jewelry that she had given to me as an heirloom. I clearly explained to him that he was not allowed in my bedroom, since that was my personal space. Again, I explained to him that people are not allowed to touch other people's belongings or their bodies. After each conversation he said he understood. He did listen to what I had said and stopped going into my bedroom. He also never tried to touch me inappropriately again. For a while, there were no other concerning events, until we moved into our new home.

It was wonderful to leave our small over-crowded apartment, and move into a four bedroom house in August 2000. By then, I had already given birth to my son David, who was born 10 months after we came home from Cape Verde. David was four months old at the time of the move, Joey was three-years-old and Adam was ten-years-old. We were all thrilled to live in a house with so much space and have over an acre of beautiful land. There was plenty of grass for the kids to run and trees for the boys to climb. We had such high hopes for raising our family on the peaceful dead end street.

However, shortly after moving in, something disturbing occurred. It was very hot one day that summer, and I put four-month-old David on my bed upstairs—to take his nap under the cool fan. When we were downstairs, putting the laundry into baskets, I asked Adam to bring one basket upstairs and dump it on my bed. Obviously, I meant for the small load of laundry to be at one end of the queen size bed—away from where the baby was peacefully sleeping. A few seconds later, I got a feeling that I had to check on the baby. I went into the room and to my disbelief, found David under several inches of laundry. His nose was just barely visible through the pile. His entire body was covered. Adam had meticulously covered every inch of David, except his nose—where there was a tiny space for him to breathe. When I yelled at Adam, he had a slight smirk on his face as if it was funny. He then tried to explain to me that he just dumped the laundry and never even saw David on the bed. Adam was ten-years-old at the time. He was too old to be making such a big "mistake."

At the time, I tried to believe that Adam did not see the baby. But I couldn't ignore my gut instinct, which was telling me that Adam did it on purpose. I told Adam he had to pay closer attention to things. Now looking back, I realize how significant the dream I had seven years prior to that day, truly was. In the dream, my baby boy was placed on a bed while taking a nap. People carelessly or purposely threw their jackets on top of him. He could barely breathe under all the coats and I raced in the room in enough time to save him. Now I raced into my bedroom to dig David out from under the mountain of laundry. If I had only made the connection between Adam's actions then and the prophetic dream I had years earlier, maybe I would have realized how dangerous Adam truly was.

Another troubling event happened about ten months later. One afternoon, Bob and I were building a wheel barrel on our porch. David was hungry, so I asked Adam to bring him inside, and give him a yogurt. Adam tried to feed him, but explained that David would not eat it. I went in to find out why he wasn't eating, and when I picked up the container, I realized it was warm. I asked Adam why he was giving a warm yogurt to the baby. He stated, "Oh, I was eating a yogurt earlier, and I didn't like it. So I gave it to David." Upon further questioning, I learned that Adam had tried a yogurt earlier in the morning. He didn't like it, so he placed it on the counter in the direct sunlight. That day was excruciatingly hot so the yogurt instantly soured and spoiled. Hours later, Adam tried feeding the same yogurt to the baby. I was furious and re-explained what we had told Adam several times before. "Food from the refrigerator has to be left in the refrigerator or it turns bad, and if given to someone—it will make the person very sick." I don't know if it was an honest mistake on Adam's part that day, since by then he had been living with refrigerated food for about two years—or if it was an experiment to watch what would happen to the baby.

Soon after the yogurt episode, there was another "accident" that happened. David had just started walking at fifteen-months-old, and was still wobbly. Since walking was a new experience, he easily lost his balance and fell on the floor regularly. One day, Bob asked Adam to vacuum the living room carpet. As I cooked in the kitchen, and Bob organized things upstairs, Adam began vacuuming. The next thing we heard was a blood curdling scream from David. Bob and I ran in to see that Adam had run over David's foot with the vacuum. The beat-a-bar had ripped off the top layer of skin, and caused the area to bleed. When David fell down from the injury to his foot, Adam ran over his hand. Adam then earnestly stated that he ran over David's foot and hand accidentally. He tried to show that he was saddened by what happened to David, but was scolded by Bob for hurting his baby brother.

Then in Christmas 2001, I came home from work one evening to find crushed ornaments all over the living room. Bob was outside shoveling snow and Adam was upstairs in his bedroom. Joey was on the couch holding David tightly, who had a small dot of blood on his bottom lip. Joe quickly explained what happened. "Mom, I was watching TV and all of a sudden, with one eye, I saw David grab a ball off the tree. Then he grabbed another ball and bit it. I knew it was an emergency so I took my one eye off the TV, put both eyes on David and turned off the TV." David had been biting the Christmas balls and shattering them into sharp glass pieces all around the room. Joey explained that Adam had walked through the room, saw what was happening, and left Joey to deal with the crisis. In the middle of the emergency, Adam casually walked upstairs to his bedroom. I raced David to the emergency room and learned that even nurses have made the same mistake of putting breakable ornaments too low on Christmas trees. The doctor said that David was fine after the exam and Bob and I removed all the breakable Christmas balls from the tree.

After the yogurt, vacuum, and Christmas ball incidents, I should have understood that Adam was not a safe person. But as time passed, we were free of additional crazy episodes that were unsafe or threatening. Adam sometimes forgot a chore or needed extra coaching to complete his homework. But overall, there were no areas of concern. Adam was doing well in school and it seemed he was becoming a responsible young man. Joey had started kindergarten, and David had started speaking in half sentences shortly after his two year birthday.

Things seemed to be peaceful for the next few months, but my feelings and instincts that something was wrong started to flood over me again. Ever since Joey was a baby, he used to constantly draw and color. Every picture he drew of the family depicted happy people, full of life. As his artwork flourished and the people were drawn with proper proportions and telling features, I started to notice something strange. In every picture, Joey always drew Adam right next to me. He also always drew himself at the extreme opposite end—the furthest point away from me. It seemed his artwork was telling me something, but I could not understand the message. At the time, he also seemed progressively distant from me, but I thought maybe it was a phase boys go through developmentally.

When Joey was four-years-old, he began asking Bob and me to sign him up for karate. When he first asked for classes, I checked the prices of a few local organizations. I found that the classes were terribly expensive and were only offered for older kids. Joey was very disappointed that we could not register him and continued to ask for classes for the next few years. At that time, Joey was already trying to reach out for help, and find new ways to defend himself.

Throughout the next year, Joey grew older and became more unsociable. I felt sad because I noticed he didn't come to me to talk about things, or cuddle like he did when he was younger. His amazing verbal skills seemed to be lost as he usually sat quietly alone. I noticed his personality and mannerisms had changed drastically. He became extremely isolated—not speaking with Bob and me as he did when he was younger. I remember thinking to myself, "Maybe developmentally these are the years that boys start separating from their mother because they would rather be with other boys or men." I could see that the more Joey became isolated, the needier Adam became.

Adam was needy from the beginning. But, as he grew older, he became unbearably demanding. He expected me to listen and talk to him every minute. Besides needing help with his homework and answering his numerous questions of the day, Adam had many other things he wanted to discuss. From the time he came home from school until it was time to go to bed, Adam continued talking without taking a break. But his questions and conversations were draining. They were not connected and seemed to be a mish mash of any ideas he could throw together. When I asked other mothers if their teenagers were so demanding on their time, they usually said Adam's behavior was totally normal.

Now I can see how Adam was using himself as a shield. He followed me through the house, talking my ear off. Any extra time I had, which should have been reserved for my young children, was gobbled up with incessant questions and complicated stories from Adam. He consciously created a barrier between the boys and me. The boys were forced into solitude and isolation. Joey didn't talk to me much anymore and didn't come near me. David was always desperate to get any attention from me that he could. He needed me to hold him constantly and had limited verbal skills to communicate.

In retrospect, I can now see how Adam intentionally set the scene. He purposely made sure I was not able to give Joey and David the love and quality time they needed to feel safe and close to me. Adam's blockade between me and my children ensured they could never tell me what was happening to them. He made sure I could never truly look at my children to see what was so drastically wrong in their lives. As I spent less time with Joey and David, Adam's control over them grew tighter and tighter and I lost my children more and more. In his artwork, Joey was clearly depicting the separation between himself and me. He was also showing how Adam never left my side. The colorful depictions showed Adam cleverly acting joyous and playful. Our happy family portraits clearly illustrated that Bob and I were blind to who Adam was and how he had taken total control over our family.

About six months before we knew of the crimes Adam had been committing, I had another dream. *Bob and I have been separated for many years. One afternoon as I'm leaving work, I see Bob outside of my office building. His hair has is sticking out all over as small dread locks and his body is emaciated. He has been lost in a world of drug use— living in bushes in the industrial park. But, he believes his life is wonderful.*

As I walk towards him, I notice he appears high on something. I suddenly remember our newborn child whom he took with him when we first separated. Through the years, I never had the chance to know the baby. As I say hello to Bob, he quickly shows me a teenager next to him. Both of them have been living in the streets. I suddenly realize this teenager is my baby I never knew. He is now 13 years old. As I look at him I realize I don't know him at all. I question, "Is this really my child?"

Months after Adam was removed from our home, I remembered this dream. The symbolism is incredible. In the dream I did not know who the teenage boy was. I knew he was supposed to be mine, but questioned if he really was. As I looked at my thirteen-year-old "son" in the dream, I understood that I really did not know him at all. Adam was thirteen years old when we confronted him about all of the stolen objects, and the mental, physical, and sexual abuse he committed against Joey and David. As the dream told me, I did not know who Adam was and what he was capable of.

As I remembered different things from the past, I realized I had other uncomfortable instincts that I could not explain. When we first moved into the house, we had originally intended for Joey and David to share a bedroom. Adam was older, so he was going to have his own bedroom. But during the second winter that we were in the house, there was no heat in Joey and David's bedroom. We decided to have David stay in our room, and Joey share Adam's room. One evening, when we were all upstairs, Bob and I told Adam and Joey to go to bed. Adam started walking towards his bedroom and instantly Joey followed behind him. As I watched Joey obediently following, I was struck with a strong instinct that he seemed to be too submissive—almost like a slave. I said to Bob, "Do you think it is a good idea for them to share a room? Adam is so much older than Joey." Bob then explained how most families have kids of the same gender sharing rooms—since there is not enough space for each person to have his/her own room. He assured me that Joey was fine.

The whole time while Adam was secretly torturing Joey and David, he was able to portray himself as a polite, courteous young man. I did not know what he was doing in secret. I could see the image he portrayed to everyone. However, my body was trying to tell me that my family and I were sinking. For the last six months that Adam was in our home, my body was falling apart. In October 2002, I became very sick. The strep throat became bronchitis, which then turned into walking pneumonia. Eventually I was diagnosed with Mono in December 2002. Since I have always been a relatively healthy person, I could not understand how I could be so sick. With all of the breathing problems I was having, Milady's, our family friend and Joey's godmother, finally stated, "Pneumonia is liquid in your lungs. Claire, You have to ask yourself, what are you drowning from?"

That question was something I pondered over and over again with no answer. I felt uncomfortable in my own home and could not understand why. I noticed I felt more comfortable going to work than spending time with my family. I constantly found myself getting more and more upset with Adam. During the last few weeks that he lived with us, I witnessed him doing things that were annoying or outright mean. He had started openly teasing Joey in front of me—something I never saw him do before. He would tease Joey to the point that he would make him cry. Then after Joey would start crying, Adam would continue teasing him. I scolded Adam numerous times and could not understand why he was acting so mean. I wondered, "Why is he purposely teasing his younger brother to the point of tears and not backing off when he can see how upset Joey is?"

Many times I would yell at Adam, yet I would still hear him pick on Joey in another room. Adam persisted, calling Joey "chubby" or any other name that would make him cry. I thought at the time, "Siblings will tease each other, but this is more than teasing." I could feel something was horribly wrong. I noticed, there was a weird unexplainable energy surrounding my family that made me feel very uneasy. As the discomfort persisted, my health deteriorated week after week.

As my health continued to fail, I became very disturbed to see that while I had to spend days in bed—no one in the family seemed to be concerned. I had raised my children to be empathetic and helpful, yet no one came in to check on me or bring me something to eat or drink. Bob did not care what was wrong with me. They all seemed so wrapped up in something I could not grasp. It was as if everyone was living in his own world and could not see me. Friends and other family members could see that I was getting progressively worse, but when

I spoke of the weird energy in the house—they had no idea of what I was talking about.

The only person who understood, was my friend Julia. A couple of months before I became so sick, I spoke with Julia. She was the only one who could see and verify the negative feelings and unexplainable instincts I had. She knew there was something wrong and believed my children were not safe. She received strong instincts about Joey, and believed a higher force was guiding her. She trusted what she was receiving and quickly intervened. Immediately, she told me to never have Adam baby-sit the boys again, because she felt that something horrible would happen to Joey. Her words were so strong—I did heed her advice and arranged for Danene to watch them. I know without a doubt that her trust in her own instincts and following through on those feelings saved my children's lives. I discuss that story with more detail in Chapter 11 "The Role of Spirituality".

For years, no one ever verified the weird feelings I had about Adam, but soon after Julia's instincts, another person helped me understand who Adam really was. One of the objects Adam stole was a palm pilot from his teacher, Robert. I called Robert right away when we learned it was his, and kept him informed as we uncovered the secrets surrounding his exemplary student. Robert had high hopes for Adam's future, so hearing about all of the disturbing things he was doing—was crushing. But, communicating with Robert helped me understand how Adam portrayed himself in school, versus his mannerisms at home. As we both tried to understand who this juvenile really was, Robert shared his observations. Adam acted similar to the way he did at home—incessantly talking, and expecting everyone to listen to him 24 hours a day. Robert also shed light on why Adam never packed a lunch for school, or needed money to buy lunch. Adam always told me he wasn't hungry during the day while at school, and would rather eat once he got home. But when I spoke with Robert, I learned that Adam bought ice cream sandwiches for lunch almost everyday. Since Adam wouldn't accept any lunch money from me, he was obviously stealing from many people for a long time. Robert also told me that Adam fit in well with the other kids in seventh grade, but by eighth grade—the other kids picked on him a lot and he often sat alone in the cafeteria.

When we learned of the scare tactics and physical abuse Adam had inflicted on Joey, I again called Robert and left a message on his voicemail. I didn't want to explain everything on an answering machine so I just said, "Adam has been doing a lot of other bad stuff. Please give me a call when you get a chance." When Robert called me back his first question was if Adam was sexually abusing the boys. I was shocked and said, "No! Why would you say that?" He responded by saying my message sounded so serious, that his first reaction was that Adam had been sexually abusing the boys. Robert was then extremely relieved to hear that was not the case.

I did not forget Robert's first reaction. I wanted to know why he had such a disturbing instinct. I figured I would settle my mind by asking Joey. I wanted to find out that it was not true and then be able to forget about it. A few days later is when I casually sat with Joey and asked him, "No one ever touches your peeper or your bum, right?" I am thankful that Robert had that first reaction! In a billion years, I would have never thought that my son would respond that he actually was being sexually abused. The idea of asking him if anyone had ever touched him inappropriately would have never entered my mind. I took it for granted that if anyone had ever touched Joey's private areas or made him touch their areas, he would tell me immediately.

Immediately after we found all the stolen items, my health began to improve. Once Adam was removed from the home, my health dramatically increased and I had more energy. My heart and body had known there was something horribly wrong and that we were all drowning, yet my mind knew nothing.

During the first few months, after learning of the mental and sexual abuse, I had several dreams of Adam coming back to the house. In each of the dreams, I would verbally abuse him, saying every horrible word possible. Then I would hit him in the face and body. The dreams would always end with him and me in a physical altercation. Each time, Bob had to jump in to defend me and fight his own son.

The dreams were extremely emotionally charged and very detailed. They were so life-like, I thought they were real. The intensity helped me understand that the dreams were serving as warnings. I knew in my heart that we would have to be prepared for the possibility of Adam coming back to the house one day. I could easily see him sneaking into the house when we were out, and waiting quietly inside for us to return. I knew if he came back, he and I would have a physical fight, since I would be protecting my children. When I told most people my fear, they told me to relax and not think about it. They thought Adam was in a secure facility and would never think of escaping or coming back to our house. One day I confessed my fear of Adam returning, to my father. It was terrifying and reaffirming to hear him agree and say he could easily see Adam coming back.

I never told my children that I was afraid Adam could return. I had to make them believe we were safe now, and no one would ever hurt them again. But, from the day Adam was taken out of the home, I kept hearing in my heart, "The system will fail, the system will fail." I had a sense that the state workers would be so taken with Adam, that they would never allow Bob and me to send him back to Cape Verde. I believed one day Adam would suddenly appear in our house. I knew if he came back, he would be there to hurt all of us. I felt I needed to be prepared and prepare my children, without alarming them.

As the months passed and Joey's confidence grew, he gained his own perspective of the abuse he had survived. He began to process some of his personal instincts. One evening, Joey told me that he had visions of suddenly seeing Adam in the house. Joey confessed that he was scared that Adam would sneak into the house and hurt David and himself. I tried to comfort him that Adam was closely watched in the treatment facility and could not escape. But I knew no facility could be totally foolproof. I told Joey I was also a little nervous of Adam coming back too. I explained to Joey that I was happy and proud he was finally in martial arts because he would be able to defend himself. That night I promised Joey and myself that I would also sign up for self defense. I enrolled the next morning and felt the fear slip away as I learned how to deal with Adam's possible return.

As my fear of Adam subsided, I began to experience mental peace. I slowly started to think of other things besides the abuse my children had suffered and the monstrous acts committed by Adam. But soon the peace was shattered by another disturbing dream. *I see Adam climb into another boy's room at the treatment facility. The boy is slightly younger than Adam and very naive. I see everything and can feel the boy's thoughts and feelings. Neither Adam nor the boy can see me. I know the boy has been raped numerous times in his life and his understanding of right and wrong has been permanently blurred. He feels uneasy and unwillingly, yet he goes along with whatever Adam plans for him. I sense the boy's confusion as Adam manipulates him and takes control. The boy knows what Adam is going to do, and he sees he has no alternative. He knows it is wrong— but it has happened so many other times by other people, he doesn't know how to stop the cycle of abuse against him. He doesn't even recognize that it is abuse. I can't believe what I am witnessing! The boy lies still on his bed as Adam penetrates him from behind.*

I woke up startled and overcome with a sick feeling. The dream was too vivid to be just another dream. I experienced the boy's emotions. I saw every detail of what happened to him. I knew his thoughts and feelings! When Bob woke up, I immediately told him about the dream and stated that I believed Adam had just committed sexual abuse against another child in the sexual offender treatment facility.

A few days later, on Mother's Day, Adam left a message on my voice-mail—even though he was strictly forbidden from contacting me. He said, "I just wanted to say Happy Mother's Day and I'm at a new place." He finished the message by saying the facility name and phone number of where he was taken. The state social service agency had been told several times by Bob and me that Adam should never be allowed to contact me. I was furious that Adam was now given the freedom to call. That night, I left a voicemail message for the social service caseworker stating that Adam is not supposed to call me and that I wondered if the facility was even watching him. The next day while I was driving, the phone rang, and I mistakenly answered. I heard, "Hi Mom. It's me—Adam." I told him, "You know you're not supposed to be calling me, right?" He responded with "Yeah, but I wanted to tell you I'm at a new place. I really like it." He said he had been in a little trouble because, "I didn't know horsing around with myself was not allowed." I understood from his fragmented explanation that he understood he was not supposed to joke around with other residents, but did not understand that he could not fool around by himself. I tried to escape from the conversation as quickly as I could and hung up the phone.

That night he tried calling me again because his phone number logged into my cell phone with the date, time, and phone number. I still had not heard from the case worker and I became irate. I left an explosive voicemail message for him, and instructed him to call me. I needed him to respond to me right away. I stated I was upset that the shelter was allowing Adam to contact me and I wanted a restraining order or no contact order put in place immediately.

A few days later, I was finally able to speak with the caseworker. I asked him why Adam was relocated to a new shelter. I thought the reason must be because he had harmed another boy, so I asked the caseworker if Adam had harmed any of the other children at the facility which then provoked the move. The caseworker explained that Adam was relocated because his 90-day stay at the first shelter had ended. The caseworker then went on to explain that the week before, Adam had escaped from the new facility for a few hours. He stated that no one knew when Adam left, how long he was gone, when he came back, how he got out and how he was able to re-enter. The day of the escape was the exact same day I had the disturbing dream. I asked him why I was never informed, and he stated he had left a message on my home answering machine. I knew he was lying since I had given him four different numbers to reach me, and never received one message. But this was not the first time he said things that were not true. He had already built up a history where I could see he never really had his facts right.

About two months later the prosecution lawyer from the Attorney General's office told me what really happened when Adam "escaped". She stated that Adam did not "escape" from the facility, "He was in another boy's room for about an hour to an hour and a half". He had been told the night before when he first arrived at the new facility, that he was not supposed to go in anyone else's room other than his own. The prosecution lawyer told me that she wanted to pursue this situation as a violation of the rules and guidelines of the facility. But everyone else just passed the situation off as not a big deal. She had originally reviewed all of the paperwork against Adam and told me, "He is a monster! I would like to see him locked up at least until he is 21!" But I could see as the months passed, she was being beaten down in court and eventually left the case entirely.

The exact day Adam had "escaped" but was found in another client's room, was the same day I had the dream of him perpetrating against the young boy. Learning that Adam had gone against the rules and was in another boy's room—to me verified what my dream had shown. In my dream, I witnessed the crime Adam committed against the young boy. Why was everyone so passive about Adam breaking the rules? Did anyone ever talk to the other boy to find out why Adam went in his room? I could never tell any social service personnel about my dream, since they could use that as ammunition against Bob and me. I had to quietly accept that I would never have answers to all of my questions.

Throughout our ordeal, it was interesting to analyze the progression of my own dreams. After surviving the first few months of shock, guilt and self-blame, I began having dreams where I was a child and several people started to sexually abuse me. The most disturbing part of these dreams was that my own children were the perpetrators who were violating me. *I know what keeps happening to me is wrong. But, I know I have to let him do what he is planning. I understand that the perpetrator has his physical and mental needs. I know I can't fight. I know there is nothing I can do to protect myself. I don't know how to refuse or fight back. I lie still, physically feeling every sexual act against me, but all I can do is wait until he finishes. At last he stops, but I'm left feeling disgust throughout my whole body. I've been horribly violated. But, I still care about this person. I cannot tell anyone. No one would believe me. I know it will happen again—and there is nothing I can do.*

As I awoke from each dream, I was sickened and haunted by the memories. In each dream, it was a different son committing the crimes against me. I never could understand why my children were the perpetrators. But the intensity of the dreams gave me a slight understanding of the emotions and feelings a child must feel when someone who is supposed to provide love and protection—is violating them on every level imaginable. These dreams continued intermittently and upset me for several months until there was a shift in my processing.

One night, I had a different dream. *I don't know how or why, but Joey just died. He either fell or became suddenly sick. I'm so lost and upset! I don't know what to do. Why didn't I see or do something to prevent this tragedy? As I sit blaming myself, Joey's spirit suddenly visits me saying everything is all right.* I was so upset in the dream that I woke up crying and continued crying for several hours. Joey had already been through the hell of being sexually abused and tortured by Adam. Now was he going to die from a freak accident or an illness? Again, the worrying wheels began to turn. What did this dream mean?

The next shift was when I started having dreams about Joey and David's safety. *For some reason I drop the boys off by the edge of a highway entrance. I tell them "I'll be back in a few minutes." As I drive for a few minutes on the highway, I realize they might not be safe alone. I quickly turn around and speed back to where I abandoned them. As I approach, I see a man with them, and several other men emerging from the trees. I run to them to protect them. As I grab them and hold them close, I recognize that the man is homeless and has salvaged some food to give to the boys. The men appearing out of the woods are friends with this man and they are homeless as well. I'm shocked to realize the people I was terrified would hurt my children are actually helping them. They have no intention to harm them in any way. They are trying to care for and protect them.*

This dream showed me that I was still battling my feelings that I had failed to protect my children and left them vulnerable to Adam or anyone else who wanted to harm them. But this dream also helped me realize that I could protect them and would be able to intervene before anything else bad happened to them. Seeing all of the men in their dirty and ripped clothes, yet so willing to help my children—helped me understand there are people who can be trusted.

I could see my progression of dreams as a process. I recalled how years before I ever met Bob, I became certified as a rape crisis counselor. My job at the time was to work with kids who were running away, homeless or involved in drugs and alcohol. Each week I had to take my turn manning a 24-hour hotline, which received calls from kids that needed help. Since I never knew what types of calls I would get, I figured I should gain some knowledge about rape. I clearly remember during the training that the instructor spoke about how an individual's healing can be tracked through his/her dreams. An adult who has been raped will initially dream of the violence and trauma over and over again. This continues until the individual starts to gain some control in his/her life. As the person begins to feel more comfortable, the dreams progress to a level where he/she starts to fight back against the perpetrator. Eventually the dreams evolve to a point where the survivor gains the control and power, and is able to defeat the perpetrator or is able to walk away from the abuse.

One of the last dreams I had concerning the sexual abuse was vivid and left a lasting impression. *I'm dating a man. We both have strong feelings for each other. I touch his lower back, just above his rear end and he yells at me, "Don't ever touch me there again!" Then he retreats into a zoned out state. He has a blank stare and is not aware of his surroundings. He doesn't remember yelling at me. I instantly understand that he was sexually abused as a child. The next thing I see is him lying down on his back—and he has two heads. One of the heads is aware of the abuse and trauma he suffered as a child. The other head is trying to live fully with peace and happiness—free from any memories of what happened to him. I know the pain he suffered physically, mentally and emotionally. I see how this pain took up permanent residence in his body. I unexpectedly understand that I can help him heal through his own trauma. I tell him, "I'm going to take care of you." I know I can blend the two heads together peacefully and bring balance to his body through Reiki— a healing form of energy. I understand that if I work on him, I will be able to balance the energy throughout his body. I know if I perform several Reiki sessions on him, the two heads will eventually blend into one. He will be aware of his past, yet able to live a peaceful and happy life.* When I awoke from the dream I instantly remembered what Barbara Absi, one of the female survivors, said when I interviewed her. She explained her internal turmoil as, "I felt like I had ten heads. When I talked about it I had less heads."

I was not the only person who had dreams foretelling the trauma to my children. Several people had dreams that they could not understand the meanings or why they were having them. About a year after buying our home, (which was a year and a half before we learned of the trauma Adam inflicted) Adam woke up one morning and reported a dream that truly upset him. He told me he had a dream that *"Joey is at the bottom of a dumping site and I'm on top of a cliff looking down at Joey's dead body. As I sit, looking down at Joey's body, his spirit comes and sits next to me. His spirit says, 'Don't worry Adam, I am still alive, I just don't have a body anymore.'* Adam was visibly shaken by the dream. I was troubled to hear that Joey was dead in the dream, and asked if Adam was upset about that too. He said he was not upset about seeing Joey dead at the bottom of the hill. He was upset that Joey's spirit was still alive and was still trying to talk to him.

The same night Adam had his dream, my friend Miladys had an upsetting dream too. Her dream was, *"We are all walking down a street, along the sidewalk. As we walk, someone secretly sneaks out of the woods, grabs Joey, and disappears. We all turn around to check on Joey, but he has vanished. Claire is so lost and filled with grief that she cannot see Joey trying to communicate with her in spirit to tell her that he is all right. Joey is very upset that he cannot reach his mother. The only person who can see Joey is me."*

Immediately after Adam's and Miladys' disturbing dreams about Joey's safety, I had an upsetting dream. *We are in our backyard, which is surrounded by woods. A man in green overalls runs into the yard, picks up Joey and starts to run back into the trees. I scream for Bob who then chases after the man.* I woke up before the dream ended. I was completely terrified. Three people had horrible dreams concerning Joey's well-being. I told anyone and everyone who came in contact with Joey to have eyes in the back of their heads. I was terrified that the dreams were a warning that someone was really going to take Joey. I was frightened to let him out of my site. If we went to a store or any public place, he had to hold my hand or hang onto my pocketbook at all times so I knew he was right with me. For days I lived in terror until things finally seemed to calm down and I could relax again.

After asking Joey about the sexual abuse and what else was happening during that time, I've been able to estimate the time the abuse began. From our understanding, the sexual abuse began around the time when everyone was having those horrible dreams. We had been worried and prepared that a stranger was going to attempt to take Joey. We were prepared to do everything possible to protect him from this stranger. But it was not a stranger. The "stranger" we were so worried about was Adam. The dreams symbolized Joey potentially being taken away or killed.

After Adam was removed from the home, I started having bizarre visions when I came home from work. Our home had two staircases. As I entered the house near the staircase, which led to my bedroom, I would glance through the living room and get a vision at the bottom of the opposite staircase. The vision was always of *Joey's motionless body at the bottom of the stairs closest to Adam's bedroom. In horror, I run to Joey and screech as I realize he is dead. I run up to Adam's room to learn what happened. Inside the room, Adam is playing on his PlayStation. As I scream in agony for an explanation, Adam casually says, "Oh, I thought I heard a loud thump, but I did not think to go look what it was."* Then *the vision backs up, as if I'm rewinding a VCR tape. I suddenly see Adam push Joey down the stairs intentionally!*

I had this vision constantly for weeks and could not understand why I kept seeing such a disturbing image. I knew Adam had forced Joey to do a summersault down the stairs closest to my bedroom. But every time I asked Joey if anything happened on the opposite staircase, he said, "No. Bad stuff only happened on the other stairs." Yet my visions persisted and I could clearly see Joey's motionless body and saw Adam push Joey with extreme force.

About one year after Adam was removed from our home, Joey suddenly remembered something. That evening, Joey and I stood at the top of the staircase closest to Adam's old bedroom. We were talking, and as we stood in that spot, it evoked Joey's memory. He explained that one day as he started walking down the stairs, he stepped down and turned to look at Adam who was behind him. Adam abruptly put both hands on Joey's back and pushed him as hard as he could. Joey was hurled down the stairs and luckily smashed into the handrail, half way down. As he hit the wooden pole, Joey reached out—and stopped his body from falling to the bottom. Joey said he hurt his back and arm from the fall, but knew he had stopped himself from getting really hurt. Upon hearing Joey's memory, I finally understood the vision that had persisted for weeks. Adam had in fact pushed Joey. Yet the vision was of Joey dead at the bottom of the stairs. At that point, I realized that was going to be our future if Adam had stayed in our home, and if he was still allowed to baby sit the boys.

As I thought about the visions, dreams and all of the stories Joey told me, I knew Adam had the intention and was trying to kill Joey. I knew it was true, but felt I had to check with Joey if my understanding was accurate. But, I was afraid and hesitant to ask Joey. I didn't want to suggest something so scary incase he had never considered it himself. Later that day, I gingerly asked Joey, if he thought Adam was purposely trying to hurt him or do something worse to him. Joey's immediate response was "Of course Mom, I knew he was going to kill me. I just didn't know when." He went on to say, "Mom, don't you remember that day on the porch when you yelled at me?" I responded that I didn't remember or understand what he was talking about. Joey explained, "We were all on the porch. Adam was sitting down on the floor and

I was standing behind him. I held a hammer high up in the air right behind him and thought to myself, 'If I hit him hard enough, he can't hurt me anymore.' That second you yelled, Joey! Put that hammer down right now! You could hurt someone!"

Throughout the process of Adam being removed from our home and then bounced from shelter to shelter—he never showed any guilt or remorse for his crimes. My parents, friends who he stole from, school officials, the police, Bob and myself all witnessed that Adam had no connection to the crimes he committed against another human being or their feelings. When we returned several stolen objects back to the school, the officials stated that Adam's cold affect was "chilling and disturbing." The police officer that placed Adam in the holding cell reported checking on him and said, "I've never seen anything like it before. Every kid that goes in there usually freaks out when you close the door. They always start screaming and crying. But Adam was calm and almost looked comfortable. When I brought him to the deten- tion center, he walked with his wrists handcuffed together and looked relaxed—like he was walking through his living room."

Even after the emotional effects on his victims were explained— Adam never showed any emotions. From my children' and my personal experience, I believe that a person who has no connection to his/her actions or how they affect others—is dangerous and capable of extreme crimes. Adam was attempting new ways to take Joey's life. The abuse my children suffered was horrible. But, Bob and I are extremely lucky that Joey and David are alive! If Adam had lived with us any longer, I know I would not be able to use those words.

Chapter 5
Survivors

When we first heard that our children were sexually abused, I was desperate for answers. I searched for information, but could not find anything that helped me to be a strong and supportive parent for my children. I needed to know what the future looked like for them. I wanted to know what signs to look for that would indicate they were progressing through their trauma, or they were regressing. I thumbed through a couple of books and found myself getting more and more aggravated. The books spoke about the perpetrator and had very little information about the survivors. The books were always very outdated, and written by therapists who seemed emotionally removed. Also, the perpetrators in the books were men and the "victim" was always a girl. Nothing could help me with the feelings I was having or the behaviors my children were exhibiting. I needed to know how to survive my own emotions, but more importantly how could I help and support my children.

I was very lucky to confide in a few friends about our situation, who then began to tell me their personal stories of surviving sexual abuse from their childhood. When I heard the personal narratives, I found I was finally receiving answers to some of my questions. I decided I needed to interview more adult survivors so I could get a true understanding of what happens to someone when they have been sexually abused. Through the interviews, I was then able to recognize themes to identify and classify perpetrators, and themes of survivors' struggles—pains, progress in healing, and the supportive role parents need to play after a child has been traumatized.

I am so incredibly grateful to all of the survivors who shared their stories. Each word, every feeling, and all the emotions they expressed helped me understand what a child, who has been sexually abused, truly survives. I learned how I can serve as a support for my children throughout their lives. In the beginning, there were many times when my sons discussed upsetting feelings, memories and disturbing dreams. Since I had already gained such valuable knowledge from the survivors, our family was able to process each trauma calmly and peacefully. We had the courage to face each horrible memory, try to process the feelings, and replace the recollection with a new positive experience. I am forever indebted to the survivors who helped me protect my children from further trauma in their lives—by giving me the knowledge and strength to help empower Joey and David. We learned how to process their abuse peacefully, honestly, and effectively.

In total, I interviewed fourteen adult survivors from across the country. A few were friends, several were people referred to me by friends or family members, and many were strangers who voluntarily shared their stories of survival. I interviewed seven male survivors and seven female survivors. The perpetrators in their stories consisted of eleven males and three females, one of which was a juvenile. While most of the survivors were assaulted by more than one perpetrator, I focused the interview questions on the first perpetrator in the survivor's life. I incorporated the survivors' statements about first perpetrators and consecutive perpetrators into this chapter and chapter 6.

The interviews were conducted over the phone or in person, and usually lasted about one and a half hours. For each interview I utilized the same questions relating to the perpetrator's tactics, mannerisms and personality and the survivors' various stages. I was especially interested in knowing the tactics the perpetrator used to silence the child and how the abuse affected the survivor emotionally, mentally, spiritually and physically. I asked questions about what helped or would have helped the child cope, and what hindered the healing process for each of the survivors. Especially helpful to me were answers on how parents can be supportive. The stories were individually unique, yet I found several common themes linking each survivor. Unlike Joey and David, most of the survivors did not receive support and early intervention. Thus, most of the children became re-victimized by another perpetrator (secondary perpetrators). Sometimes the secondary perpetrator violated the child soon after the first perpetrator. In other accounts, the child had grown into a young adult before he/she was violated again. Of the fourteen survivors I interviewed, twelve were re-victimized by another perpetrator. Sixteen of the secondary perpetrators were men and seven of the secondary perpetrators were women. One of the female survivors was even sold into sex slavery and estimates the number of secondary perpetrators against her was about 70 males and 4 females. Her first perpetrator, who initiated and then sold her into a fierce world of hell, was her own mother.

The crimes took place in over 7 different states. The survivors were from various ethnic groups and races and experienced the range of extreme poverty, middle socio-economic levels or complete affluence. The races of the perpetrators were various as well as their socioeconomic levels. Surprising to me, several of the perpetrators were extremely wealthy and maintained positions of great respect and admiration within their communities.

I was shocked to learn that the most common theme throughout all of the interviews pertained to the questions: "Did the perpetrator ever show signs of guilt/remorse at what he/she did to you? Did the perpetrator ever try to apologize?" Each survivor who was interviewed answered these questions without hesitation. Every response was a clear "No" or "Never." There was an odd sense that these questions did not even belong in the interview because the answer was always the same. I quickly understood that none of the perpetrators ever showed signs of remorse. Survivors have knowledge about people that most non-survivors do not have. They understand the disturbing reality that there are people living all around us who have no conscience. Each of the survivors experienced and witnessed as children—the true mindset of a predator. They have observed and lived through the self-serving, controlling and painful ways a perpetrator will violate another human being without any hesitation, guilt, or remorse. Most people, who have never been victimized, patiently wait for perpetrators to "come to their senses" and feel sorry for what they have done. Yet survivors know that day will never come. As one of the male survivors, Dan, clearly stated regarding people's knowledge of sexual abuse and the evils of perpetrators, "The general public are sheep." He explained that people walk around blind to the wolf in sheep's clothing that is right next to them. Once exposed, they still can't see a perpetrator.

Another upsetting concept for me was to learn about the self-questioning torment each survivor experiences for years after the abuse. In every single case of sexual abuse, the perpetrator is at fault, yet many of the survivors repeatedly asked, "Why me?" "Why did I get singled out for this?" "What did I do to encourage or allow this to happen?" It was disturbing for me to learn that the survivors didn't always know that what was happening to them as children was wrong, not their fault, and that each perpetrator should be stopped and incarcerated immediately. It was heartbreaking to listen to the years that these children struggled with feelings of guilt and did not understand where to place their blame and anger. A criminal, who should have been incarcerated, violated them. Yet these children were left questioning themselves, blamed by loved ones, and not protected by the legal, social service, medical, educational and faith-based institutions in our communities. The adults and systems that were supposed to be instilling a sense of safety and pride into the children—had failed each survivor.

The ages that the survivors were first attacked ranged from newborn to 14-years-old. Some of these assaults happened once. However, most of the survivors were sexually abused for several years. The longest amount of time any perpetrator violated any of the survivors was throughout a period of 16 years. The average length of time that the survivors were sexually abused was over a 5 year period.

Since we were able to intervene to protect Joey and David, I was curious about survivors who disclosed and were or were not supported by family members. Two of the survivors who disclosed the abuse to their families as children, were supported and were not re-victimized. Yet the other twelve survivors, who disclosed or did not—were violated by an initial, secondary and in many cases, several more perpetrators. The time span between the first perpetrator, and additional violators committing crimes against the survivors, ranged from—immediately after the first trauma to up to 20 years later. The average number of total perpetrators each individual had to survive was 3 perpetrators. Of the 12 survivors who were re-victimized, none of them received support from their families. Some did tell family members and did not receive support and others remained silent. The survivors did not feel they had anyone they could turn to for safety. The few who told their families watched as the adults turned the abuse around—by blaming the child, supporting the perpetrator, and leaving the child feeling exposed, vulnerable and alone. Despite surviving the sexual abuse, the children were now re-victimized by the same people who should have immediately worked to protect them.

Tanisha was eleven-years-old when she delivered newspapers for a local apartment complex. The janitor always said hello to her, but in a way that made her feel uncomfortable. He was friendly, helpful and "flirty." She soon saw his personality change into someone who was aggressive and "demonic." One day, he grabbed her, dragged her near the stairwell, and brutally raped and sodomized her. Years later, she often felt re-traumatized by family members who would say, "It was a long time ago, forget about it."

As adults, people do not understand the trauma that continues to haunt survivors and hinder them from healing. Linda stated she felt hindered by, "Judgmental people who say, 'you should just forgive and move on. You don't have to go through all that.'" But how are children supposed to "forget about it" when they are bombarded by memories and feelings from every level of their senses? Years later, a particular sound or smell can instantly drown a survivor with complete memories of their trauma. They are suddenly not only remembering—they are re-living!

All of the survivors knew their attacker. Four of the survivors had a family member (mother, father, cousin) attack them. Five of the survivors were violated by priests, and five survivors were perpetrated by predators that were not family members, but were considered close to the family (babysitter, mother's boyfriend, friend of the family). Being close to the child and his or her family is what gave the perpetrator access and power over the child to remain silenced.

When I asked about the "immediate effects on you as a child—physically, emotionally, mentally and spiritually," the answers varied. The female survivors seemed to differ from the male survivors by having more reports of physical trauma, such as stomach problems, ulcers, head trauma, urinary and throat infections, panic attacks and shame of their bodies. Angie remembers, "I became aware and ashamed of my body. I felt if someone could do that to me, I didn't deserve to be on this earth. I was a dirty horrible person with this secret. I felt like I was living a lie." The male survivors differed from the females in that they admitted more reports of acting out against family members, problems with school, and breaking/destroying property or objects. The women turned inward while the men acted out.

I needed to understand what survivors experienced or what helped them survive while the actual abuse was taking place. Two of the survivors reported having outer body experiences during the violent acts against them. Kim explained "I could feel myself slipping further away like an outer body experience. I was in the shell or outskirts of my body." As I continued with the interviews, I found a complete separation from emotions—seemed to be the only initial way any of the children could survive the abuse. Don Asbee remembers his feelings of disconnect from the abuse he suffered at the hands of a priest. "I can recall a feeling of separation from myself—disassociation. When I look at a picture of my confirmation, I look like a dead person. I was in another world. It is a scary place. I don't know who that person is."

Linda's abuse began when she was four-years-old. Her mother was the perpetrator. She explained, "I escaped every way I could, into books or music. People and relationships were too much for me, because I had to hold down so much pain. I couldn't really experience relationships with people. I was a character in a play, but I wasn't really there. The lights were on, but no one was home." Isolating, withdrawing, being afraid of adults and people in general was common for all survivors. Understandably, these children completely lost their trust of people. Peter remembered his experience as a 12-year-old surviving sexual abuse committed by the local priest and the coping mechanism he used, "Isolating myself from everybody else. I thought I was different from everybody else because I had this big secret." Marigrace was violated by many adults and added, "I never trusted anybody. I never knew who was worthy of trust and who wasn't. I was afraid of everyone."

Confusion, guilt, shame, depression and fear were the overwhelming feelings of these children surviving sexual abuse. It was difficult for me to hear how the abuse would mentally affect a child. The amount of worry these children had to deal with was so unfair. Dan stated,

"I was always thinking really bad things might happen. I was always preparing for the worst." As I listened to the different stories, I was amazed at how no one in the community ever picked up on any signs that there was something wrong. The children were forced to live their lives, while skillfully hiding their painful secrets. They were not able to tell anyone of the abuse, and were forced to live a lie. Angie, whose perpetrator was a 15-year-old female and an "all American sweetheart" babysitter, stated, "Just as the perpetrator appears normal, the victim appears normal. But inside is havoc." John explained, "The sexual abuse gave me dysfunctional coping skills and helped me to learn how to hide things. I could keep up a front that everyone would like. Your mind is a pot of boiling soup, but people can't see that."

Several of the survivors told me they did not tell anyone about the abuse because they thought others would blame them or not believe them. From the accounts, it seemed that fear was often what helped keep the children silent. Beth recalled, "I was trying to keep it a secret. I didn't want people to think I wanted it, that I was at fault or that I brought it on."

It was not surprising for me to learn that almost half of the survivors turned to drugs and alcohol to cope and escape from their trauma. Six of the fourteen survivors recalled using drugs and seven of the fourteen survivors stated they used alcohol to cope. Five survivors used drugs and alcohol together. Yet for others, the fear of being re-victimized kept them in abstinence of any substances. Six survivors stated they did not use drugs or alcohol. As David Clohessy explained, "Then you are not in control. What could people do to you?"

Something disturbing for me to hear was that some of the survivors cut, burned or pierced their body parts in an attempt to gain some control over their internal feelings. Self-inflicted cutting and burning of the body took place in two female survivor stories and piercing body parts took place in two male survivor stories. One of the female survivors explained the act of cutting and burning herself. "I was so disassociated from my feelings and emotions, I could not feel anything. Burning and cutting became forms of relief to express my feelings." Another female survivor stated, "I used chemicals to burn my vagina to try to clean it out."

I was saddened to hear of the children who developed an eating disorder as an after effect from the sexual abuse trauma. Five of the female survivors and one male survivor reported developing an eating disorder. One survivor stated, "I would eat my emotions by stuffing food." Another female survivor stated, "The heavier I got, the less attention I got from men and boys. I never wanted to look sexy at all." Another female survivor indicated that for her, "Anorexia was a subtle attempt at suicide."

It was upsetting to hear that many times the desperation and hopelessness were so overwhelming, that the survivor started contemplating suicide or wished that he/she did not exist. Juan remembered, "I prayed to God for years to take me. What did I do to welcome that kind of situation?" Eleven out of the fourteen survivors experienced thoughts of suicide. Actual suicide attempts plagued four of the fourteen survivors. In total, the four survivors who attempted to end their lives tried between 2 to 20 times each. Unfortunately, a few of the survivors expressed during the interviews that they knew other survivors who could not gain any form of internal peace, and did eventually complete their suicide attempts. One of the male survivors said that he recently lost 4 survivor friends to suicide—three of them were alter boys who were abused by priests.

Similar to Joey and David, severe sleep disturbances were common for most survivors. For the survivors who were abused in their home, they reported going to bed very late and getting up early. Terrified of further abuse, these children would often sit in other parts of the house while everyone else was sleeping. Many of the survivors were haunted by dreams of violence or sex into their adulthood. Eleven out of the 14 survivors stated they were plagued by dreams of violence and 4 of the survivors reported being traumatized by dreams of sex. In the dreams of violence, it was common to see snakes or knives. Also, several survivors dreamed of cutting up the perpetrator or feeling the perpetrator use a knife against them. Seeing dismembered body parts was also common in many of the dreams.

Some of the survivors reported having disturbing sex dreams as adults. In the dreams, their current sexual partner's anatomy (it was usually males in these dreams) would change. The male's penis would turn into a snake, or the partner would turn into the childhood perpetrator. As adults, the survivors' interest or lack of interest in sex was very clear. Four of the survivors (both men and women) stated that they went to the extreme opposite of desiring/enjoying sex—they avoided sex and sexual relationships. Three survivors (all men) stated they became obsessed with the idea of sex and often found the sexual dreams pleasurable. Three of the survivors (2 men and 1 woman) stated that they ultimately became promiscuous as a result of the childhood sexual abuse. For the remaining four survivors, promiscuity, or abstinence was not an issue.

An alarming thing to learn was out of the fourteen survivors, five mentioned their thoughts of harming the perpetrator. This also points to the statements several survivors made, "The victim becomes the perpetrator." But the survivors who thought of harming the perpetrator soon realized revenge would not help them. Juan explained, "Some things are not meant to be questioned or blamed. When is enough pain—enough? When is righting the wrong, right? If I could shoot him, it wouldn't replace anything and wouldn't make me feel better. What is the point? It wouldn't miraculously heal the wound. It was obviously supposed to happen because it happened. I'm tired of playing the victim. It is exhausting. Enough is enough."

It was heartbreaking to hear that from childhood into adulthood, the survivors mentioned how difficult it was to maintain relationships with other people. Since trust and boundaries had been broken, they did not have stable relationships to measure what a "normal" relationship should look like. Since Linda's perpetrator was her mother, the abuse, "Affected everything about every relationship. Your mother is your window to the world. I didn't have enough trust to share myself with anyone on any level. It affected my ability to have an emotional relationship with anyone, especially with a female."

Several survivors indicated they had, as David Clohessy stated, "A long series of failed relationships. If things became too serious and intimate, I would sabotage the relationship." Juan explained, "I never felt like a man or felt adequate. I always had to out do or over do. To leave a relationship, it had to end violently in a fight." Barbara Absi explained, as a young woman, "I became very co-dependent. I couldn't stand on my own two feet. I didn't trust my gut." Many of the survivors had experienced divorces or many failed relationships, and were still wondering if they would ever find someone to "settle down with." There were a few survivors who were lucky enough to find a spouse who would help them through their personal struggle. However, many survivors felt hindered in relationships by all of the internal issues they were still battling. Peter's struggle with relationships was explained as, "You got dealt a bad hand, play it, and make the best of it. I can't figure out how to settle these issues. I don't want to be a 40-year-old bachelor. I want to get this shit over with and put it behind me."

Some of the survivors stated that as adults disclosing childhood sexual abuse, they often experienced other people judging how they should or shouldn't feel years after the abuse. I realized that the judgments from others seemed to deny the survivor the right to experience what he/she needed to feel in order to progress through the stages of healing. Erick stated, "I never gave it merit how it does influence people's lives. People don't understand the impact it really has. This event in my life was huge."

After conducting the interviews, I found there was no defined pattern or steps of healing. Each individual experienced his/her own personal progression in different ways. Each stage was crucial to that individual's awareness and turning points. To an outsider, it would seem some of the stages would not serve a purpose—such as denial. Yet, as Kim explained, "Denial was my greatest gift. I had the ability to shut off all my emotions to survive. Through healing, you have the courage to look at what you were denying. It makes you feel like a fighter when you can think, 'what they did to me is not going to ruin me for the rest of my life.' " David Clohessy stated that the most important aspect for him to survive was, "Repression—the ability to block it out until I was older, stronger, independent, away from my family, and with a wonderful spouse. If I remembered it as a kid, I don't know where I would be." When I asked the question about stages of healing, several of the survivors gave similar answers. Peter stated, "I don't know what stages are. Any progress is good progress." Dan summarized progress as, "It is a journey. You have to find out yourself—if there really is such a thing as 'healing'. It always is going to be there. If the scar is there, the memory is there. There is no 'healing'—you just become a better person."

When I first began with the interviews, one of the first accounts I was deeply moved by was Kim's story. She had survived horrible mental, physical and sexual abuse by her father for years, only to be re-offended by her own mother. Her insight and ability to express deep feelings and emotions into words, was invaluable for me. Throughout the interviews with other survivors, no matter how difficult it was to hear their pain, Kim's words resonated with me and served as a continual reminder. "There is no advice you can give to someone. You'll never get over it. It changes the rest of your life. There is no wrong way to survive." This message became very clearly embedded in my mind. No matter how dysfunctional the coping methods used by each survivor seemed, the important thing was that they lived through the experience and were triumphant by not committing suicide!

If a survivor goes through a period of drug or alcohol abuse, self injury such as burning, cutting or piercing, or any other period or behavior that seems "dysfunctional" from other peoples' point of view—that is what that individual survivor needs to experience at the time. To get through to the next stage in an individual's personal recovery, a survivor cannot be denied the point he/she is currently experiencing. Anything a sexual abuse survivor has to do in order to avoid killing himself/herself, or hurting others—and try to wade through a stormy sea of emotions, cannot be judged. Every survivor has the right to his/her own individual coping mechanisms and processes as long as he or she is not violating other people.

As I listened to the many interviews and witnessed my own children's progress, I learned that the stages a survivor progresses through can become blurred. Often a survivor can go through several stages or stay in just one or two categories. Different events or periods of time in a survivor's life can trigger the person to re-visit a period already traveled. A survivor can also skip different phases. There is no defined order in which a survivor must go through the processes, as some survivors may stay in one healing area throughout their lives. The most important concept is that it is not important which stage a survivor is in—what is important is that the person is still alive! I found there were five phases or stages survivors pass through: Awareness, Acknowledgement, Anarchy, Assertiveness and Acceptance.

Awareness begins when a child, or an adult who is remembering or experiencing the abuse—knows what is happening, understands the dynamics of who is offending and who is being violated, and what the predator expects. Initial coping mechanisms are: shock, paralysis, denial, and dissociation. Confusion, fear and guilt are often the overwhelming feelings a survivor experiences at this stage. Awareness happens on all levels: sight, sound, hearing, feeling, taste, emotion, energy, and thought. The survivor is not aware mentally of all that he/she has experienced. But the body, mind, heart, soul and spirit all absorb the situation and store it to analyze and re-experience in the future.

Acknowledgement is when the survivor can mentally comprehend what was done, but cannot understand why or how it happened. At this stage, the survivor can only comprehend that the event that happened was bad. An understanding of who the perpetrator is or was begins to develop and the survivor begins to analyze and re-live his/her position of powerlessness in the situation. Secrecy, fear, depression, sadness, and questioning of self and God seem to be common emotions and thoughts at this phase. This period can often take years for the survivor to remember details of the abuse, retrace the beginnings of the predator's tactics, and re-think how and why the crime happened. Many survivors at this point, are plagued with self-inflicted destructive behaviors and/or acting out and being disruptive to others. Alternatively, several survivors at this stage go in the opposite direction and become perfectionists. They push themselves to extreme limits to show their abilities or to keep some form of control in their upside-down lives.

Anarchy is a period when the survivor is bombarded with thoughts, feelings, emotions and memories of the abuse. The survivor tries to mentally make sense from everything being thrown together in a whirlwind. At this point, there is a struggle to gain clarity and peace over the trauma, as the unruly emotional and mental storms persist. As the survivor works through these extreme emotions, he/she begins to see, re-live, and acknowledge what was done to him/her. Anger begins to settle deep within the survivor. Often times the anger is towards the perpetrator or the institution that allowed the perpetrator to continue committing his/her crimes. For many survivors, this is a juncture that keeps resurfacing throughout the individual's progress.

Assertiveness is when the survivor can clearly see and accept that he or she was and is not at fault—and that total blame and wrongdoing lies with the perpetrator. This is the stage when many survivors become active in pursuing their own situation legally. The survivor may begin to see his/her personal trauma as a motivating source for sexual abuse prevention and/or activism—stopping perpetrators through exposure and legal processes. Others get involved in community education or advocating for stricter laws and legal enforcement. The survivor also begins to recognize the value of self-awareness, and talking to others. As the survivor accepts what has happened and how it has affected him/her—many personal strengths and insights are gained.

Acceptance is the stage when a survivor sees the abuse in his or her life, and knows the personal growth gained through such trauma. The survivor no longer feels that he or she is drowning and experiences true feelings of peace and joy. The survivor is able to see the abuse as something that happened, but he/she is no longer controlled by it. At this stage, survivors may develop a stronger spiritual connection to a higher power and understand a fundamental purpose in their life.

In the first few years after the abuse and into adulthood, all of the survivors had periods of personal questioning. Dan recalled thinking, "Why is this happening? It seems like it went on forever but I can't remember any of it." Many of the survivors were harsh and blamed themselves that they must be a horrible person to have this happen. Most of the survivors questioned God and the existence of God. A common question survivors had was, if there is a God, how could He allow these things to happen? Linda recalled, "God's love was a vague concept. It wasn't very personal. I grew up with the idea that I had to depend on someone else. My idea of God was that He was very nice to everybody else, but He didn't really care about me." Beth stated, "It got to the point He wasn't listening. Why was He letting this happen to me?"

Many survivors believed facing the abuse was the first step and continued to be an integral part of their own healing. As Dan stated, "It's not your fault. Don't do anything to take your mind off of it. Deal with it. Stare it in the face and beat the shit out of it." David Clohessy realized, "I'm a less trusting, less outgoing, less happy person than I would have been otherwise. I look at some easy-going relaxed adults and think 'wouldn't it be good to be like that'. I'm also not naïve enough to believe, 'gosh, this maybe didn't have that much of an impact on my life.' "

For children who were abused by several perpetrators, they could not understand why the abuse kept happening and began to question if they were at fault for "attracting" perpetrators to them. Peter remembers, "What is it with me? Why do all these sickos come after me? Am I gay or what? Why are all these things happening to me?"

All of the survivors reported being "triggered" by different things that would send them back into stages they thought they had already completed. As Linda stated, "I will think I'm through and then something will trigger and I'll go through it again on a deeper level." Even though survivors acknowledged they would probably always be "triggered", an understanding and acceptance of the fluctuating process is what seemed to bring survivors a sense of peace. Marigrace stated, "I don't see things as being stuck. They are opportunities to work through something. If something resurfaces, it is there for a reason. There is still something else to work on." Barbara Absi summed it up by stating, "It was personal choice. I was stuck at stages because I was supposed to be at that stage."

I was interested to know what emotions, actions or thoughts made survivors feel that they were not progressing through their personal healing process. Several factors contributed to survivors feeling "stuck" in a stage or phase. These factors were: not talking to others and not actively pursing their own growth. The survivors told me that a common reason why they did not talk to others about their trauma was their fear of what people would think. Many times the survivors acknowledged they were hindering their own progress by holding onto the secret. Often they were silent because they were still battling internal feelings of self-blame or fault, feeding themselves negative self-talk, and feeling hopeless. John recognized how, "Not talking about it, keeping it squashed down and not dealing with it," was an impediment to his progress. Angie stated what hindered her from healing was, "A sense of hopelessness. All the damage had been done and now—knowing I had to live with that. I got tired of all of the self doubt and not doing things I knew I would be good at." Marigrace realized, "When I was not searching for help or soul searching, I was acting out against myself. I was not able to grow and was perpetuating the abuse." David Clohessy admitted, "I didn't know what I needed and was not comfortable asking, or didn't ask in an effective way."

The factors that foster survivors to feel "stuck" as adults are varied. Survivors, who were abused by priests, feel stuck in anger and sadness—because of "the secrecy and denial by the Church. They never said they were sorry. The perpetrators are a small part. The major problem is the institution sheltering them. God's emissary was doing this. If it felt bad, then YOU were at fault. It was in a sacramental context. You had to go along, because God wanted you to do this." Don Asbee also added what he currently struggles with, "The anger and outrage of looking now as an adult—watching the Church back peddle over helping victims." Erick recalled how a priest, habitually gave him alcohol before the abuse, and said things like, "Don't be ashamed, others wouldn't understand" or "Keep your mouth shut". As an adult, Erick realized, "Before, there was no separation between Church and God. Now there is a huge separation." Peter recalled how a priest took advantage of his pre-teenage emotions of "feeling like you don't belong to any group—then comes someone who is nice and makes you feel good about yourself." As an adult, Peter believes, "Organized religion is a joke. I don't believe how anyone can go through what I've gone through and still believe in the Church." Words that were very painful for me to hear were David Clohessy's, when he stated, "I don't have a faith—it was stolen from me as a kid."

All of the survivors reported feeling triggered, or affected at different times, but only three survivors reported severe flashbacks or intrusive memories. Similar to what Joey experienced in the beginning, these survivors who were attacked by priests, found themselves back in time, re-living their abuse.

A flashback or intrusive memory can come as a shock to the survivor, since his/her reality seemed free of all painful memories. Yet the mind carefully tucks all recollections away to uncover later in life. Usually, when the trauma is too intense or happened at a young age, the survivor's mind automatically blocks out the experience and helps the person forget. Then later in life, without any warning, the survivor can suddenly see things from his/her past and not know what the re-living experience means. As Don Asbee explained, "I would be awake and go into another reality. It was as if I was watching CNN and then I would be viewing Days of Our Lives." For a while Don Asbee thought he was going crazy. He explained that he would be fine and then suddenly the room would change. He would suddenly find himself seeing everything from the viewpoint of a young boy—as if he was lying on top of a table. His mind was replaying the scenery he saw from his childhood—while he was helpless, and being raped by two different priests. His brain had completely protected him from the memories for 35 years! But the sudden memories helped uncover the reason why Don had always felt extreme physical pain throughout his entire life. Amazingly, when he remembered what happened to him, the intense anal pain he had suffered, now suddenly disappeared.

I believe the reason why the survivors who most often had these severe experiences of intrusive memories were survivors of priest abuse, is because the idea of the "Hand of God" doing this to them was more than a child could bear. If another person is committing the abuse against a child—the child knows it is a person committing the crime. But if the abuse is coming directly from the "Hand of God"—who are you to question what is happening? It would naturally cause too much internal mental strife, knowing "God" approved and was doing this to you. Such a traumatic experience would naturally make the mind shut down the memory and hide it away for a long time. For most of the priest survivors, the idea of questioning a priest would have been equivalent to questioning God. As John stated, "The way my family treated the priests, with such high esteem—it would be my fault. It is your word against a priest. Priests can't lie. They can't do anything wrong. After all, they are chosen by God." Since these children could not possibly challenge God and "God's chosen representative", the only way to survive was to totally block it out of their minds. For years, they would forget the abuse, until the survivor was in a better situation to start facing the trauma.

Other survivors explained that they believed they were personally responsible for keeping themselves from personal growth. As Peter stated, "It was myself—thinking I could do it myself". Marigrace could see what hindered her was "not recognizing my own responsibility. The world was not responsible for healing me. The world didn't owe me any-thing." Several survivors recognized how not thinking about the sexual abuse or not processing the emotions served a purpose at a particular time, but didn't help in the long run. Trying to keep control over a flood of various thoughts, memories and emotions became a large contributing factor in why survivors felt they could not grow. John stated, "If you don't think about it, you can't get past it. I never let it go and still have not let it go. I haven't surrendered it. Even through the faith I have in God, my humanity won't let it go. It's like losing a part of you. I've lived with it so long—I don't know how to live without it."

While some of the survivors believed feeling "stuck" and "reverting back" were signs to revisit and strengthen previously gained skills, other survivors were upset that they had emotions and feelings they could not stop or shake off. Kim stated, "I still cannot get rid of that black hole in my chest—that heavy feeling that is always with you." David Clohessy said he finds himself pondering, "I will never know how my life might have been different. I wish I knew how my life would have been different." Juan stated, "Sometimes I don't feel productive. I don't feel successful—emotionally, professionally and financially. Sometimes I catch myself playing the 'victim' and not making decisions when I should make decisions." Linda admitted how the abuse still affects her today, "I dissociate frequently. I go off in my mind and forget what is going on. I never wanted to say, 'Oh, poor me, I'm a victim.' I would rather say this happened, it was really bad and this is a strength, or some good that has come from this. I don't like the victim thinking. I don't want to go there."

To be a support to my children, I needed to learn what factors helped the survivors to heal. The most common things were individual counseling, support groups and writing. Whether it was journaling, poetry, or some other form of expression, survivors identified writing as the factor most contributing to their personal healing. Marigrace recommended, "When journaling, use your own hand writing, it makes you get more real with yourself." Linda stated, "I write poetry for emotions so deeply buried, I can't express them in regular words".

Besides writing, counseling and support groups were the next factors that helped survivors. Thirteen of the survivors sought out professional counseling, with an average time of 10 years in therapy. The average age the survivors went to counseling was 23 years old. Barbara Absi stated, "I would take one step forward and two steps back. Counseling helped me understand why I wasn't trusting my instincts." Of the thirteen survivors who went to counseling, ten stated it dramatically helped, two stated it helped a little, and one stated it did not help at the time. Many of the survivors indicated that they had to go through several counselors until they found someone whose style matched their personal needs.

A few survivors mentioned, if the counseling was not directed and did not accurately address sexual abuse, the survivors reported few benefits. As Linda stated, "The counseling was for an eating disorder. It didn't help. It just kept me alive. The abuse was still going on at home." She also added, "Everybody heals in their own way. You have to find it. Don't depend on another's view of how you should heal. If you have to go through 100 therapists, find a therapist that feels safe."

Nine out of the fourteen survivors also attended an in-person or on-line survivor support group. The average age of those who sought out support groups was 34-years-old, and the average time spent in a group was 4 years. All of the nine survivors who participated in a support group, found it to be helpful.

Sexual abuse survivor groups are more difficult to find than other support groups such as Alcoholics Anonymous, Gamblers Anonymous, and Cancer support groups. However, the benefits of participating in a group seemed gigantic for survivors. Most of the survivors who were attending a group at the time of the interview, planned on staying in their group for a while. A suggestion was, if an individual is not ready to talk openly in front of others, he/she should participate in an on-line group. Linda explained how she benefited from an on-line group, "It helped me talk about it without watching people's reactions."

I believe other factors that help survivors heal, are found within the individual. Tanisha stated what helped her heal was the, "Understanding that I had choices. I didn't have to be a victim forever." Angie recalls, "Somehow I knew I was worth so much more than I was feeling inside. Finding the courage to heal, knowing my truth, and not being ashamed of my truth. Owning up to what happened to me. I would have protected myself if I knew it was wrong. It wasn't my fault." Marigrace realized her turning point in healing was, "When I made the decision that suicide was no longer an option. Until then, I didn't know peace and happiness in my life. Now even stuff that is hard, I know I'll work through it and another day will come." Barbara Absi acknowledged that the most important aspect to her survival and healing was, "Trusting in myself—not doubting how I feel, and allowing myself to heal, grow and allow the process that I would get through it."

I asked each of the survivors what advice they had to give to other survivors. Barbara Absi stated, "Don't allow a perpetrator the opportunity to choose your path for life. You can choose what path you want to go down—the negative path or the positive path. Take control of it and don't allow it to control you. Choose how you are going to live the rest of your life, as a 'victim' or a 'survivor'". Peter commented on his view of the sexual abuse as, "I don't want it to be the all encompassing thing in my life. It was bad what happened to me, but let's move on here. This is something that happened. It's not something that rules your life or something to dwell on. I wouldn't let this get in my way of doing what I want to do." Tanisha summed it up as, "With time and perseverance, you can survive. You'll never be the same person, but you can survive."

It was interesting to learn that the survivors, who continued with counseling, often found internal peace—if they concurrently became actively involved in preventing childhood sexual abuse, or exposing perpetrators. They were able to define their personal trauma in terms of a higher purpose and develop a higher form of spirituality. Marigrace explains, "During the abuse, it was total survival. I was just trying to live. When the abuse stopped, it was almost the same. I was still living as if the crisis was still there. It was a matter of life and death only now I was afraid I would take my own life. I believe there was some purpose for it. If someone survives and doesn't kill themselves maybe there is less evil in the world and they can now help others. God was keeping me alive."

After hearing about the trauma and struggles each survivor went through, it was gratifying for me to hear how each individual was able to find a turning point—allowing the survivor to take action or understand his/her growth despite the abuse. Peter found resolution in his life when "I filed suit, it felt like the right thing to do. After me, five others filed." John stated, "I think it has strengthened my spirituality. People are evil, and people change. People go from being good to bad. God never changes. God is consistent day in and day out." Angie realized,

"I'm happy that I have taken all the steps needed and will continue to survive this. I feel lighter now. When I think about the actual acts I had to perform and being manipulated—they are reminders of what I've experienced. Now I can switch into a confident person. It has helped give me the skills in communication, and the confidence and drive to help others. I can really read people because now I trust my instincts so much more."

Talking about the abuse and finding other survivors was recommended by most of the survivors. This support helped the survivors regain control in their lives, and gave them power over the abuse. As Juan stated, "Talk freely. There is no shame. We've hid it for years. Voice your opinion and trust your instincts. Trust yourself." Don Asbee advised, "Talk! Tell your story. Find somebody you know you can trust and tell them. It is the only way the cycle will be broken." Marigrace added, "Listen to those who have gone before you, if you have the chance. I never had anyone telling me suicide was no longer an option." Angie explained, "Just knowing you are not alone is a wonderful feeling." John said, "Talk to other people who have gone through it. Find other survivors. That way you know you're not alone, and it helps you understand it's not your fault. You were manipulated by the other person and taken advantage of."

When the survivors began to view the abuse as an obstacle that they could conquer, it added to their personal feelings of strength. Angie voiced, "Don't give up on yourself. You have coping skills. Some people have a great sense of humor. Others have a highly evolved sense of instinct. Listen to yourself and don't give up." David Clohessy recommended using three steps: "1) Break the silence - silence is deadly, 2) get into therapy or a support group, and 3) take some kind of action to protect other kids. It is the only way you can make lemonade out of lemons."

One of the most crucial pieces of information I needed to learn, was how I could support my children. I was desperate to know what a child, who has been sexually abused, needs—to help him or her heal properly. Juan explained, "Parents always own it like they did something wrong. It is not your problem. Don't take it personally. You didn't do anything. You couldn't do anything. The child pushes everyone away and the parents become the outsiders. Parents are then on the

106

opposite side of the bridge and there is no happy medium and no equal ground. It is not your fault." Just as parents can hold onto unnecessary self-blame, the survivor can drown him/herself in self-condemnation. Erick explained how survivors feel, "Every cell in their body tells them they did something wrong. The parents have to give affirmation to the child that they did nothing wrong." Linda added, "Validate the child's feelings. Encourage the child to talk. Do creative things to value him or her. Children take ownership of situations they have no control over. Many times they think, 'this is my fault.' Help them deal with knowing—some people are just not safe. They can then determine for themselves if they feel someone is not a safe person."

The survivors strongly recommended two things: stressing to the child that it is not his/her fault and open communication. Kim expressed, "Get rid of the perpetrator, apologize to the child. Let them know it is not their fault. Have open honest communication in the family. Constantly reiterate that the person who did that was wrong, and the most important thing is to teach the child to hear his/her own intuition." Tanisha stressed, "Take time to listen to the child and never blame." Beth added, "Let your child know you love him/her unconditionally and he/she can come to you with anything." John commented, "Let the children know there is nothing they can say that will shock you. You will be there for them and support them 100%. Never let them think you will doubt them." David Clohessy recommended, "Believe them. Ask what they need over and over again. And follow through on these requests even if they don't make sense to you." Angie stated, "Just listen. Give them time to heal. It's finding out what they need to feel safe in their home and with other people. Teach them those skills. Encourage them to be open and honest—to face those things within them." Marigrace summarized the advice for parents as, "Be there and listen to your child. Never ever, ever say 'how could you have gotten in this situation' or 'how could you have let it happen.' The child is already asking these questions. Take your personal anger and use it toward advocacy. Use the energy to help your child heal, and be honest with your feelings. Tell the child, "I'm frustrated, I'm scared for you, or I don't now what to do but we'll go here for help and we'll do this."

From the interviews, I learned that having a higher spiritual connection or higher understanding of the sexual abuse, became a contributing factor to eventually finding some form of internal peace. The survivors who had some form of spirituality or higher knowledge, seemed to question themselves less and have less turmoil. Kim explained, "Sexual abuse breeds an intensely spiritual person who is constantly searching: Where is God? Why is this happening to me? Why was I born into this life? Are bad things always going to happen to me? Where is the justice?" Marigrace noted, "I'm alive because I held onto my own belief in God. I thought my life would be – 'just getting through.' Now I have really great days and sometimes down days. But, it is not as bad as it used to be. The fact that I did wake up is all worth it." Linda recalled how, "The pain drove me to seek a spiritual life for myself. There is so much more to life that I am experiencing now because I am healing. It is like a tunnel widening. I am widening my horizons spiritually. I'm realizing God is a whole lot bigger than I thought. The abuse has deepened my spirituality which has given me solid ground beneath my feet in the craziness of all of this."

I believe any parent, guardian or caretaker of children should know the warning signs for a child that may have been or is currently being sexually abused. The more knowledge adults gain, the easier it is to identify children who are being sexually abused—to help prevent or end sexual abuse in its early stages. From the interviews with the adult survivors of childhood sexual abuse and our own family tragedy, I have been able to list several signs of a child who is possibly being sexually abused, or has been abused. (see *Chapter 8 "Is My Child At Risk For Sexual Abuse"*)

As we learned of the sexual abuse Joey and David had suffered, we began to remember small signs, which should have served as warnings that something was wrong. However, we were not able to make the connection until after the abuse was disclosed. Joey had increased periods of isolating from everyone. Then at times he tried to grab everyone's attention, by running around the house showing off his naked rear end. I used to tell him, "Put your pants back on! Why do you always have to show off your butt?" Even after Bob and I would tell him to stop exposing himself, he continued to strut around dropping his pants to be a comedian.

One day, I walked past Joey and thought I heard him groaning in a sexual manner. I stopped and listened carefully. I was shocked to realize he was mimicking sexual groans. I was horrified, and wondered where he would have heard that type of sound. I immediately told him to stop, and asked where he had heard that noise? He stood with his eyes wide open and could not say anything.

There were many evenings Joey would go to take his bath and we would find that he had raw skin around his anus. It was as if he had been sweaty all day and ran for hours—rubbing off the top layer of skin. It happened so many times I was thinking I should bring him to the pediatrician to figure out what was wrong. Then, we rationalized that it was probably because he was a little chubby—so the sweat in that area caused the damage to the skin. We also thought maybe Joey was not wiping himself completely after each bowel movement. After checking that Joey was wiping properly, we noticed if he showered everyday—his skin would not get raw. We concluded the skin was disintegrating in that area, because of the excess sweat. The daily ritual then became making sure Joey took a shower everyday to avoid getting raw skin. But the truth was—if Joey skipped a shower one day, then Adam's bodily fluids were left in that area from early in the morning into the next evening. We had no idea that showering everyday helped Joey's skin from being raw, because it was washing away the acidic evidence of the crimes Adam was committing.

After the initial disclosure and removal of Adam from the home, both boys were confused and nervous. Joey then realized it was what needed to happen and stated he finally felt safe and free from being paralyzed with fear. One of the first things he said was, "Mom, now I don't need to eat junk food anymore since Adam is gone." But, soon Joey was thrown back and forth with all of the emotions he had hidden and suppressed for the two years he was abused. Those intense feelings did not have to be hidden any longer—so they came out whenever they could. He would suddenly lose all control and have a total meltdown—flopping his body down on the floor or couch and sobbing uncontrollably. Things that for us, seemed to have no connection to Adam, would send him into a complete rage and emotional breakdown. It was difficult for me to understand how the abuse had ended—yet he was still so emotionally distraught several months later. He would scream, yell, sob and many times wanted to be left alone. During these episodes, we could not touch him or speak to him. There was no way to console him as he would sob and thrash his body from side to side. These meltdowns happened weekly for many months. We understood that we just had to leave him alone, and let him cry the emotions out. As the months passed, eventually these incidents became less frequent and less intense—until they finally ended.

Joey was then able to explain why he purposely isolated and stayed away from Bob and me. He said he was terrified that he might slip and say something accidentally. He knew if he mistakenly said a tiny portion of the torture he was suffering from Adam, the "beings" would instantly come to kill him. In his mind, the safest thing was for him to stay far away from all of us and make sure he never said a single word.

A few weeks after Adam was taken out of the house, David began taking his clothes off in front of other people to get a reaction out of them—similar to what Joey did when he was younger. David would dance around to purposely show off his private areas. No matter how many times Bob and I would tell him not to do it, I would still get reports from other people that he continued to expose himself during the day while I was at work. The only thing that helped him to finally stop exposing himself was when I explained privacy, private parts. I also told him that part of the reason why Adam was taken away was because he showed his private parts to David and touched David's private parts.

In the beginning, Joey, David and I discussed every memory. I was desperate to understand what my children had suffered, what signs I had missed, and how Adam had fooled both Bob and I, and everyone around us. After several months, both boys went through a period where they did not want to hear Adam's name at all. Anything that reminded them of Adam had to be taken out of the home or destroyed. It was a cleansing period for all of us. We discussed Adam less in the home and for a while I think we all tried to forget about everything that happened. But then the horrifying dreams began to haunt Joey.

Since I had just given birth to my third son, Paul, and was recently home from the hospital, Joey did not want to disturb me when I was sleeping. He kept having bad dreams each night, but told no one. Finally, after about two weeks of trying to hold the dreams inside, he told me what he was experiencing.

"Adam sneaks into the house. He takes a machete and cuts everyone's head off. He even cut off the baby's head!"

"Adam is behind the bushes, waiting for me and David. He has us run a race and kills us with a gun. He hides again because he is waiting. When Mom and Dad get home he will kill them too."

"David and I went out to the sandbox to play. Adam had been above us, hiding in the tree branches. He jumps down and kills us with knives. He starts walking towards the house because he is going to kill Mom and Dad who are inside."

When Joey was finally able to tell me the dreams, they immediately stopped. We learned that talking about everything helped to get the fears and emotions out, so it wouldn't bother him in his sleep. I told him to tell me every dream or memory he had from that point forward that scared him in any way or reminded him of Adam.

For about a year, Joey didn't have any other bad dreams until he started being haunted by huge raindrops, letters, and numbers. One morning Joey woke up and told me that he kept having the same nightmare, but each morning he forgot to tell me. The dream was that *the whole family disappears and leaves Joey alone by a pond. Huge raindrops, start to fall and land in the water. As the drops hit the surface, the ripple affect expands to a larger area. The place where the drop hits becomes darker—like black water.* The dream was terrifying for Joey, but I could not understand what was so scary about it. Then, Joey stated, "When I'm awake, if I see any signs with large letters or numbers, I go back into that dream." We could not understand the terrifying connection, but I knew it must be related to Adam. Finally as I asked Joey endless questions, until we both remembered that Adam used to wear a pajama top that had letters and numbers on it. As we spoke, Joey recalled a day when Adam sexually abused him. As Joey lay still—praying it was over, he could hear every raindrop as it fell on the roof. When we discovered the connection, we packed ourselves into the van during the next rainfall and parked next to a local pond. After talking about fun, silly things, Joey developed new positive memories so he would no longer feel afraid. Soon, Joey's raindrop dreams ended and he did not feel nervous when he saw signs.

As time went on, the boys were able to discuss their memories and fears with more detail. We started to understand why David, from when he was very small, was super protective of Joey. Several times David would actually hit anyone that teased Joey or was not nice to him.

Around this time, David was obsessed with the Hulk. What he loved about the Hulk was that he was an ordinary person and when there was a bad situation, he could become bigger than life and could take total control. Unfortunately, since David was a baby when Adam was in the home, David witnessed much of the mental and physical torture Joey suffered. He saw Adam force Joey to roll down the stairs, he saw Joey crying and afraid. He witnessed Joey getting chased through the house with a knife, and witnessed Adam choking Joey. One day when Joey and I were talking about a few more things that Joey remembered, David stated he never could help Joey and it really bothered him. He could remember not being able to talk and having no power to stop the situation. I assured him that he was a brave boy for wishing he could help Joey and that he should never feel guilty or responsible since he was a baby and really could not have done anything. I apologized to him again that Adam had done such terrible things.

Unlike Joey who readily discussed the trauma he had suffered from Adam, David usually kept his trauma private. He did not want to talk about Adam and avoided any conversations about the past. He was so young to see such unspeakable things happen to his older brother, Joey. But, we soon realized the tortures he also experienced.

I remembered a day when Joey and Adam had gone to the neighbor's house to play with their friends. David and I sat at home, and I was happy to have some quality time with him. We sat in the living room on the floor, playing with his toy piano. As we sat playing music, suddenly David began pointing to the top of the stairs and screamed, "There's a monster." I looked and saw nothing. I assured him, "There is no monster." He was adamant with what he saw, and his whole body was shaking uncontrollably. He kept screaming, and pointing to the top of the stairs. He wanted both of us to run out of the house. He was so terrified, I found myself getting spooked that maybe he could see a spirit or something I could not see. I tried to assure him that monsters do not exist. But he was so convinced of what he was seeing—he could not hear anything I said. I finally told him, "I'll get rid of the monster." We walked room to room and I yelled, "Hey monster! You have to leave! This is not your home! Get out of here!" It seemed to help David for the moment. But, for many months after Adam was removed from the home, David would shake in his seat at the dinner table. He was so terrified, he would wedge himself in between Joey and me so that the monster wouldn't come and get him. All of these times he would say the monster was at the top of the stairs and was coming to get him. That same spot at the top of the staircase, where David could see the monster—was the same place where Adam pushed Joey down the stairs. At the bottom, is where Adam tried to choke and suffocate Joey. Poor David had witnessed the whole thing. He had seen a real life monster!

Learning what the boys had been through, made it very obvious that they needed to learn some form of self defense to re-claim their bodies and minds. I thought about how the abuse had taken a toll on Joey's spirit, and witnessed the progressive isolation from everyone. During the abuse, Joey became a quiet child who had no confidence. His warm friendly personality of charming everyone as an infant and toddler—was totally wiped out. Several friends often commented how withdrawn Joey had become. They noticed he never wanted to talk to them on the phone anymore. During visits, he barely spoke a word. Once we learned of the abuse, I hoped that Joey taking classes in martial arts would help him feel safe again and bring back his confidence. I wanted him to become assertive instead of withdrawing inside himself. If Joey could learn self-defense moves in class, he would never have to suffer from any type of abuse again. He could now re-claim his body as his, and be proud of his own strength. David would also learn just by watching Joey in class.

I can clearly remember when Joey first joined the Tae Kwon Do class at the local YMAC. His instructor told him to yell when he kicked or threw a punch. At first, Joey let out a peep of a sound. For a second time, the instructor told him to yell loudly. Again, Joey made a whisper of a noise with absolutely no power. The instructor stopped the class and asked Joey, "If we looked outside this window and you saw your dog out in the parking lot, how would you yell for him? What if he was running away? How would you call him?" He then demonstrated how yelling for the dog quietly would not be effective. He explained to Joey that the same intensity to get his dog's attention had to be used when practicing martial arts. Joey had to call his dog at the top of his lungs and then at the same volume, give a yell for self-defense. Within minutes I witnessed how the instructor was able to transform Joey from a quiet timid child, into an assertive strong individual. Adam had squashed Joey's voice for so long through fear and torture—Joey did not know how to re-gain his own personal power. With every yell, I could see Joey's body stand more at attention as he lifted his head with more confidence. He remembered how to be assertive and feel proud of his body. He re-discovered his voice and was able to use it at full volume. As the months continued, I felt completely blessed to see Joey's hard work and appreciate his miraculous transformation. He found himself! He became an exemplary student who was usually assigned to teach all the new kids when they entered the class. His commitment to martial arts has never wavered and I know this is what has helped him—to never be a victim again.

As Joey gained confidence, he was able to share his insight into his own experience. One day, he explained to me, "When someone has touched you in your private areas, it feels like dirt is filling up your whole body little by little. But when you talk to people—it feels like the dirt is going away." He said before he started the counseling, "My whole body was filled with dirt, but now it has almost all cleaned out and there is only a little left in my foot."

Another day, Joey stated that he thinks, "Everyone has a God spirit and their own spirit. When someone drinks alcohol or takes drugs, it feels like the God spirit goes away and the person's spirit is left alone. Then it is hard to walk around because then it is just one spirit trying to control your body." He added that when he was sexually abused, "My God spirit was trying to help me tell, but my regular spirit was telling me, 'No, something bad will happen.' " He then explained what was happening with Adam. "Adam's spirit was going crazy because he was doing bad stuff. His God spirit was trying to tell him to stop it. But he would not listen, because his spirit was thinking, 'Yeah, I don't need the God spirit—it's OK, I don't need anything. All I need is my own spirit and myself.' He didn't believe in his God spirit and he ended up doing worse stuff. He couldn't stop it because his spirit was going crazier and crazier."

Sexual abuse survivors learn the difference between the words "victim" and "survivor." A "victim" would be anyone who is still mentally imprisoned by the abuse he/she suffered. A "survivor" would be a person who doesn't let the abuse control them and feels in control of their own life. I disagree with these terms. I believe anyone willing to use a child's body for their own satisfaction—is capable of murder. Sexual abuse is horrific—it not only invokes incredible fear and confusion within the survivor, but also leaves the survivor with mental, emotional, physical and spiritual baggage that he/she carries throughout life. I see anyone who has been forced to endure sexual abuse, as a "Survivor."

As discussed earlier, any mechanism a person uses to cope and survive from sexual abuse—whether it is constructive or destructive, is a personal choice and a right of that individual. If the person is not harming others, and he/she needs to use drugs or alcohol to escape the memories, or cut or burn to "feel" emotions—who can say whether that is "right" or "wrong." As each case of sexual abuse is unique to that individual person, so are the methods he/she will use to cope. Ideally we would hope that all survivors could find constructive coping mechanisms, but sometimes people need to experience the destructive mechanisms before they can progress to a more positive way of survival. As long as the person does not end his/her life, does not harm others, and continues to struggle searching for inner healing and peace—that person is a survivor.

Chapter 6
Perpetrators Among Us

Sexual abuse is a crime about control and power. Early in my career, I worked as a Detoxification Counselor. While working with people who were battling serious drug and alcohol problems—I heard ghastly stories of sexual abuse. In writing this book and listening to the survivor's descriptions of their perpetrators, I realized perpetrators enjoy the process of planning, fantasizing and eventually executing their plans. It is not a simple situation where, as some of the counselors we met stated, "Adam was playing out what was done to him." Sexual abuse is an intentional action. The goal for each perpetrator is to strip a child of all rights and freedoms—so the person committing the crimes can experience the power of having total control over another human being.

How a perpetrator is created is a complex concept. When I was trained to be a Rape Crisis Counselor, years before I ever got married and started a family—we had to watch a disturbing video. The movie "Child of Rage" (1992), which was directed by Larry Peerce, documented a true story which depicted a young girl and boy, whose parents were involved in drugs and other dysfunctional behaviors. The mother died when the daughter was two. The baby boy, who was only a few months old, had been beaten and left in a crib, in a dirty diaper for days. Eventually, the state's social service department rescued the children. However, the two-year-old daughter had been so seriously sexually abused by the father—it destroyed her. The two children were adopted into a family by a loving minister and his wife. But the girl's thought patterns were so distorted from the abuse, it ruined their chances of having a "normal family". At night, the two-year-old would sneak into her adoptive parents' room with sharp objects. When they asked her what she was doing, she would state that she had to kill them. They had to immediately hide all knives, scissors and anything else that could be used as a weapon. They learned that she had poked her brother with pins and said she had to kill him as well. The loving parents then had to lock her in her room at night, since they were so fearful of her. She also killed any animals she found in the yard. Her intention was to take any sharp object she found and stick it into anyone who was near her—and kill the person. Finally the parents had to send her away to a school since there was no hope of helping her. The treatment facility where she went was similar to a jail, where they stripped the kids of their own identity, and tried to replace the shattered thought processes with new patterns. After a few years, she had the chore of taking care of the animals on the farm-like setting. The video showed her giving food and water to the sheep and she did not attempt to injure them. Did the therapy work? Or was it temporary? Would she ever be a "safe" person? Or would she always be a threat to all people?

I found from the interviews, that most of the survivors go through a period where they question or blame God. But sexual abuse is not Gods' fault. Sexual abuse comes from men, women and juveniles. It is torture that is methodically forced upon and taught to another human being. At this point, society is ill- equipped to deal with the survivor and the perpetrator—and the "education" continues to be passed down from generation to generation. Another human being—my stepson, Adam, brought our family's tragedy to us. He had received the "education" from his relatives who raped and abused him in Cape Verde. But throughout the trauma, God, our Spirit Guides and our Angels were with us during the entire process. They were patiently waiting for us to ask them for help. Many times they were intervening, however we were so embedded in the quagmire, we could not see their subtle messages for protection.

To strip a person of his/her rights, independence, control, peace, and body is the goal of each perpetrator who commits sexual abuse. To manipulate another person into total submission is the highest success for the perpetrator. Yet, once the perpetrator has acquired the total submission of another human being, it is no longer a challenge or interesting, and he or she will search for other prey—another child. In our case, Joey's submission was not enough to quench Adam's thirst. As Adam got more violent with Joey, he began to "groom" and mold David to be his next victim—by implanting horrible fears into his mind to keep him silent.

Perpetrators are masters of disguise. They can portray a kind, generous loving person. They can be CEO's of companies. They can be trusted community leaders. But they have hidden lives and secret desires for control. Of the adult survivors I interviewed, all of the primary perpetrators carried full-time respectable jobs and were considered "good people" by those around them. The words used by survivors to explain the perpetrators' image and personality shown to others in the community were: friendly, caretaker, caring, outgoing, social, supportive of others, helpful, respected, likeable, fun, thoughtful, intelligent, kind, sweet, and loving. Only two of the perpetrators were described as showing "likeable" personalities as well as other personalities in public: tough, rough and aggressive.

The interviews revealed several tactics that were used by the perpetrators to commit their crimes and keep the children silent. The various types of tactics were: bribes, fear, putting the survivor down, making it a special relationship between the perpetrator and survivor, power, control, fear, and the threat that the perpetrator would start abusing the survivor's siblings or others if the child did not surrender to the abuse. Regardless of the types of tactics used, most survivors suffered similarly. Each survivor had to struggle with facing what happened, and eventually realize that the perpetrator was at fault. Each survivor was then left with a lifetime of soul searching, why this happened to him/her and face the immediate and lasting effects. Angie recalled, "I knew something was wrong, but I couldn't put my finger on it. No one would believe me if I told anyone. I repressed everything. She turned off my voice and left me powerless."

From all of the survivor interviews, four of the primary perpetrators were family members: 1 father, 2 mothers and 1 cousin. Of the other interviews, the perpetrators were people known to the child: 5 priests, 1 babysitter, 1 babysitter's brother, 2 mother's boyfriend, and 1 building janitor.

As I conducted the fourteen interviews, I began to piece together three basic descriptions of perpetrators. Many times a perpetrator will fit into one defined category. However, some perpetrators have almost a double personality—showing a combination of mannerisms and tactics from more than one category. In all cases, the perpetrators will spend weeks, months and years preparing the child to be a victim. The stories point to the fact that a perpetrator's thought processes are so skewed—they can never be "cured" and will always be a threat to children's safety.

The Buddy - Teacher Perpetrator

These perpetrators seem to be less violent and threatening against the child—serving as a "big brother," "big sister" or "buddy" type of person. They spend quality time with the child, buy valuable gifts, and take the child on special trips. Any time together is made to be "special time" together or "classroom time"– where the child receives his/her sexual education. These perpetrators use various tactics, which cannot be easily identified as "wrong" by the child. Since the perpetrator acts caring, the survivor struggles with internal, mental confusion.

These perpetrators act nice to the survivor, but continue to do inappropriate things. These perpetrators will play with the child, create a special bond between them, foster open communication, and make the survivor feel protected or privileged to be with the perpetrator. These perpetrators use tactics to quietly trick the child into submission. Dan remembered his perpetrator saying, "If you don't want it, I'll stop. He was using it as a teaching method." Erick recalled his perpetrator explaining, "There is nothing wrong with it. Don't be ashamed. Others wouldn't understand." Angie stated, "She made it feel like it was a good game to play and she chose me. I looked up to her. She was like my older sister. I wanted to be like her. She was the all American sweetheart." Erick recalled how his perpetrator, "Made me feel special, important in my life. Kind of like everyday was your birthday."

Many of the Buddy – Teacher Perpetrators develop strong relationships with the parents and other family members of the child—so he/she can have unlimited access. David Clohessy said, "He relied on my sexual naivety, confusion and innocence. He abused their trust (parents) to get access to me and my siblings. All feelings with him feel polluted. Was he nice and liked me or was it manipulation and all a sham?" Others use their position in the community and a child's need for a parent figure to commit their crimes. John remembered, "Here's the man of God, listening to me and taking the place of my father. He explained that as priests, God gave us our bodies and we're not supposed to be with a woman. He made you feel like you were number one important and gently listened to you. He seemed genuinely concerned how you felt and made you feel you were more mature than your age. He made me feel I could be trusted more than any other boy in school." John also stated how the community viewed the perpetrator, "He is such a good man, such a pious, holy and sacrificing man."

Survivors from these types of situations were often left feeling confused and searching through early memories to understand conflicting emotions. As adults they understand they were violated during their childhood. However, they also recalled childhood memories of quality time with the perpetrator with whom they felt a special relationship. They often questioned, "Was it abuse?" "Did he really care about me or was he just using me?" Survivors who were abused by violent, controlling and angry perpetrators do not seem to suffer from these types of confusing and mixed emotions.

The Sugar Daddy – Threatener Perpetrator

These perpetrators start out as the "Daddy" or "Grandpa" type of caretaker role by buying gifts, and buying things for the family. Then the personality progresses to highly volatile and full of threats against the child and his/her family. The Sugar Daddy – Threatener Perpetrator has to show he/she is in full control. No one is allowed to question him/her because the individual is too powerful. The sexual abuse from these perpetrators seems to be more violent and vicious–causing enormous physical pain to the survivor, which affects the physical body years after the abuse. Kim recalled how her perpetrator manipulated her from a very young age, "'This is something between us.' He had a criminal brain. He was always trying to get something and his solution to everything was violence." Beth remembered, "I had to protect my sisters. He knew he had a hold over me by saying my sister looked cute or touching them. Every look and touch always had a sexual overtone." Linda recalled, "I was expected to know what I could tell and couldn't tell. I was not threatened or bribed. I just knew it was something I couldn't talk about. Everyone thought the world of both of my parents. She was very changeable. I walked on eggshells a lot. As a teenager, I never knew what she would do or be like next."

The Mind Control "Monster" Perpetrator

These perpetrators use rituals, fear and implanted beliefs to terrorize their victims. They create such a concrete belief system for the child that he/she cannot think independently. The thought patterns become so ingrained in the child's mind—there is no escape from the implanted beliefs. Marigrace explained how her perpetrator, "Would use violence or threats that she would do it to other children if I told. Or she would prove how crazy I was and used humiliation and degradation so I was beaten down, and no one would believe me. No one could believe someone that 'sick' (me). She never recognized me by my given name. She used a terrible nickname for me during the abuse. I was confused and if people called me by my name, I didn't know if I should answer or acknowledge them. Others would say, 'we wish we had a family like yours.' She was a complete monster—night and day personality. My therapist said, 'She was more monstrous than any man could be. I've never heard of anyone as evil and scary as your mother.'" Marigrace knew exactly when her abuse started—since family videos of her first day of life clearly document her mother committing crimes against her as a newborn.

Adam was a Mind Control "Monster" Perpetrator. A few days after Adam was removed from the home, Joey explained to me who Adam really was. He stated, "When adults were around, Adam acted so nice and polite. As soon as he knew no adults were around—he acted like he had no mind, like a crazy person. That is who he really was." Shortly after Adam was removed from the home, Joey explained to me, "It was like he was a king and I was his slave. I had to do whatever he said all the time."

I had educated Joey from when he was very young about people touching him or hurting him and using things against him. I told him if anyone ever threatened his family's safety or his family member's lives, he needed to tell me. But there was no way I could have prepared Joey for the terror he faced with Adam. Adam's tactics for silencing Joey were unimaginable. He studied Joey, found any fears and magnified the fears against him. Adam built the fears into dimensions beyond comprehension to ensure his constant power and control over Joey.

Almost one year after Adam was removed from the home, Joey was triggered by a very early memory. One evening before I gave birth to Paul, I sat with the boys and we discussed how it would be when the new baby came home. Joey suddenly became very fearful as he remembered a conversation he had with Adam four years earlier. Right before David was born, Adam had taken Joey aside and said, "Now that the baby is coming, Mom and Dad will give me almost all of their attention because I'm the oldest, and the baby will get some of their attention. So you won't get any attention because they have to give it all to me and the baby." This was when Adam first began mentally manipulating Joey.

Looking back through the years, I can remember when Joey's fear of specific things started. I can now comprehend how Adam carefully studied Joey to see what made him frightened. He would then explode the fears into monstrous proportions to have control over Joey. He would constantly discuss the "beings" and reiterate the power he had to mentally call them to appear anytime he needed them. The "beings" were so powerful, they could mentally hear Adam and immediately respond. They had the mental power to know if Joey told anyone or if he was crying. If they heard Joey crying, they would instantly come to kill him. If Joey didn't do exactly what Adam wanted, Adam had the power to mentally call the "beings" and they would come within seconds—knowing their job was to kill Joey.

As Joey told me how Adam mentally terrified him and the tactics he used, I was able to retrace in time where Adam got the ideas and how long he was using the "beings" against Joey. During the summer of 2001, when we suspect the sexual abuse started, I was taking the boys to a particular babysitter's house, which was far from home. The woman, who and her husband who were recommended to me from a previous babysitter, seemed very attentive and caring. However, I remember feeling a little uncomfortable leaving the boys there. Joey told me that a neighbor, who was a teenage boy, became friendly with Adam and the two of them spent a lot of time together. One day the neighbor was mean to Joey in front of Adam, and Joey told me Adam did nothing to protect him. Another day, the babysitter allowed the teen and Adam to watch the movie Chucky while Joey was in the room. Joey was too young to see such a terrifying movie, and it truly scared him. But Joey was assertive and told the babysitter he did not want to see that movie, so they allowed him to watch cartoons in another room.

At the time, I remember seeing that Joey was very frightened by the movie. I sat with him and told him I was happy he asked to go into another room. I stressed to him that the mannequin was not real and the whole movie was not real. I remember telling him if he was ever afraid of something, he did not have to listen or watch—he could always walk into another room. Little did I know that Adam was also noticing how terrified Joey had become of Chucky. That is when Adam began developing his tale that Chucky had a knife the size of a staircase railing, and would come to chop Joey into pieces. Adam convinced Joey that *Chucky was real and had super powers. Chucky and Adam were able to communicate through their thoughts. Chucky also had the power to hear if Joey told anyone or if he cried.* This is how Adam first started manipulating Joey's mind. This is also the time period when all of us had the horrible dreams about losing Joey. I believe this is when the sexual abuse began. Adam was also able to add Dracula, Killer Bees, and rabid cats to his stories from the summer of 2001 to the winter of 2002.

Soon after we moved into our home, Adam met a teenage neighbor who was left alone for many hours each day. During our house warming party, the boy and his younger four-year-old brother decided to search through Adam and Joey's belongings. I later learned that a couple of my friends told the teen and his brother to go outside several times—but they did not listen. Bob and I became very cautious around that family. As time went on, Adam told me that the boy had started stealing from people in the neighborhood. Adam diligently told me everything the teen stole, the trouble he caused in school and bad things he did on the bus. When I banned Adam from being friends with the boy, he was furious and could not understand why I did not want them together.

Finally in the summer of 2002, we met a neighboring family that consisted of a mother, her boyfriend and her teenage son. They all seemed nice, and Adam and the teen got along well. At the time, Bob and I were relieved to see that Adam was forming a friendship with a "nice" kid, since a number of the local teens were already getting into drugs and legal trouble.

One evening we visited the family, and the mother told Adam and Joey to be careful in the backyard—not to go near the grill, where some wood bees had taken up residence. Joey was extra cautious and later said he was afraid. I told him bees usually don't bother people unless you step on them or bother their homes. This is when Adam added fuel to the fire and began terrorizing Joey with yet another tale. Adam invented the story that *there were Killer Bees that were the size of buildings. They, just like Chucky and Dracula, could hear Adam calling them mentally and could hear if Joey told anyone or ever cried.*

On another occasion, neighbors told us that a white cat had followed and tried to bite one of the young men in the yard. We all suspected that this was a wild cat and probably had rabies. I told the boys to be careful and if they were outside and saw a white cat in the yard, to come inside immediately. Joey became overwhelmingly frightened. Every night when I brought them home from the babysitter's, he would cry in terror at the doorstep until the door was opened. Adam saw this intense fear and developed his newest story. *The white cat did have rabies and also had the super powers of Chucky, Dracula and the Bees. If summoned, the White Cat would come to bite and claw Joey to death.*

After many months free from Adam, Joey remembered another scare tactic used against him. With a teenage boy in the car, sometimes I would leave the boys inside and run into the store for a gallon of milk and bread. Each time I was going to run in, the boys would ask if I could get them some candy. I would explain that if anyone was fighting or crying when I returned, I would not be able to give them any candy. The boys understood they had to be nice to each other. I would then quickly run into the store, get the few items and come back to the car. Every time when I returned, the boys were like perfect angels, patiently awaited their candy.

Joey recalled the experience David and he endured each time when I was away from them for those few minutes. Adam had a blue rock, which he told the boys had powers. He explained that *if the rock touched either of them, they would instantly die.* He also told them that *if the rock touched them on the head, their head would shrink and then people would eat their bodies*. Adam would then terrorize them by coming close to each of them—threatening to touch them with the rock. As they screamed in terror, Adam would keep a careful eye for me coming out of the store. Joey explained that as soon as Adam saw me coming towards the car, he would say, "Oh, here comes Mom! You're not going to get any candy if you're crying." The boys would quickly dry their tears and I would hand out the candy—knowing nothing of the mental torture they had just suffered.

It was many months after Adam was gone that I understood the connection to this bizarre tale he was using against the boys. During that time, Adam had said that the kids at school were teasing him because his head was very small. Adam's head was noticeably small in comparison to his growing body frame. He had become adamant to grow his hair as dread locks. He said longer, bushier hair helped make his head appear bigger. In retrospect, I could see that Adam had taken the frustration he had at being teased in school about his small head—and used it against his brothers.

Another way Adam traumatized Joey was to use his fear of losing his mother against him. Almost on a weekly basis, Adam used to try to sneak up behind me to scare me. Luckily, every time I knew he was coming and did not give Adam the reaction he was seeking. I told him many times, "Adam, don't do that. If you scare someone bad enough, you can give them a heart attack!" After Adam was removed from the home, Joey recalled how Adam closed the bathroom door one day and told Joey I was in there. He then told Joey "I'm going to run in there and give mom a heart attack." Joey pleaded and begged him not to scare his mother because he was terrified I would die. Adam then dramatically swooshed the door open laughing, as Joey saw that I was not in the room.

Adam showed no compassion towards the boys. If he ran past them and accidentally knocked one of them over—it was as if he had knocked over a chair. He would not say he was sorry and would not check if they were all right. The only time he would apologize to them, was if Bob and I screamed at him after knocking them to the ground.

One day, right before Adam was removed from the home, the whole family was walking to the local YMCA. The boys were very excited because we were all going to play basketball. David ran up ahead followed by Bob and then Joey. I was behind Joey and Adam followed behind me. As we hurried down the sidewalk, Adam suddenly ran past me. He ran right up to Joey and jumped on his back with full force. Joey was five-years-old and his small body could not support the weight of a thirteen-year-old boy. Joey's body collapsed face first onto the cement. Adam comfortably sat on top of him and then jumped to his feet. I could not believe what I had just seen! Bob had looked back at that moment, and also witnessed the whole thing. We were both so horrified and filled with intense emotions! Bob was ready to hit Adam and demanded an explanation of what he could be thinking to just jump on top of a small boy like that. Adam made an excuse that he was trying to run around Joey, but at the last minute Joey moved in front of him. Adam stated he was trying to jump out of the way from hitting Joey—and landed on him instead. Bob and I knew it was a lie since we had witnessed the entire event. Since we were out in public, we could not make a huge scene. We were so upset, neither one of us could speak with Adam that day.

Right around the time when I started getting sick, which was a few months before Adam was taken out of the house—Bob came in the house one afternoon telling me that one of the baby bunnies looked sick. Later that day, Adam went out to find that the bunny had died. Adam then went outside and brought the bunny into the house to show us that it had died. As he held it up in the air, the head dropped. I was very upset by the whole thing and was worried if the other rabbits would soon get sick as well. Bob too was concerned why this bunny had died. As Adam stood there holding the corpse, he laughed out loud and purposely moved the body so the head bobbed from side to side. It was entertaining for him!

In hindsight I can see that Adam had become extremely arrogant during the few months before he was removed from the home. He would use the stolen objects right in front of the person he had stolen it from. He had started calling Joey "chubby" in front of me and even after several times of me scolding him, he continued. He had even started to use his controlling tactics on Joey while in the car with Bob. Joey recalled a day when Bob was driving to the store. Bob realized he had gone the wrong way, and turned the car around. At that moment, Adam leaned over to Joey and whispered, "Oh, see! We had to turn around because the bees were waiting for us and they were going to kill you and Papa. Papa knew it—so that is why he turned around."

Joey later reported other ways Adam showed his arrogance. One evening, Adam climbed out on top of the porch through a window, while I was cooking dinner downstairs. He wanted to show Joey, he could break any rule Bob and I had in the home. Joey later remembered that the sexual abuse had even progressed from just during the early morning hours while Bob and I slept, to during the day—while I was in the yard feeding the dogs, rabbits and chickens.

A few weeks before we found the stolen items, Adam started a conversation about "deep dark secrets." He said, "I have a deep dark secret that I would never tell anyone." Intrigued, I asked what the secret was. I got the sense from him that it was something that really bothered him. So I asked again, "What is the secret?" I explained to him that deep dark secrets are not good to keep because, "Those are the secrets that make us feel uncomfortable and bad." I said, "Talking about things we are embarrassed about, can make uncomfortable feelings go away." Hesitating during each sentence, Adam finally said that his deep dark secret was, "I had a dream that I was having sex with an older woman." I immediately got a sick feeling that the dream involved me. I quickly told him, "Sex dreams are normal to have as a boy is getting older and there is nothing to be embarrassed about." But I quickly changed the subject. This was his "deep dark secret?" He was worried about having sexual dreams with his step-mother—but never believed the torturous acts he committed against his brothers were deep dark secrets. He had no intentions of ever disclosing the horrible abuse he had inflicted on his two younger stepbrothers.

Besides the mental fears, Adam terrorized Joey with knives. Joey could not clearly remember the details of the day when Adam chased him through the house, threatening him with a knife until much later. All he could remember was running in the rain with no shoes to Danene's house for safety. Almost a year and a half after Adam was removed from our home, we sat watching TV one evening and Joey suddenly remembered. Adam stood in the living room cutting an apple. As he moved to sit on the couch, he instructed Joey to sit quietly on the stairs. He was not allowed to speak. As Adam cut the apple in half he said to Joey, "If you talk, this will be your head," symbolizing that he would cut Joey's head in half. Adam stared at Joey as he dug the knife into the apple—implying he would make the same incisions in Joey's body if he moved or spoke. After sitting for a long time, Joey told Adam, "I have to go to the bathroom". Instantly, Adam jumped up, furiously threw the apple to the ground, and screamed, "What!" Adam then chased Joey up the stairs with the knife in his hand ready to stab him. Joey ran upstairs, through the bedrooms and down the other staircase. He quickly opened the closet to get his shoes and realized he had no time. At that second, he threw open the door and ran as fast as he could to the neighbor's house. He could not care that it was freezing and raining outside. He ran—dressed in shorts and a t-shirt, with no shoes or jacket. Joey told the neighbors that Adam chased him with a knife. A few minutes later, Adam arrived—smiling, and carrying David. He laughed and explained to everyone that he was only joking.

Another day, Joey tried to escape again. He asked Adam if he could go outside to get his football in the yard. When Adam said yes, Joey quickly went outside and started to run down the street. But Adam saw Joey escaping and ran faster—catching him in his arms. He grabbed Joey and shoved him back in the house. Joey could not remember what happened once inside the house.

Long after Adam was gone, I could not stop thinking about something. I finally asked Joey how he knew what was expected of him each morning. I needed to know what this monster had done to my child. Joey told me that the way Adam would wake him up each morning, was that he would hurl his entire body on top of Joey with full force. When Joey would wake up, Adam would stare at him with his lips pinched together. His eyes would give a furious stare that would look right through Joey. From the possessed look, Joey instantly knew what he had to do. Joey would then pull his pants down and Adam would lay on his side behind him. Joey had to lay there helpless, and wait for Adam to finish. Once Adam finished his crime, he would push Joey away. As I heard this, I suddenly realized why Adam had such a hard time getting up for school each morning in seventh grade—despite getting a full night of sleep. Each morning I would shake and poke him, as he would lie there in a comatose state.

Joey's rawness around his anal area went unrecognized for months. Since we had convinced ourselves it had to be a problem with cleanliness and being chubby, I bathed Joey myself several times—to make sure he was totally clean. As I bathed him, he would scream in excruciating pain from the water hitting the sensitive area—where the top layer of skin was removed. His screeches were unbearable to hear! Since I had to listen if David was all right downstairs or in the next room, I usually left the bathroom door open during these traumatic times. Adam was always right outside the door. At the time, I thought Adam was equally concerned why his younger brother Joey was suffering so greatly. Adam was concerned. But, his worry was not for the welfare of Joey. His apprehension was that Joey might say something. Adam hung around the bathroom door every time Joey had to take a bath—to make sure he never told anyone the real reason why his skin was raw.

Joey remembered portions of other tortures, but it took two years for him to recall everything that happened to him on the staircases closest to my bedroom. Adam demanded, "Do a summersault down the stairs or else I'm going to call the bees!" Adam stood half way down the staircase and told Joey he would catch him as he rolled. David, who was two at the time, stood at the bottom of the stairs watching as Joey was forced to roll down. Once Adam caught Joey, he grabbed Joey and pulled him through the house to the other staircase. Again he demanded, "Roll down the stairs or else I'll call the bees!" Then as Joey rolled, again Adam caught him half way down. Then Adam screamed, "The bees are coming! The bees are coming!" Joey quickly ran upstairs and hid himself in the bathroom under a towel. Adam ran to the outside of the door and yelled in, "Joey! The bees are in there! They're in there!" Joey ran out and stood shaking and sobbing with fear in the hallway. "Joey, the bees are out here! The bees are out here!" Adam grabbed Joey, and led him down the staircase where he had just tumbled. In the living room, Adam sat behind Joey, wrapping his arm over Joey's shoulder and around his four-year-old brother's neck. He placed his other hand over Joey's nose and mouth. Adam said, "Pretend that you're dead so the bees can't smell you and they won't come." Joey understood he had to be almost dead for the bees not to come. As Adam's hand covered Joey's nose and mouth, he squeezed his other hand against Joey's neck to choke him. For what seemed an eternity, Joey was being suffocated—to the point that his eyes filled with tears from not being able to breath. Then, Adam finally let go. Joey later explained that he knew deep within himself why Adam stopped that day. "He didn't know how he would explain how I had died. When you would come home from work he wouldn't know what to say."

I finally understood the visions I kept having of Joey dead at the bottom of the staircase after Adam was removed from our home. Adam did develop a plan of how he would explain Joey's death. But Adam did not have enough time to execute his plot. Miraculously, we learned of his secret torturous behavior before he was able to carry out his demonic design.

Juvenile predators perpetrate against young children. The children usually do not have the verbal skills to explain what is happening, or are too afraid to tell anyone. When a disclosure is made, or adults recognize that sexual abuse has taken place, children are often dismissed as credible sources. Legally, the focus then shifts to physical evidence. However, since the skin in private areas of the body has a rich supply of blood, any rips or wounds usually heal within a few days. Thus these cases are very hard to prove and the crime continues.

From the survivor interviews, I was able to analyze which tactics the perpetrators used most often. The survivors indicated that the most common scheme the perpetrators used to silence the children was power and control. The next most common method was to make the abuse into a special game—or a valuable secret. The perpetrators implied that it was something that should remain private and between two people— since no one else would understand. Fear and the survivor feeling that he/she had to endure the abuse to keep other siblings protected was the next most common strategy used against survivors. Putting the child down by degradation and insults was the next most common factor. Another device used, was making the child feel comforted or protected from other children who were mean, or bullying. The last tactic was using bribes such as money, gifts and excessive toys or special trips.

A sexual abuse perpetrator will use any maneuver to get his/her next victim. A perpetrator cannot feel compassion for a victim or guilt for his/her crimes. There is no longing for recovery or a feeling or need to stop the "addiction." After interviewing survivors and understanding Adam on a deeper level, I believe it is rare to find a perpetrator who seriously yearns for recovery. I think most perpetrators never feel guilt or remorse. In a twisted way, I feel perpetrators believe they have a right to commit their crimes. They can also easily rationalize why they should continue.

A perpetrator can be a man, woman, or a child. Perpetrators can be family members, friends, other children in the neighborhood, older cousins, siblings, stepsiblings, parents, stepparents, aunts, uncles or grandparents. They can be teachers, coaches and medical professionals. They can be parents' work colleagues, youth group directors, clergy, company presidents, or any other community leader. Perpetrators are everywhere. They are constantly plotting how to have access to kids—through church, school, the local youth facility, by meeting other parents with children, through the internet, at the park, at the zoo, at the bus or train station, through their own children or others' children, or younger family members. Any place where children may be—a predator can always be lurking.

Until our society begins to see sexual abuse perpetrators for whom they really are—predators, and until we are able to develop systems that stop empowering them, the best defense is to teach children how to protect themselves. Children must learn how to identify, respect and trust their own instincts. They need to know signs of potential perpetrators and they need to be able to communicate openly with their parents and other loved ones.

A predator studies a person and plots how to gain access to that person to commit his or her crimes. They plan how they will gain personally from the victim's vulnerability. They usually look for someone who is defenseless —like a lion hiding behind a bush, studying which deer in the herd is young, old, sick or weak. Or they may look for a potential victim who is strong—so the process of gaining control and power is more interesting and exciting.

Through the interviews, work experiences and our own trauma, I believe there are ranges of predators. On one end are the psychological predators. These people thrive in the workplace. They are determined to ruin colleagues through rumors, lies, and gossip. They believe other people are threats to their own advancement, so they plot how to remove their colleagues. I have seen this type of personality several times in different work environments. These people are usually so caught up in their own ego and need for control, that they cannot see how toxic their language and actions are against others. I've witnessed how they get their victim when the person is vulnerable, gather information, and then use the information to hurt the individual. They plot how to succeed, how to make individuals fall around them, and ultimately how to have power over others.

Another perpetrator is the <u>possession predator</u>. This predator will steal things from someone or intentionally ruin relationships between their victim and others. The woman who wants to steal her friend's boyfriend—to hurt her friend is a predator. There are also predators who will seek financial gratification. Telephone scam artists who prey upon unsuspecting senior citizens are predators. Identity thieves are possession predators. They study and analyze a person's vulnerabilities and then strategize how to feed their personal hungers for finances, personal recognition, and power. I believe these perpetrators are in the middle of the range of predators.

At the other extreme from the psychological predators are the <u>life predators</u>. They use psychological and physical abuse against their victim. These perpetrators operate on an animal level of consciousness. They will murder their victim for the "high" feeling of torturing someone and having the ultimate power to terminate another person's life. Similar to other perpetrators, they look at people and weed out potential victims. They look at a person and evaluate how easy it will be to manipulate the individual mentally, use them physically, and then discard them when they are done.

Very close to the life predators, I believe, are the <u>sexual predators</u>. A sexual predator uses a vulnerable person's body for his/her own mental, emotional and physical gratification. Predators of this nature use rape or sexual abuse as a way to feel power and control over another person. Much like a cat will play with a mouse. Often times, the cat will play with the tiny creature and not immediately kill it. The cat enjoys the power it has to manipulate the mouse to run in different directions. The cat enjoys the power—knowing it can terminate the life of the small animal if needed. Sexual predators enjoy playing with a person's life by using body and mind. They violate the person's body, strip the individual of pride, confidence, and dignity, and craftily create total mental havoc for the victim. A sexual predator knows he or she has the power to squash the life out of the victim—but is entertained by the chaos they have created. The tactics to silence the victim, the physical act, the art of finding new prey—it is all a game for a sexual predator. It is fun for the perpetrator to gain total submission of a child. Once the submission is gained, the hunt is no longer interesting. Then it is time to search for a new victim. At that point, the person can either be discarded or not—it is not really important to the sexual predator. What is important is that the game continues.

Eight of the fourteen survivors reported that the perpetrator used drugs or alcohol before or during the abuse. Four of those survivors reported that others considered the perpetrator a total alcoholic or drug addict. The other four were considered social drinkers. Seven of the fourteen survivors also stated they were given alcohol or drugs by the perpetrator prior to the abuse.

Six out of the fourteen original perpetrators committed their crimes while under the influence of alcohol or drugs. Yet, the other eight perpetrators did not use any substances during the abuse and were violating children with completely clear intentions. This indicates that sexual predators will perpetrate with or without the use of substances. Perpetrators plan their actions, alcohol or drugs do not influence their crimes. The actions are intentional and the crime is committed without a conscience.

As mentioned in the earlier chapter, all of the survivors stated there was no indication from the perpetrator of any feelings of guilt or remorse. All of the survivors indicated that the perpetrator did not seriously attempt to apologize for his/her actions. Just as an animal will not mourn the death of its prey—a perpetrator who commits intentional and planned murder or sexual abuse, will not feel remorse or guilt. It is similar to asking a shark to feel sympathy for the person it just bit. It is a ridiculous concept. This is the clarity survivors have. Survivors know and have been forced to accept the true nature of perpetrators. They are true predators with no remorse for their actions.

We observed the callous, cold affect of a perpetrator, numerous times with Adam. When we returned all of the stolen objects to the rightful owners, and when Bob and I confronted Adam about the physical, mental and sexual abuse of Joey—he felt nothing. Adam was removed from the home on a Sunday and that Thursday called me on the phone. He said, "Hi Mom, I really like it here. I like this place better than the last one. I want to stay here. If we do one chore per day, we get $10.00 each week. If we do more than one chore, we get extra points. The other day I went bowling and a 26-year-old woman took me to Newport Creamery. I got a vanilla shake." He was so happy to tell me how wonderful this new and exciting place was. He had no connection to his actions and why he was taken out of our home. He felt no remorse, guilt, or embarrassment. There was no sadness that he was ripped out of our family. It was as if he had never lived with us before. He did not feel bad about what he did. He did not miss us in any way. He was happy in his new place. It was hurtful to think the support, nurturance, guidance and love we had given him for almost four years, meant nothing.

When Bob dropped off a bag of clothes for Adam one day, he said, "Papa, I've been here a month and it only feels like two weeks!" This was a kid, who came from nothing—yet with our family, he had constant support from his parents, brothers, grandparents (my parents), friends of the family, friends in the neighborhood and at school, and supportive teachers. He had everything imaginable that a 13-year-old boy would need: a bike, TV, toys, a great yard, a position on a winning soccer team and a home. But not one person or thing was missed. He was completely content with his new surroundings. It was as if he went away to camp for exciting new adventures.

I thought back to when we first brought Adam to America—and he never showed any signs of guilt or remorse when he hurt others. One day our family went fishing with my parents. At the time, we were visiting relatives who lived on the ocean. Joey and Adam were ecstatic to go fishing with my mother. They cast their fishing poles out several times to learn how to use the equipment and what to do in case they got a bite. Then, during one of the initial attempts, Adam brought the rod back and the hook became embedded in my mother's leg. My mother screamed for him not to hurl the rod forward—since it would rip open her leg. He stopped right before whipping the line forward, and saw the hook stuck in her flesh. We got the hook out, and Adam immediately picked up his rod to keep fishing—as if nothing happened. Meanwhile Joey, who was about three at the time, was so traumatized to see his grandmother in pain and bleeding—he immediately said he did not want to fish anymore. Since Adam showed no signs of remorse or guilt for hurting my mother, we immediately stopped fishing. Adam never made any attempt to see if my mother was all right or to apologize. If we had not stopped fishing, he would have continued and not acknowledged what he did.

Once we returned all the stolen objects, family members, friends, school officials, a few social service personnel, and a few law enforcement and legal representatives concurred with Bob and me. Adam was completely removed from his actions and the consequences of his actions—he felt nothing. After learning of the kleptomaniac behaviors, and returning the stolen objects to school, the officials there stated that it was extremely "chilling and disturbing" to see that there was no emotional response from Adam. He remained unmoved, cold and completely calm. It was unnerving to watch.

The police officers, who were involved in the case, both witnessed Adam's demeanor. They told me that they had worked in the adult male prison for years and saw Adam's type of personality regularly. It was the same personality they witnessed in the men who kept coming back to prison who never learned from their actions. I already knew from deep within me—how dangerous Adam was, but having my instincts affirmed by law enforcement officials, helped me accept that Adam was a true sociopath. When I told one of the officers that I was afraid of him coming back, he encouraged me to always lock all doors to the house and call the police immediately if Adam ever showed up on our doorstep. He also hinted that if he ever broke into the house—we would have to use any means necessary to stop him because he would not be there for a friendly visit.

I clearly stated to each of the mental health professionals involved in the case, that I truly believed Adam was a sociopath. The police officers and a few mental health workers, who seemed to be more educated in the field, all nodded silently in agreement with me. As the nodding ended, we stood in uncomfortable silence, accepting the unthinkable. The idea that a teenager could potentially be a complete sociopath at such a young age, was a tragic and terrifying concept.

We knew Adam was dangerous to society, but I quickly realized there were many more like him and they were everywhere. One afternoon I sat in a doughnut shop with my children. For some reason, Joey wanted to sit at his own table separate from David and me. As we sat eating our food, I noticed a man that passed by and looked at Joey.

About a minute later, the same man passed by again and looked at Joey. When the man walked by a third time and looked at Joey I realized, his eyes never scanned the rest of the doughnut shop. He was not interested in knowing what adult was supervising the child, was the child alone and where are the parents? He was interested in the possibilities. It was not a quick glace when he gazed at Joey. It was a look of possession.

Perpetrators view victims as their possessions—things they can use for a certain time and then discard when no longer needed. The day in the doughnut shop convinced me I had to understand that other perpetrators were always lurking. I had to empower my children so they would never be victims again.

Sexual abuse is about control and power. For some reason, the perpetrator needs to feel in control. He or she uses other people as objects to satisfy those needs. The word evil comes up in our culture very seldom except in religions. We are taught that evil is the devil, or horrible spirits that we cannot see. We are never taught that there are people around us in our everyday lives who are evil and will attempt to do evil acts against us. We have trouble believing that someone can be so wicked. The idea of a young teenager or a mother being considered evil seems repulsive and unrealistic, but it is exactly the word needed to describe these predators.

When we cleaned out Adam's bedroom, I found a picture of him under his entertainment center. He had taken a red marker and colored his eyes so they looked bloody. He drew a large red protruding nose for himself. He added thick red eyebrows on his forehead making them look heavy and angry. He drew horns coming from the top of his head and filled in a long red pointy beard. He made his own picture look like a picture of the devil. Was this a true reflection of his self-portrait?

As I stated earlier, Adam showed no remorse. However, he was able to show emotions quite regularly, as all perpetrators can. They are incredible actors who can show emotion, appropriate for specific times—when it is to their advantage. They will show emotions to manipulate a child, and to protect themselves. From the time we first brought Adam home as a nine-year-old boy, until the time he was taken out—I saw him cry three times. He never once cried about leaving his grandmother—who raised him from when he was an infant and with whom he was very close. He never cried with guilt when he would "accidentally" bump into one of his younger brothers knocking them to the floor. He never cried when he was scolded, or privileges were taken away.

The three times I saw Adam cry were: when he first came to America and had blood drawn by a phlebotomist, when he was sick one day with a high fever, and when Joey disclosed the sexual abuse. When Adam had the blood drawn, I tried to assure him that it was all right and the phlebotomist was taking a small amount just to make sure he was medically healthy. Adam screamed in terror. At the time, Joey was two-years-old and looked at Adam as if he was a lunatic. Even Joey understood that the blood needed to be drawn and never acted so ridiculous. The screeching cries Adam made were similar to an animal whose leg was caught in a trap. All of the hospital staff could not believe Adam was so out of control. When Adam cried during his high fever, it was because he felt extremely sick and had never experienced flu symptoms before. When I confronted Adam about the sexual abuse he had committed against Joey, he did not cry. But when he heard Bob screaming that he was going to send him back to Cape Verde for ruining our family—Adam suddenly cried. He realized he did not want to be sent back to a country that did not have the same comforts as life in America. He conveniently began crying and stated, "I just remembered, my uncle used to do it to me."

Studying a perpetrator's motives for selecting certain victims and using specific tactics for silence, leads to many questions. Adam perpetrated against young boys. Did he perpetrate against them because those were the children he had access to? Had the scare tactics he used been used against him? Did the ideas come from his own memories, imagination or did he get the ideas from movies or some other source? The other question was why did he perpetrate against boys and only steal from men? Why wasn't he actively stealing from women?

The objects Adam stole did not make any sense. He stole after-shave from a neighbor, and at the time was 12-years-old with no facial hair to shave. He stole valuable things and took them apart in his room so they would not work again. Why would he steal things only to destroy them? Why did he take the broken pieces and carefully hide them so no one could find them—instead of discarding them into the trash? When

Adam stole objects and then used the items in front of everyone, was it arrogance or forgetfulness?

Adam had stolen my father's Walkman, which was a gift from my mother. He explained to Bob and me that he borrowed it from a friend. Then one day he had the audacity to use the walkman in front of my mother. She looked at it and thought "Oh that is the same brand I bought." But, knowing the set she had purchased was lost, she forgot about the incident. At the time, she didn't realize the set Adam was wearing was the gift she had given to my father. Was Adam hoping to get caught because he knew he would never stop stealing on his own? Did he use the objects in front of people because he truly forgot that he stole it? Or was it arrogance to show how in control he was? He had done such a great job of manipulating everyone around him. Everyone thought of him as a truly innocent, sweet, polite, respectful and responsible young man who was beyond suspicion. Many times he used to tell me that he wanted to be an actor when he grew up. I would just listen and say, "That is a good idea." But, each time I secretly thought, "How could he be an actor? He doesn't show any emotions. To be an actor you have to have a dramatic personality." Little did I know he was giving Oscar winning performances every day that he was living with us.

Almost all of the electronic objects recovered from Adam's room were in pieces. He had obviously tried to take them apart to see how they worked. I later found out from his counselor that taking apart electronic objects is a common sign of a child who has been severely sexually abused. She explained that it is almost as if they were not in control over what happened to them during the abuse, so they try to understand material objects. Perhaps their mind believes, if they can put the electronic gadget back together—then they can master their trauma from the abuse.

But, I knew Adam would never heal from his past mental, physical and biological trauma. He was already too far gone. I understood and knew that Adam's brain did not function normally and he would always be a threat to our safety. Since he was sentenced to sexual assault in the second degree, it carried a 10 year period where he had to register as a sex offender. I was never informed if this would take effect immediately or once he became eighteen. Eventually, I checked with a police officer to verify if Adam's sentencing automatically listed him with a criminal record. It was extremely saddening to learn that any youth offender, such as Adam, will remain totally protected. Juveniles' records are sealed and even law enforcement personnel cannot have access to those records.

What concerned me was program staff encouraging Adam to find a job in the community. They had requested Bob's signature to give permission for Adam to work. It did not matter that Adam was a convicted criminal. His record was not accessible to allow a background check. I even asked a friend of mine who is a police officer, to double check if Adam's record was accessible—and if his criminal activity was listed. The answer was exactly what I was afraid of. Adam's record was inaccessible and he could get any position of employment where juveniles were allowed to work.

As I witnessed the dysfunction in Adam's mind, from when he lived with us and was ultimately removed. I worried about my children's futures. I was terrified if Joey and David could potentially become perpetrators. I was completely attentive when the adult survivors mentioned anything regarding the difference between perpetrators and survivors during their interviews. Kim stated, "Sexually abused kids need to learn empathy. A perpetrator is reactive, impulsive, and selfish and needs immediate gratification. A victim is reflective." Juan stressed the link, which is apparent when someone does not seek therapy and does not introspect to understand him/herself more intricately. "A victim and a perpetrator walk a fine line. One can become the other." Angie was forced to see her own potential as a perpetrator. She explained that she had a child come up to her one day and he looked at her in a very peculiar way. Angie believed the child could see her on a much deeper level than anyone else could. "He saw that I was a monster. I possessed all these horrible thoughts and abilities. I know how to manipulate because I've been manipulated. I know how to silence because I've been silenced. The healing part is the consciousness of really knowing that it is not OK and understanding what happened to me." The perpetrator had given Angie an education she normally would not have received. The perpetrator had given her an education, which she could then use and teach to another person. The survivors I spoke with mentioned— the potential of becoming a perpetrator is within each survivor.

Through conscious self-reflection, understanding the wrongs of the predator, and acknowledging the acts committed as abuse which should have never taken place—the survivor can remain a survivor without becoming a perpetrator. The survivor must realize that he/she now has the self-control and power to consciously choose never to re-enact the manipulative tactics and crimes that were committed by the perpetrator. Survivors can accept the responsibility of educating and advocating for prevention. Before finding her own personal healing, Angie stated, "I believed she (the perpetrator) was forever inside of me. But now there's no room for her anymore. People who have been sexually abused have a deep sense of compassion and understanding. You can help others if you have the courage to tap into it."

Preventing the crime from happening is the best way to keep children safe. It is imperative that parents know the potential risks for abuse and the ways a child can be manipulated. However, it becomes difficult for a parent who is protecting his/her children to still embrace the concept that there are many relationships between an adult and a child that are healthy. Quality time with a safe adult can be a bonding experience that helps create strong individuals.

The following lists serve as warning signs of potential sexual abuse perpetrators. The information should be considered in conjunction with all instincts, feelings, thoughts, emotions, and dreams. If internal negative messages are accompanying any of the following signs, you may be receiving warnings that the person is not a safe individual. Also look for combinations of behaviors from the list of children who have been or are being sexually abused in the Survivor Chapter.

Warning signs of an adult perpetrator

Special interest in children – work situations often involve children
Taking on a role of care-taker of a family that is not his/her family
Excessive need to be near younger children
May or may not have other adult relationships
Seeking a spouse or partner who has children from a previous relationship
Appearing as the ideal person your child should be with
Excessively planning quality time or "special trips" with a child

Giving gifts to a child

Giving gifts to family members to win over parents—they become less on guard

Pitting children against each other

Having an extreme focus on one child

People who openly show their anger, jealousy of children, and controlling behavior

Knowing too much about kids' things: games they play, music they listen to, and styles of clothes they wear

Warning signs of a juvenile perpetrator

Stealing behavior

Easily playing with children of a younger age for long periods of time

Excessive need to be near younger children

Touching of younger children (head, shoulders, back)

Excessive talking—distracting adults through words

Trying to appear as a "buddy" or "helper" to the parent—never leaving their side

Wanting to sleep with younger children

Taking apart objects—especially electronic gadgets

An individual who is picked on by other kids at school

Does not express any personal emotions

Does not show signs of bonding to other people—no strong relationships

Aggressive behaviors

School or social behavior problems

Damaging body parts

Anger problems

Severe mental health issues

Hurts or kills animals

Setting fires

Since our case involved a juvenile perpetrator, who was a victim of sexual abuse himself—the mental health and judicial systems immediately viewed the crime as less severe and automatically sided with Adam. They convinced themselves that, "Adam really didn't know any better since he had it done to him." By accepting the distorted concept, they did not have to face true evil. They did not have to look at Adam for who he really was.

When Adam was ten-years-old, he began mentally torturing and manipulating the boys. By the time he turned eleven, Adam had completely trapped Joey and David into a world of terrifying tales with no escape—and began sexually abusing both boys. He had actively attempted to murder Joey in several different manners, yet the mental health professionals in the case felt sympathy for Adam. They downplayed the situation as Adam's counselor clearly stated, "I know it is hard now and seems impossible, but you will see that in time, he (Adam) will do better, and then your family can be re-united."

It is difficult for people to see a juvenile and believe that he/she can do such evil acts against another human being. If there was any truth to the idea that a perpetrator will do what was done to him/her without knowing that it is wrong—then Adam would have committed the sexual abuse against our children in front of Bob and me. He would have openly discussed the horrible stories that he used to terrify Joey and David. He would not have gone to such lengths to manipulate their emotions, exacerbate their fears, and forbid them to disclose what was happening. Adam found every devilish way possible to keep them petrified in fear. He was supposedly abused in a one bedroom home where no one had any privacy. Yet, Adam learned how to commit his crimes secretly, at night, in different rooms—while Bob and I slept. He took advantage of any seconds or minutes that Bob and I were not physically close to the boys, and did everything imaginable to ensure his crimes remained hidden. He knew what he was doing was wrong—but he continued to commit the crimes and silence his victims.

Chapter 7
Prevention

The most fundamental conversation all parents need to have with their children, as soon as they can understand words—is that people might try to take them or do things to them that no human being has permission to do. A child needs to understand that every person's basic right is the right to his/her own personal space, body and mind. No one should ever attempt to take that right away from a child. Children need to learn from very early ages that their bodies are temples. Their bodies are to be respected by themselves and by others.

The next conversation to have with your child is about fear. As parents, if we know what makes our children afraid, we can help them understand their own fears. Once parents know a child's terrors and where the ideas are coming from, then the parents can help their child develop new thinking patterns. The best way to prevent sexual abuse is to constantly check in with your child. Ask your child if anything made him/her scared or upset during the day. Ask if anyone said or did anything, which frightened him/her. When a parent knows what specific fears a child has, such as spiders, the parent can ask, "Does anyone usually talk about spiders with you?" This will give a parent clues as to who around the child might be purposely building up the child's fear. Anyone who is purposely feeding fear to a child should be suspected of attempting to do much worse—and a child's time with that person should be closely monitored or eliminated completely. Encourage your child to report immediately to you, anyone who scared or frightened him/her during the day or anyone who made him/her feel uncomfortable.

As I explained earlier, I warned Joey from when he was very young that there are people who may try to hurt him. From when I was first pregnant with him, I had instincts to protect him from rape or being taken. I felt I did a good job preparing him and educating him that people can sometimes do bad things to other people—especially to children. I did not know to tap into his fears. I did not know that an advanced perpetrator would methodically use a child's fears against the child.

Adam was extremely sophisticated in his ability to analyze a child, study what the child's fears were, and then incorporate those fears into monstrous new dimensions. Joey knew no one should do anything to him, which hurt him. He knew he should tell Bob and me if anyone ever threatened a family member's or his personal safety. But he did not know that people should never frighten him by manipulating his imagination. He did not know that he should immediately report anyone purposely scaring him. Since Adam was able to convince him of the terrifying "beings" and Joey was not able to tell anyone, he could not escape from the mental, physical and sexual torture.

Children need to know the proper names of each of their body parts and the body parts of a person from the opposite sex. Since perpetrators can be either male or female, a child needs to be able to explain the perpetrators body parts in relation to his/her own body parts. A child should also be instructed to report if he/she ever sees any private areas of anyone who he/she spends time with.

Many discussions of good touch and bad touch should take place in your family. Good touch should be explained as a touch that makes you feel comfortable and safe. A bad touch should be explained as a hit, slap, punch or a touch in any of the private areas—either by someone's hand, body part, or an object. The child needs to understand that the only reason why anyone should ever touch his/her private areas is if there is a medical or hygiene reason. Parents need to explain to a child that he/she should never have to touch someone else's body parts or look at someone else's body parts. A child should not be watched while changing or going to the bathroom. A child should not secretly be shown pictures of adults without clothes or other children without

144

clothes. Rubbing up against another person's body is also something that needs to be stressed as reportable behavior. Even a touch on the shoulder, arm or back that makes the child feel uncomfortable—needs to be reported immediately.

Good and bad feelings need to be a part of daily household conversations. Children should be encouraged to openly ask any questions, and state any concerns or worries with their parents. Parents need to encourage children to tap into their feelings and openly discuss comfortable versus uncomfortable situations and instincts. Anytime a child feels uncomfortable, he/she needs to know that a parent/guardian should be told right away. The responsibility then lies with the parent to listen to the child and fully hear what he/she is saying.

Many perpetrators will "test" their potential victims. They will touch the child's back, shoulder, arm or waist and wait to see how the child responds. If the child does not move away, or communicate verbally, or physically that this is not welcomed touching—it becomes a green light for the perpetrator. He or she will then start "grooming" or preparing the child for more advanced touching and silence. Children need to be encouraged to listen to their inner voice and feelings. If they get a "yuckie" feeling, strange feeling or a heavy feeling in their tummy or heart—it is a way to know something is wrong. This feeling needs to be openly discussed and respected. If the child ever experiences the feeling, he/she should not be forced to be near the person who made them feel uncomfortable. If contact with that individual is unavoidable, then all interaction between the individual and the child needs to be closely monitored.

Help your child learn to trust his/her own instincts. If your child is frightened by something, trust that he/she may know something you do not know. Learning to feel what their heart is telling them is imperative. A few months before we learned of everything, I wanted to teach my children how to be more in tune with their own instincts. I was told to practice two different exercises with them. One exercise is to have them listen inside of themselves to guess who is calling on the telephone before the phone is answered. Another exercise is to think of a number or color. Then the child has to listen to his/her heart, or tune into any visions he/she sees in their mind to guess the color or number. The heart and stomach are great places to tune into feelings. The forehead is a great spot to actually see things that the normal senses don't pick up. It is also known as the "third eye" in many spiritual teachings.

Another discussion related to good touch and bad touch would be **green flag** people and **red flag** people. Joey and David's counselors explained that a **green flag** person would be someone that the child instinctually feels is safe and has never shown any reason to feel uneasy or nervous around the person. A **red flag** person would be anyone who has demonstrated in some way to the child, that he/she can act "mean", "wrong" "uncomfortable" or "not nice". Children learn very early what are right and wrong behaviors. Listen to your children when they say someone did not act "right" or was acting "wrong." Anyone that frightens a child should immediately be seen as a **red flag** person. Children will probably not be able to make the connection—that is why it is so important to truly listen to their words. Once their words have helped you as a parent define someone as **red flag**, tell the child to be very careful around that person and to immediately report anything uncomfortable, weird or bad. Any person, who is defined by your family as a **red flag** person, should not be allowed near your child. But, if contact with the person is unavoidable, give your child the power and right to report anything odd to you immediately. All time near the **red flag** person should be closely monitored and supervised. Children also need to understand that sometimes people can appear to be a **green flag** person but may become a **red flag** person or vice versa.

Green flag or **red flag** just means to always pay attention to people. But once something is said, or done that clearly indicates that a person is a perpetrator either by your child or any other child, your plan with your child must change dramatically to reflect the severity of the situation.

Validate your child's feelings. If he/she does not like someone—good! It seems very contradictory to our culture. But, you would rather have your child not like someone who is a good person, than to force him or her to like everyone. If your child says he/she doesn't like someone, ask what is not liked about the person. Did he/she witness the person doing something, or is the child getting a feeling? If it is a feeling, help your child tune in and see where it is coming from—the mind, heart, stomach or forehead. Each of those locations will help you as the parent understand what senses your child is experiencing.

146

Explain that it is all right if he/she does not like someone, because there are so many people in the world. You don't have to like everyone. It is important for your child to get familiar with his/her own instincts. Reaffirm to your child that he/she has the right to meet people and if something (a feeling, emotion, vision, instinct) tells them not to like that person, their innate instincts will always be respected.

Don't ever force a child to hug or kiss someone if they do not feel comfortable! That teaches children that they do not have a right to their own feelings, emotions and bodies. If they feel uncomfortable, nervous or shy—that emotion needs to be respected. Culture plays a large part in this aspect. When we traveled to Cape Verde, my husband and I would get embarrassed because Joey would not allow the old women to kiss him or touch him. Culturally, the proper greeting is to shake hands as you give a kiss on both cheeks. If you do not greet people in this manner, you are going against cultural etiquette. Joey did not want to shake hands or kiss anyone, yet Bob and I still encouraged him. By us following the "cultural norms" we were forcing Joey to do something he was not comfortable with. As the old women bent over to kiss him and he hit their hands and faces, Bob and I scolded him. We taught him that he did not have a right to his own body and his feelings of discomfort were not important.

Study your child to know his/her mannerisms and look for slight changes in his/her personality. Spend quality time with your child (reading books, listening to his/her ideas, playing games) and talk openly about things that you remember being scared of as a child. This will show the child that everyone has fears and that you can relate to his/her fears. The child will then understand that you are accessible to him/her for future conversations.

My advice to parents is that you need to develop your own instincts/feelings and trust the information. If you get weird feelings from someone, you don't have to rationalize or study where that feeling is coming from or why you are experiencing such things. You do not have to wonder how you could think something so horrible about a particular person. Empower yourself to understand that many instincts and feelings come to us naturally. They come as gifts from a higher source—so respect your senses! They may serve as warnings, reminders, or connections to other people. You don't need to over analyze them. Accept any instincts/feelings as your own antennae that help you navigate through your day. If you ever get a feeling that your child may not be safe with someone—trust that feeling. You do not have to explain your feelings to anyone. Just as everyone has the right to his/her own body—everyone has the right to his/her own instincts and feelings.

Chapter 8
Is My Child At Risk For Sexual Abuse?

All children are at risk for sexual abuse. No child is safe. You may think your child is safe, but he/she might be more at risk than you think. There are several factors, which may pose more of a threat of your child being sexually abused. These factors can be found in many sexual abuse cases. However, a child may also be sexually abused even if none of these factors are present:

If you believe your child is safe – If you believe your child is safe, your child is more at risk of being sexually abused. By believing in false "safety," you will not be on guard—watching for any signs in people around your family, or indications from your child that something could be wrong. There are perpetrators everywhere—every race, gender, age, culture, and socio-economic level. It is safer to have a small percentage of fear that your child may be sexually abused—which will automatically trigger your defense mechanisms and put up your alert antennas. You will be operating in a totally different mode than if you believe your child is safe. You will watch for signs of perpetrators. You will be more cautious—monitoring where your children are and whom they are with. You will tune into your own and others' instincts and you will communicate openly with your child.

If you do not believe in instincts/feelings – If you do not believe in instincts and feelings, you will not pay attention to the warnings you are receiving, or the warnings your child receives. In my situation, I did not listen to the instincts and dreams I was receiving. If I had paid attention, I could have intervened earlier and perhaps—kept my children safe.

If you believe children do not have a right to their own opinions/instincts - If you believe children do not have the right to: "not like" someone, not want to kiss or hug someone, or not want to be near someone—you are telling the child their instincts and wishes are not respected. The consequence is to have children who do not trust themselves, and who continually find themselves in situations where their opinions, or they as people, are not valued or respected.

If you have any type of addiction – Any addiction to drugs, alcohol, medications, gambling, shopping, sex or any other type of addiction—takes your attention away from your children. When an individual has an addiction, his/her focus is on self and self's needs. If you're addicted to something, you are tuned into your next fix, your next high, your next winning or your next outfit. You are not tuning into your own instincts or your child's fears as closely as you would without substance use or addiction problems.

If you are currently involved in a dysfunctional relationship - If you are involved in a relationship with someone that is not a healthy relationship, similar to addiction—your focus usually is on the other partner and his/her actions. Whether the other person has an addiction, a mental health problem or is simply not acting fair or nice—your energies are going to that other person who is upsetting you, and not to yourself and your children. You will not be paying attention to your own instincts and the instincts of your children.

If you are a single parent - Perpetrators can be attracted to your children and see a relationship with you as a way to have access to your children and your children's friends. A single parent who is overwhelmed with work and the responsibilities of a home and raising a family—is a perfect playground for a sexual predator.

If you are a workaholic – Similar to an individual with an addiction problem, a workaholic is focusing his/her energies on the work projects, agendas, schedules, and time limits. Even when the workaholic is not working, his/her mind is still on work—not on his/her children. As most families need one or two people working to "pay the bills," many children are put into daycare or babysitting situation. Babysitters and daycare providers will usually not be tuned into your child's fears, or instincts. A workaholic parent/guardian will probably not find the time in the day to sit with his/her children to ask how their day was, if anyone made them afraid or uncomfortable, and if they had any weird feelings or thoughts.

If you see the good in all people – If you think all people are "good"—think again. Perpetrators are professional chameleons. They can mold themselves into anyone you want them to be in order to gain access to your children. Perpetrators do not sexually abuse children by accident. It is a process that starts with a plan, goals, tactics and action. They are on a mission to conquer any child they want. The ideal place for a perpetrator to get his/her victim is anywhere there are children: churches, youth agencies, schools, youth groups, kids' camps, children's choirs and any home with children.

If a child has a poor relationship with his/her mother or father – If a child has a poor relationship with one or more parents, he/she is more likely to seek love, appreciation, and approval from any adult that makes the child feel special. Six of the fourteen survivors I interviewed stated that the perpetrator bought special toys, or gifts, and took the child on great vacations. These perpetrators gave the child a lot of attention and made the child feel special.

If you do not know the warning signs of a child who is being sexually abused or signs of perpetrators – If you do not know the warning signs of a child who is being sexually abused, read the following section entitled, *Know the Signs*. If you do not know the warning signs of a juvenile and adult sexual predator read *Chapter 6 "Perpetrators Among Us."* Most of the survivors interviewed, indicated similar effects on their bodies, minds, and spirits. There were also common themes pointing to telling traits of perpetrators. It is important to know what the warning signs are—to then identify a child who is/was abused and help the child become safe immediately. Then therapy can be introduced as soon as possible. Parents who know the signs of perpetrators can keep their children away from potentially dangerous people and thus keep them safe.

If a child does not receive an education on perpetrators, instincts, fears and his/her body – A child that does not receive an education from his/her parents that there are good and bad people everywhere (outside and inside the family) is more at risk of being sexually abused. A child, who has not received any education on trusting his /her instincts and discussing instincts and fears, will be more at risk. A child, who has not been taught that his/her body is a temple that needs to be respected by him/herself and others—will not know to tell anyone if inappropriate things occur.

A child who has no one to talk to – A child who has no safe supporting adults in his/her life will not be able to disclose any uncomfortable feelings. He/she will be forced to suffer through the abuse—feeling alone, not believed and abandoned.

Know the signs

The following is a basic list of possible signs of sexual abuse. The items were taken from the interviews with survivors and things I witnessed with my own children.

Behavior problems—acting out in school or acting out against family members
Getting picked on by older siblings or other children
A child who feels uncomfortable with his/her body
A child who feels uncomfortable with his/her gender
Stealing
Taking apart objects/toys
Isolated/withdrawn
Perfectionist
Violent outbursts against others—breaking things intentionally (windows, doors)
A child who avoids certain people with no explanation
Overly emotional around certain people
A child who does not have many friends
Actively burning, cutting, piercing body parts
Purposely setting things on fire—furniture, objects, buildings
Seizures
Using drugs/alcohol
Suicide ideation/suicide attempts
Torturing or killing animals
Ulcers, stomach problems
Pain in areas of the body— anus, vagina

Raw skin in areas of the body—rectum, vagina
Trouble sleeping
Going to bed very late and waking up very early
Anxiety/fear
Losing control of bowels
Diarrhea
Excessive touching or self-harming of private areas (accidental/ intentional)
Excessive eating / under eating— Bulimia, Anorexia
Shifts in personality— Talkative to shy, outgoing to isolated, good student to poor
Purposely showing off private parts of the body without embarrassment
Making sexual noises, groans, grunts
Excessive fear of things (real or imaginary) or certain people
Blood from any body openings
Urinary tract infections, throat infections
Unexplained gagging
Any sexually transmitted diseases

Chapter 9
Confirming Suspicions / Creating Safety

The best method of prevention is open communication with your child. Daily check-ins to see how the child's day was should be incorporated into your family's routine. What made him/her happy, sad, angry, or fearful during the day? As your child communicates with you, if you feel something could be wrong, follow your instincts. When thinking about your child's personality, mannerisms and behavior, try to mentally review the list of warning signs listed in the previous chapter. If your child demonstrates one of those signs, you need to pay much closer attention to your child. Who has access to him/her? Who has had access in the past? On a regular basis it is good to ask the questions, "Did anyone scare you today? Has anyone scared you? Has anyone ever touched your… (list each private part)? Has anyone made you look at or touch their private parts? Has anyone watched you take your clothes off? Has anyone showed you pictures of people with no clothes or said weird things to you that made you feel uncomfortable?"

The key to getting a child to tell is making sure you are ready for his/her answer. When you are going to ask the question, you must be mentally prepared that you may get a positive response. To learn that your child has been sexually abused is a life changing and family changing event. A disclosure will throw your child, your entire family, your support network, and you into dynamics you never dreamed of. Your initial reactions to any sexual abuse disclosure and actions throughout the process, are crucial to your child's healing.

For a child to disclose that he/she has been sexually abused, he/she must be able to spend quality one-on-one time with you. The child needs to have moments where he/she feels completely safe. Quality time together should be a normal part of your on-going relationship with your child. Since I had three children and was working several jobs, I did not spend much quality time with my children. Adam constantly dominated any of my extra time for himself—I was not able to consistently spend quality time with Joey and David. Joey had disappeared so far into the background, he would have never been able to disclose to me. I know Joey telling me what was happening to him was truly a miracle.

There were a few factors that helped Joey disclose. The first thing was that Adam was caught stealing. Up until that point, Adam had convinced everyone he was perfect. But now that everyone knew Adam was not the wonderful child he projected, Joey could see that Adam did not have complete control anymore. The next reason why Joey was able to begin disclosing was that we meditated together. By giving him the chance to imagine and feel all of his worries, fears, angers and any other negative feelings move away from him, fill a pink balloon, and then float far away—was what helped Joey to feel lighter. He was then able to initiate disclosing the scare tactics Adam was using against him. After the meditation, Joey felt safe enough to explain his darkest most terrifying fears, which were keeping him enslaved in the mental, physical and sexual abuse. Joey finally felt safe enough to tell someone about all the horrible bees, Chucky and everything else that was supposed to come and instantly kill him.

After the disclosure of all the fear tactics Adam had been using, I intentionally had Joey overhear when I confronted Adam with his horrific lies. Joey heard as I warned Adam that every adult in his life was now watching him very closely. The last factor that led to Joey finally disclosing, was that I asked the simple question, "has anyone every touched your peeper or your bum?"

One of the most important ways to find out if your child has been sexually abused is to simply ask the direct question, "Has anyone touched your ___?" And then list the various private parts that someone could potentially harm. As a parent, I believed I had given my children enough education to protect themselves. I had warned them of some of the tactics a perpetrator might use. I had drilled into them an understanding that if anything ever happened, they needed to tell me immediately. But, that was the problem—I was relying on them to tell me. I've learned it does not work that way. The parent has to ask the child directly.

Luckily, when Joey disclosed the sexual abuse he had suffered, my instincts took control and my reaction was to remain calm and reassuring. I told him I was happy he told me, and that Adam was wrong for doing what he did. I told him Adam had taken advantage of him and made him do horrible things because he knew Joey was a young child and was not be able to protect himself. I instilled in Joey an understanding that for the rest of his life he needed to always remember—Adam was wrong. Joey needed to understand that he will forever be totally free from any guilt or fault. All blame and fault would always lie with Adam.

During the first few days that Adam was removed from the home, Joey became a flood of memories. I told him that I wanted him to tell me everything he could remember so I could help him. He gradually remembered more and more with each passing day, and candidly reported each memory to me. As he told me the details of the sexual abuse he said it in a very matter of fact manner, as if this was an everyday occurrence for most people. My role was just to listen and encourage him to say as much as he could remember. Of course in my mind I was more and more horrified, but I did not want to show my reactions. Since we did not analyze the memories thoroughly and spend time discussing what a horrible person Adam was, Joey was allowed to speak freely and move easily from each memory to the next. I purposely did not judge the situation with him by saying things like, "Adam was horrible." I knew if I added to the negativity of the situation, it would be more traumatic for Joey and stop his process of disclosing.

When David began disclosing the mental abuse and the sexual abuse he suffered from Adam, I again tried to be calm with no intense reactions. I was very proud that he was learning to put words to the horrible things he had witnessed as a baby. His delay in speech was more than likely due to the extreme abuse he had seen. To finally be able to explain his feelings was freeing for him.

If a Child States He/She Was Touched Sexually

If a child discloses sexual abuse, the first thing to do is make sure you control your reaction. You have to put aside your anger and other emotions, and calmly get as much detail as the child will give. The conversation has to be non-emotional and quiet—the same way the two of you would discuss a project the child is working on at school. You want as much detail as possible to make sure you understand your child completely. If he/she says someone touched his/her buttocks, it may have been to help the child clean up after a bowel movement. You need to remain calm to get all the details and see the situation clearly—to know if it really was sexual abuse or not.

Ask the child to act out what happened by using other family members to play the role of the perpetrator and the child. Have the child explain and show what each person did. If from the details you are able to determine that your child was in fact sexually abused—leave your emotions for later. The important thing to remember is to show your child you are calm, stable and able to hear him/her comfortably. If your child has been sexually abused, he/she does not understand how horrible everything is that he/she has been through. It will take years of processing until the child realizes the depth of the crimes committed against him/her.

As an adult, you know what a devastating crime sexual abuse is, but intense reactions will terrify and overload the child—forcing him/her to recant the story and shut down. If a child sees his/her parents crying constantly, screaming or yelling, he/she may internalize the behavior and think he/she is causing the distress in the parent. This is why it is so important to remain calm and try to have the child tell you as much as possible when the memories will be most fresh. When you need to scream, and cry, do it later and away from the child. If the child sees you crying, just explain that you are sorry and sad that this has happened to him/her. Assure your child that you are sad that the perpetrator did the acts to him/her. But try to keep the number of times he/she sees these emotions to a minimum.

• Calmly communicate with your child that you are happy he or she was brave enough to tell you and is in no way at fault. At any age, children understand you love them and you are happy they told you. Apologize to the child for not knowing, and for not keeping the child safe. Tell the child that you know now, and from this point forward—he/she is safe. Don't re-traumatize the child by saying the perpetrator is a monster and evil, even though this is what you know to be a reality. At this point, the child usually feels an attachment to the perpetrator—especially if the perpetrator is a family member, close friend of the family, or has been the Buddy – Teacher type of perpetrator.

• Encourage open communication. Allow the child to talk as much or as little as he/she wants about the situation. If the child states what happened and does not feel a need to further discuss every detail, don't force the child to speak. Communicate to the child that you are always available to talk when he/she is ready. I told Joey if I was ever too busy with something and he wanted to talk to me, he could tell me he needed to have "a serious conversation." If I could not talk at that moment, I would quickly finish what I was doing so he would not forget what he wanted to discuss. I also told him if I ask too many questions or start talking about it and he didn't want to, he could just tell me he did not want to discuss it right then. Joey and David understood that we openly discussed the abuse at home. But, I believe they liked that their grandparents' home was a place where the abuse was brought up only if they initiated the conversation. At Grandma and Grandpa's house, they could still be kids without thinking about all that they had been through.

• Ensure the child, he/she, is safe and the abuse will no longer happen. Tell the child that the perpetrator was wrong for doing what he/she did. Explain to the child that temporarily he/she will not be around the person, until you can make sure this cannot happen again. If the child gets upset that he/she won't be able to see the person, ensure him/her that it is only temporary until you figure out what should happen next. Let the child know that you need to discuss the event with people who work in these types of situations.

Your priority is making the child feel safe and comfortable. The perpetrator should not be allowed near the child at all. The beginning stage of a child disclosing sexual abuse is not only traumatic for you, but children instinctively know their disclosure will potentially: rip apart families, cause distress for everyone around the survivor, and make them more vulnerable to be blamed or not believed. Since sexual abuse often happens within families—isolating a child away from the perpetrator is usually very difficult. This process is the beginning of families separating, arrests being made, or individuals leaving homes.

If a child sees his/her perpetrator immediately after the disclosure, it can be extremely detrimental to the child—since many perpetrators communicate with their victims through slight gestures, facial expressions and eye contact. At this point, you probably do not have any idea of the vast tactics the perpetrator used to keep your child silent. A child should never be re-victimized and re-traumatized by seeing the perpetrator after disclosure has just taken place. It would be similar to escaping from a concentration camp and then having to immediately sit calmly near the captors who violated you in every way imaginable.

• Call the police, the local child protection agency and a local rape crisis center. A formal report has to be made to initiate the legal process and begin the legal protection of your child. Many states have mechanisms in place so children do not have to repeat their stories to several different people. These programs offer the opportunity for a child's statement to be videotaped while all the appropriate professionals stand behind smoked glass and witness the statements being made. If such a service exists, this will benefit your child and yourself tremendously. Joey had to tell his story to seven different professionals within the first few days. In the beginning, it was fairly easy for him to retell the story since I braced him that he would have to tell the story several times. But, after telling the story a few times, it quickly became more and more difficult for him to discuss. As he began to discover the severity of the situation, it became overwhelming, and he began to clam up. Luckily, we were able to get the police statement recorded before he found he could no longer discuss the abuse.

If any statement is recorded and played back to the child—it can make the child freeze. When a child hears his/her own voice and the seriousness of the situation, they can easily recant their story. Joey had to tell his story to the arresting officer as he taped the session. When the officer played the tape recording back to make sure Joey had answered all the questions, Joey was traumatized to hear his own voice. With each playback, I witnessed Joey turning more and more inside of himself. His story progressed from the sexual abuse happening all the time, to once or twice, to maybe it didn't happen at all. In the end he began to recant the story because he was so overwhelmed and wanted the interrogation to stop. If we were able to take advantage of a service which protected children, he would have been able to tell his story once. It would have made the disclosure less distressing for him.

• It is important for you to have a support network. If you are blessed by the continued support from family and friends—count yourself as lucky. If you gradually start losing friends and family, seek out other parents in similar situations. Some states do have parent support groups, which help make you feel less alone and isolated. Seek out professional counseling for your child and yourself. Sexual abuse is so traumatic it needs to be discussed to help the individual and the family members' progress through their pain. You need to find people with whom you feel comfortable discussing the trauma. Talking about it is an enormous way to make sense of the raging emotions.

When figuring out who makes up your support network, be very careful whom you initially disclose to. You want to only tell people who will keep the information confidential and who will be strong supporters of you. If you think someone may possibly blame you for not protecting your child, or blame/not believe the child—do not tell that person. In the beginning, you need to recognize that you are vulnerable and fragile. People may try to convince you that the abuse did not happen, or that you are unstable for having such intense reactions. Therefore, be very careful who knows in the beginning. Your strength will increase in time, but at first, you are weak and can potentially be further victimized by others who are unsympathetic and more interested in placing blame.

Many times people lose their immediate support network of friends and family members when others learn that sexual abuse has happened. Knowing a family has been affected by sexual abuse can frighten people, and make them turn away from the family. People feel more comfortable staying in a naive state—thinking their family is totally protected from such a horrendous and unspeakable crime. Before our family's tragedy, if someone told me that sexual abuse occurred in their family, I probably would not have felt comfortable having my children play with their children. I probably would have limited the amount of contact I had with the family. I would have been so uncomfortable, it would have been very easy for me to rationalize that those dysfunctional things happen in other people's families. I would have walked away and falsely comforted myself—believing something like that would never happen in my family.

In our situation, we were very lucky to have total support from family and friends. Everyone empathized with us since they themselves were equally traumatized by the whole situation. Since all of us together really had no idea what sexual abuse was, why someone would do that to someone else, and what the effects were on a child who had been abused—we all worked through our understandings and emotions together. Having such a huge support network of people I could call to discuss each emotion and memory—was what helped me. With everyone's support, I was able to see through the trauma and recognize my purpose. I totally appreciate all of our family and friends who were there for my family and have continued to support us from the beginning to the end.

• Any child who has been sexually abused should be physically examined as soon as possible. Depending on the time when the abuse occurred, sometimes there can still be signs of physical evidence. As I was told during the physical exams for both boys, the private areas have very rich blood supplies. This allows the body to heal those areas quickly, and consequently, the physical trauma cannot be seen. In case there is damage to the area, which can be seen with a high-powered microscope specially designed for analyzing children's skin, or physical evidence from the perpetrator, a physical exam can prove vital to a case. The physical evidence will then prove the case instead of the child being questioned over and over again. If the abuse happened weeks ago or more, the child should still be examined to ensure there is no lasting damage and that no sexually transmitted diseases were given to the child.

Since the perpetrator against our children lived in our home, we were in a difficult situation. We had to worry about physically separating Adam from the boys. We did not want the boys to be intimidated by him in any way, and we needed to ensure our children were safe. That first night we were in total shock and locked the children in our bedroom with us. Adam stayed in his room at the other end of the house. During the night, we were afraid Adam might set the house on fire in retaliation while we were all sleeping.

I did not know who to call or where to go with this unbelievable situation. The first day Joey disclosed the sexual abuse, the only thing my husband and I knew to do—was to keep the children away from Adam. The next morning I was very lucky to speak with a woman who confided in me that she was also a survivor. She told me not to worry about what we were going to do with Adam, but to focus solely on making sure my children were safe and were physically examined. I then called the boys' pediatrician and asked if they could be examined. Since we were colleagues, he instructed me to contact the police, the local child protection agency, and the major children's city hospital since they had the advanced equipment to see any tissue damage. He later followed up to make sure all the phone calls had been made.

If you experience a mental dilemma whether you should or should not press charges, consider this. If there were a crocodile crawling down the street into your neighborhood, would you call the animal rescue control to come and get the creature? Or would you just hope the ferocious animal would slip out of sight and not hurt anyone? Most people would not second guess themselves about calling for help with a crocodile, yet many people will contemplate whether it is the right thing to do when pressing charges against someone who has sexually abused a child. By not pressing charges, you are allowing a predator to enter into your neighborhood and potentially harm other children. You are also setting up your child for more victimization.

• From the beginning, you need to become a strong advocate for your child when dealing with law enforcement, social services, mental health and legal systems. Often state social service systems work with negligent parents who don't understand that sexual abuse is wrong. I have found that many states do not have adequate resources for the families who understand the devastating effects of sexual abuse and are desperately seeking support and assistance.

• Work hard to find an expert in the field of sexual abuse to be a counselor for your child. Empower your child to understand he/she is "trying out" the counselor. If he/she does not feel comfortable after a few sessions—it is time to find another expert. When we were first looking for a counselor for Joey, I told him, I wanted him to think about finding a counselor as if he was going shopping. I gave him the scenario of him going to buy a shirt in a store. He would first see what types of shirts they had, and then decide if he wanted to make a purchase or not. We talked about how he would want to touch the shirt and make sure the material was comfortable on his skin, not scratchy or an ugly color. We discussed how if he didn't like what they had in the store, he could always go to another store.

This is how I explained the process of finding a counselor. I told him to see how he feels with the person. If he did not feel comfortable, we would keep "shopping." We even discussed the idea of going to several different counselors until he found one he liked. But, when it came time to find a counselor, it was next to impossible. It was very difficult to find anyone who specialized in pediatric mental health—especially focusing on sexual abuse. Fortunately for us, the counselor we ultimately found was highly recommended by a few people and had many years of experience in the field. The boys liked her and her male colleague and were very excited to continue going to therapy.

• Survivors can easily be "triggered" by anything. "Triggered" would mean that an object, smell, sound, or word—anything can cause the survivor to remember the sexual abuse and feel re-victimized by the memory. You may want to consider removing anything from the home that reminds the child of the perpetrator. However, be careful not to change or remove things without the child's permission. Abruptly destroying or getting rid of things could cause more trauma for the child. Immediately after we knew what happened to Joey and David, our friend Miladys, and I instinctively wanted to get the couch where Joey had been repeatedly raped, out of the house and set it on fire. For both of us, we felt fire would somehow cleanse the energy and our own emotions. Of course, I did not tell Joey I wanted to set the couch on fire, but I did ask him how he felt about me removing the couch from the home. It was an old beat up piece of furniture that probably should have been thrown away a long time ago. But, when we first set up Adam's room to be like a studio apartment—the couch helped make it a great room for a teenager. When I asked him, Joey said we didn't have to throw out the couch and we could keep it. As time progressed and I asked him what things to discard, he realized he liked the idea of removing all objects that reminded him of Adam—including the couch. For a while, Bob thought I was insane because I was adamant to move all of the furniture out of Adam's room. I felt that the heavy furniture had absorbed the negative energy from Adam and his torturous crimes. For me, the desk, bed, couch, dresser and entertainment center all carried the negative energy and served as a continual reminder of Adam.

As time went on, Joey found items throughout the house that triggered him with traumatic memories. He felt empowered to ask me to get rid of the object and see that it was instantly thrown in the trash. It was freeing for Joey to determine what things remained in the home and what things were eliminated. I think it was also freeing for me to clean up the house and get rid of anything that was Adam's. It was a way for us to re-claim our personal space and symbolically state that Adam would never be a part of our lives again.

• Re-victimization needs to be another conversation with children. Out of the fourteen survivors I interviewed, twelve stated they were re-victimized by additional perpetrators. When a child has been sexually abused, their boundaries have been violated, their personal instincts frozen, and their understanding of right versus wrong skewed. Children who have been sexually abused have witnessed the evil side of another human being. If a child does not develop a strong sense of boundaries, personal rights, his/her own instincts and proper behavior—he/she is vulnerable to being violated again. Since predators are always on the prowl for new prey, they have a keen sense for who would be easily conquered. A predator recognizes a child, whose boundaries have been shattered by sexual abuse. Once a child has been sexually abused, a parent's instincts need to go into overdrive to ensure that the child is never violated again. A parent must also give a child, who has been sexually abused, the tools to protect him/herself from being re-victimized.

I soon realized my children were easy prey for another perpetrator. Shortly after Adam was removed from our home, I had the boys with me in a group situation. The room was filled with adults and one other child. The boy, who we had not seen in years, was now eleven-years-old. From the second we walked into the room, the boy was asking Joey, who had just turned six-years-old, to go into another room with him. Joey did not know him, yet the boy persisted until I finally said, "No, I want him to stay with me." The teenager then proceeded to follow Joey and David around the room for the entire time we were there. If they made a few steps, he was "innocently" following behind. His intensity to be with them was disturbing. He kept touching their shoulders, arms, and backs—anywhere he could.

My instincts were screaming to me to get him away from my children. My eyes never blinked as I watched intensely. Then my suspicions were suddenly confirmed when I saw Joey, who was sitting only two seats away from me, get up to go use the bathroom. The teen immediately jumped up and ran down the hall after him. I quickly followed behind, without the boy knowing. Joey had walked into the men's' bathroom, which consisted of a resting area, with a chair and table, and a small individual bathroom. Since the door was open, I was able to see that the boy had followed Joey into the large resting room and was proceeding to follow Joey into the private toilet area. As Joey was entering the private toilet stall, the boy was right behind him with every intention of following him inside. When the teenager suddenly saw me in the men's bathroom, he quickly backed away from Joey and let Joey go in alone. If I was not there, the boy would have followed Joey inside the private bathroom! At that moment, I realized Joey did not know about privacy and did not understand that the boy should never be allowed to enter with him. I realized my children were easy prey for any other perpetrator since their boundaries had been so violently shattered. I knew I had to give them powerful skills quickly.

I began a process of teaching them privacy, personal space, and rights to their own bodies. Since they were young boys, they often ran into the bathroom without remembering that others should not see them. Most of the time when they bathed, we were all together in the same bathroom. I then implemented a new family rule for our family when using the bathroom. "Privacy showers" became the new highlight for the boys. Joey enjoyed the fact that now he was old enough to shower on his own. David loved the idea of being a big boy that could bathe himself. I still had to help David clean himself, but usually walked to the other end of the room so he felt he had his "privacy". Soon both boys understood that their personal space should always be respected and they had a right to privacy.

Chapter 10
Road to Reform:
Legislative and Social Services

If you are pursing a sexual abuse case legally, in most cases, you will be your only advocate. As Bob and I found, we were fighting a system that was much larger than us. I found that the systems are designed to protect children, but if the juvenile is a sexual offender—he/she will receive more protection than the children he/she violated. In our case our children, who were victimized, and my husband and I—were all left alone, without any resources or guidance.

As I have witnessed in our family and with other family's situations, the perpetrator will probably have more rights than the survivor. All information about the survivor and the survivor's family is totally exposed and open to the court, social service systems, and mental health systems. However, the perpetrator's identity, confidentiality, privacy and other rights are securely protected. By the end of any sexual abuse case, the final result is usually that the perpetrator has all of the rights and the survivor and survivor's family have none.

If you are in this type of situation, and need to meet with social service personnel, legal authorities, court officials, and others—jot down everyone's names, titles and contact information. Find out if there is a victims advocacy group that can help keep the parents informed of the situation and offer necessary resources. And make sure they keep you informed about the case.

We were blessed to have amazing support from family and friends. However, the support we expected to have from various agencies became a continual source of pain. We were first traumatized to learn that our children had been sexually abused. But we were re-traumatized continually by the legal, social service and mental health services.

Many times when sexual abuse happens within a family, the social service systems push for family re-unification. This is because it will cost the system less if everyone lives together, than to provide housing, food and educational services for anyone removed from the home. However, family re-unification is not a solution when the situation involves sexual abuse since most perpetrators will re-offend.

As I learned from the survivor interviews and Adam, perpetrators do not feel remorse. They are disconnected from their actions. A perpetrator is like a rattlesnake. A rattlesnake may look calm, and peaceful when basking in the sun—just as a perpetrator may appear to be gentle and kind. But a rattlesnake will bite you when you are too close, and can ultimately be lethal.

If you are considering reunification for your child and a perpetrator because you believe the perpetrator has received appropriate therapy, ask yourself—would you allow your child to sit with a rattlesnake? As the "professionals" try to convince you that the perpetrator is "cured" and will not re-offend, realize they are trying to convince you that the rattlesnake is now a cute bunny rabbit. As they use the bunny costume to convince you—understand that it is still a rattlesnake underneath, just as the "reformed" individual is still a predator who will strike again.

In our case, Adam took a Sexual Offender Evaluation, which would show his risk for possible re-offending. Since Adam's rights and confidentiality were so protected, his own father, Bob could not get access to the test to know what his son's risk of re-offending was. When his actual hearing date came, of which we were not notified, I was told that Adam had two lawyers representing him. One lawyer was there, as his guardian, and the other was his defense lawyer.

My husband and I used to get compliments all the time from strangers in restaurants, and from family members, and friends that they had never seen children so well behaved. Both Bob and I believed in giving our children love, nurturance and guidance, as well as an understanding of respect, rules, and consequences for inappropriate behavior. But when we learned of the sexual abuse, we suddenly found ourselves under the scrutiny of state workers regarding our parenting skills and our competence as parents. It was terrifying since the workers who were involved in the case, did not seem qualified, acted unprofessional and disorganized, and showed no empathy toward us. Yet they had complete sympathy for Adam. We realized incompetent people now had the power to make decisions, which could put us at risk of losing Joey and David even though everyone around us knew we were great parents.

From early on, the prosecution lawyer from the Attorney General's office took Adam's case seriously. She reviewed all of the documents and called me very concerned stating, "This kid is a monster". Her belief and her recommendation was that Adam should be placed in a locked treatment facility until he was 21 years old. She believed the charge of first-degree sexual assault should stick and not be decreased to a less severe charge.

Despite her recommendations, Adam was sentenced to second-degree sexual assault and sent to a treatment facility for up to one year. The prosecution lawyer's disgust over the case was apparent. At that point, I think she lost total interest in the case, and soon after moved to another department, without informing me.

After two years of seeing how the legal, mental health and social service systems operated, I realized it would have been better if Bob and I had quietly sent Adam back to Cape Verde without ever involving the courts. Then we would have known that we would be safe from Adam ever returning. However, at the time we felt we had a moral responsibility to protect other children and families. To knowingly send Adam back to unsuspecting families in Cape Verde with absolutely no therapy did not seem right. However, the State was not only interested in giving Adam therapy, the system strongly advocated for Adam to remain in America.

Our situation and the many stories I heard from survivors lead me to the conclusion that the legal, mental health, social service, educational, political and religious institutions—keep re-victimizing the survivor and the survivor's family, yet they refuse to acknowledge how dysfunctional the organizations truly are. People from within usually do not stand up and speak about the dysfunction they witness on a daily basis—for fear of losing their jobs. If those individuals would speak up, it would cause internal strife within the organization. But the final price for everyone's silence to our society—is children's lives and children's futures.

As soon as we learned of Adam's stealing behavior, we found a counselor for him. After an initial visit, she was very taken with him. When I called her a few weeks later to inform her of the mental, physical and sexual abuse he had committed against Joey, she was concerned for Adam. She felt he should go to a shelter instead of the detention center since he was a victim himself. During the next visit for Adam, I arranged for the agency to administer a Clinical Psychological evaluation to see how mentally disturbed he was. Before the evaluation, Adam's counselor took Adam, my husband and me into her office. She stated with confidence, "In about one or two years, you will see the progress Adam is making and then you guys will all be able to live together as a family again." I was horrified that she was saying this and shook my head no. Then she stated, "I know it doesn't seem like a possibility at this point, but you'll see after he is doing well with his program." I jumped into the conversation and explained, "No we are not considering re-unification. Adam to me is a lion who has been sitting behind bushes studying who his next victim will be."

After we left her office, Adam was taken into the other room to be evaluated. I asked the counselor if I could speak to her alone in her office. When we went in the office I told her, "Adam is very dangerous, he shows no remorse or guilt for his actions and I believe he is capable of murder". She calmly responded, "Could be" and that was the end of our discussion. It was very easy for her as a counselor to recommend family reunification, since her children would not be affected. Her children had not already been victimized and she did not have to worry that they could possibly be re-victimized and potentially murdered.

During the first two weeks when Adam was taken out of the home, we had about three caseworkers from the social service department. One day as I was walking in the hall at work, my cell phone rang. When I answered the phone, the woman on the other end stated that she needed the form signed and sent back by fax immediately. I asked her what form she was talking about and who she was. She said she was from the state social service department, stated her name and again told me she needed the form. I finally had to ask her if she was our new caseworker and she said, "Yes." She then abruptly stated that she had spoken with Bob the day before in court, and needed the form signed and returned. I explained to her that I did not know about the letter since I did not have a chance to speak with my husband who works the night shift. I told her that she could send the form to me and I would sign it and fax it back.

The dialogue changed and she began to tell me about her meeting with Adam. She explained, "What a handsome and respectful young man he is." Then she asked me, "Why did you move where you did?" I was baffled by her question and asked what she meant. Again she asked, "Why did you move there (in the country) instead of staying in the city? Did you have family or friends which made you move out there?" I still did not understand what she was trying to ask me. Her question was not in a tone of someone trying to have a polite conversation. I felt like her questioning was with a tone of accusation, or that it was an interrogation. I hesitantly replied, "Because we got a good deal on the house and wanted land." She then responded with a superior attitude stating, "Oh, because I couldn't understand why you would move out there. Adam told me he was the only black kid in his whole school and I think he felt very isolated."

In her derogatory tone, she was trying to put blame on Bob and I for raising Adam in a rural community instead of an urban setting. Since Adam was black, she believed his family should have stayed in the city. Her words were forcefully stating that Adam was acting out because Bob and I had made him feel alone and isolated, as the only black kid in his school. I was appalled with her accusatory nature and told her, "Listen lady, I don't care if he was the only blue kid or green kid in school. There is no excuse for what he did." I told her she should make a note in her files that there will be no family re-unification in our case and I was concerned that so much attention was being placed on Adam instead of my children who were the true victims. She then abruptly stated, "OK then" and hung up the phone while I was in the middle of a sentence.

I could not believe what I had just experienced and quickly called Janene, a friend of mine who was familiar with the social service department. She said, "Claire, I have seen that type of behavior from the state workers all the time. I know it is horrible for you, but it is really not a surprise for me. You need to call her supervisor immediately!" I called the woman's supervisor a few minutes later and stated I did not want that woman to handle our case—I did not want her to touch a single paper regarding my family. The supervisor was upset that the caseworker had acted so rudely and stated she would have to bring the situation to her manager, since they had never had a case where a family demanded a different caseworker. (Several months later, I spoke with a friend who worked for the same social service agency and told me they had that type of request on a daily basis throughout the state). The supervisor apologized profusely and stated she would speak with her manager and contact me the next day. The next day, the supervisor called me and told me I would have to participate in a formal meeting with her, and her manager to formally request a change of caseworkers. I asked if I could just speak with the manager over the phone so I would not have to take time out of work. The supervisor then responded in a tone that was no longer apologetic or sympathetic. Now her tone was demanding and cold. She stated, "No, that is not possible, you must come into the office."

The media is filled with stories where the state social service system goes into a family and takes children away from good, hard working parents. This was my immediate fear. The terror at the possibility of the state stepping in, twisting things around, and leaving my children as pawns in a game—ripped through me. At that moment I knew, if I was a horrible parent who abused my children, that same agency would advocate for me to have visitation rights with the long-term goal of family re-unification. But since I was an educated, assertive parent who was looking out for the best interest of my children and my family, they could not understand me. I was so scared I quickly called two friends who are lawyers. After listening to what had transpired, they both recommended I get legal assistance. After scrambling for hours how I could get a lawyer for the next morning, I finally realized I could meet with them in the morning and if the conversation started turning too scary—I would excuse myself and inform them I was seeking legal counsel.

The next day I drove to the state social service agency to meet with the supervisor, manager and the accusatory caseworker. During the meeting the caseworker was given a chance to explain her side of the story and I was given a few minutes to explain my perspective. The caseworker's explanation demonstrated to everyone that she could not comprehend how insensitive she had acted. She foolishly stated, "I needed the form sent back. And I could not understand why they moved there." Everyone in the room quickly understood that she was not capable of handling such a severe situation. The caseworker blankly stared at everyone. She still could not understand what she had done wrong. She did not think there was anything wrong with asking me why we bought the house where we did, or accusing Bob and I of making Adam the only black child in school—forcing him to be out of control and commit the crimes he did. The caseworker was escorted out of the room and the manager immediately apologized to me.

I was then given a male caseworker that was supposed to be the best they had for handling sensitive and difficult situations. I was told he was very empathic and would be able to understand the complex issues faced by everyone in the family. They introduced him to me and he informed me he would probably call me to come out to the house to speak with the boys directly.

About a week later, the caseworker came to our home and briefly spoke to the boys. When they left the room, the caseworker stated that he had visited with Adam. He said, "Adam is very scary. He has the advanced perpetrator skills of an adult." He explained that he had studied and worked with perpetrators for many years and could see that "Adam has very developed tactics for committing his crimes." He felt Adam should be in a locked facility for a long time. I thought to myself that we were lucky to have him as our new caseworker. It was affirming to have someone involved in the case that could see what Bob and I had witnessed—Adam was a dangerous person.

However, as the weeks progressed, this new caseworker who was supposed to be the best, proved to be completely incompetent. When Adam hurt his finger and needed surgery, we were not informed. Days later, the caseworker suddenly called us stating he needed the release forms signed immediately. Another event that the caseworker mishandled was when he informed me after the fact that Adam had escaped from the shelter. He never informed me at the time of the escape, yet stated he had left messages for me. He also never clarified the event to inform me that Adam did not actually escape, but had gone into another boy's room.

When I was desperately looking for a counselor for the boys and myself, the caseworker gave me the contact information for a therapist who had ended her practice three years prior! When I asked numerous times to have a no contact order or a restraining order put in place so Adam legally could not come near my children and me, he ignored all requests.

Later, I learned from the attorney who was prosecuting the case that the caseworker never came to court prepared and never had the necessary reports available in a timely fashion. She told me that he was absolutely the worst social service caseworker she had ever worked with and could not wait until she did not have to deal with him.

The same male caseworker continued to keep open files on Joey and David for many months after Adam was removed. With open files on our children, Bob and I were terrified that any little thing could trigger the state to attack us. We lived in total fear—Adam possibly returning, and the state social service agency taking Joey and David from us. It was an extremely unfair and upsetting situation to be in.

Finally after keeping the files open for ten months, the caseworker finally closed the cases for Joey and David. How he closed the files was not by interviewing Bob and me to make sure we were fit parents, or by taking character references from our employers and close friends. He finally closed the cases by speaking with one person, Joey and David's counselor. When she said we were good parents, the caseworker closed the cases. I found this very scary that our value and skills as parents was based on one person's opinion who really didn't know us as well as she knew our children. What if the counselor did not feel comfortable boasting about our wonderful parenting skills? How long would the cases have remained open?

The two social service caseworkers were not the only "professionals" who handled our situation poorly. I witnessed other mental health workers use our situation as gossip and entertainment. Privacy and confidentiality should be respected in such a difficult situation, yet I observed those values being completely compromised when I confided in a colleague.

I had been sick for months from all of the stress and had to report any used sick days and vacation time to a colleague at work. I was amazed to watch my body become progressively sicker, as my instincts increased and I could sense there was something seriously wrong with my family and home. When we learned of the sexual abuse and Adam was removed from the home—my health immediately began to improve. Once I gained my strength and was back to work, I was no longer using all of my sick time. One day the woman who handled my personnel benefits asked how I was feeling. I briefly told her what had happened and could see how the overwhelming stress had compromised my health. As I confided in this woman, she told me I should really talk to some of the social workers in the department since they were used to dealing with difficult personal situations. I told her we already found a counselor that was going to work with the entire family and did not need any other form of support. I specifically told her that I did not want anyone from work to know about my situation. She again suggested that I speak with the head of the department for support. I strongly stated that we already had mental health services in place and needed my family situation to remain confidential.

A few weeks later, the woman's boss came up to me in the hallway and asked how I was doing. I said I felt much better and was getting my strength back. Then she said, "No, I was talking about your son." She openly discussed my family's situation as if I had confided directly to her stating that her assistant had told her everything. My privacy and confidentiality was not only violated by the secretary, but also by the Director who openly discuss my personal situation in the hall for everyone to hear.

Throughout our trauma, I found that the professionals who should have the qualifications, education and common sense, to handle such a difficult situation—many times did not uphold the professional values and ethics that are expected in the human service field. Our privacy, confidentiality and personal recovery were to be safeguarded—yet were not. If your family has been traumatized by sexual abuse, the last thing you need is unprofessional social service personnel who can violate your privacy and confidentiality and make your situation worse.

I quickly understood that the therapists I went to were more interested in diagnosing Bob and I as parents with a dysfunctional marriage, than to place any blame on Adam. I personally went to a therapist for three weeks to help me with the stress of learning that my children had been sexually abused. By the third session she thought she had everything figured out and stated, "Your marriage is doomed to end, and I seriously suspect you are having such an extreme reaction to the whole situation because you were also sexually abused as a child." I told her I really did not think I was sexually abused as a child, but she insisted. She also believed since Adam was himself a victim, I should be able to separate from my anger and work towards supporting him with services. She stated, "It is common for people to demonize the perpetrator, but you are invoking this whole other spiritual level which I have never seen before."

At the end of the third session, she gave me a homework assignment which was to identify the telling behaviors of Joey, Adam and myself—indicating we were all victims of sexual abuse. I left her house feeling the usual feeling I had when I left—like she was going to kick me in the rear end if I didn't get out quick enough. Thank God, as I drove away, I had a strong sense to call Julia. When I explained what the woman had said, Julia was furious and stated, "What is she trying to do? Throw you over the edge! If you were or were not sexually abused as a kid—this is not the time to explore that. You need someone to help you be strong for your children! Claire, don't go back to her!" I followed Julia's advice and called the woman's voicemail stating I would not return. As I hung up the phone, I suddenly felt empowered—I was no longer going to allow people to judge me, my husband or my family during a time of such extreme vulnerability.

Several weeks later I tried to enroll my children in a play therapy group. In order to register Joey and David, I had to meet with the therapist, who ran the group—to make sure it was a good match. As I drove to the appointment, I received a phone call from Adam. By the time I arrived to meet the woman, I was visibly shaking from hearing Adam's voice. I explained that I was upset because I had just received a phone call from the person who committed crimes against my children. Yet, I could see that it was of little importance to her. Since she needed to know what kind of abuse my children had been through as a prerequisite to entering the group, I told her our family's tragedy. As she asked questions about our family heartbreak, she began to shift focus from my children and their abuse to my marriage. She started asking more and more questions and I naively answered, until she summarized everything by stating, "It does not sound like it is a very balanced marriage." The reason I was there was to register my children for a group, not to receive an approval or condemnation of my marriage! Luckily by the time I went home and explained the group to my children, Joey said he really was not interested in attending.

What I found with the therapists I met with and the many that I called to screen to see if they were qualified to work with my children—they, like most people, were living in a bubble regarding sexual abuse. They studied their textbooks, reviewed case studies, and believed they understood sexual abuse. They could easily explain a perpetrator's behavior as "sexually reactive" and empathized with the perpetrator who must have been a victim in his/her life and was now innocently re-enacting his/her previous abuse on someone else. The four therapists our family worked with were more interested in explaining the perpetrator's actions or excusing the behavior instead of looking at the perpetrator as a predator. By explaining, justifying and looking for the roots of the problem, they did not have to place blame on the perpetrator.

The two therapists that worked with Adam casually said to my husband and me, "He is just repeating what he experienced as a child. Can you imagine what horrible things were done to him?" It did not bother them that Adam had made several attempts to kill Joey. They were fascinated with the tactics Adam had used to silence Joey and David. They saw Adam as a frail child who needed constant reassurance and love. They did not have to worry about Adam coming back, breaking into the home while everyone slept, and hurting each family member inside—so it was easy to make statements about family reunification and Adam needing our support.

I was losing hope in ever finding a therapist that could truly understand what Joey and David had been through. We needed someone who could treat the situation with respect, professionalism and diplomacy. After weeks of frantically searching, I was finally able to find two real professionals in the field. I realized it was a huge task to find them, but professional therapists do exist. We were very lucky to find a female and male counselor with extensive experience in sexual abuse therapy.

The first few sessions were a little weird for both boys, but eventually they became more comfortable and were happy to go to each appointment. I could see that the therapy was helping them and it gave Bob and me a sense of stability—knowing that professionals were involved. However, getting reimbursed for the services became a constant source of stress. For each mental health visit, I knew we would have to fight to get reimbursed.

The health insurance company was supposed to reimburse us at a fixed percentage of each visit. Yet the company routinely ignored every reimbursement request. Customer service did not assist the situation, so I was forced to constantly threaten that I would expose their dysfunctional reimbursement system. On three separate occasions I had to send letters to the President of the company to inform him that I was going to go public with the fact that "his company did not support mental health for children who had been raped."

Unfortunately, fighting the health insurance company for reimbursement was one of the many struggles I had in a long list of battles that followed. Along with fighting the health insurance company, I was constantly battling the state social service department. From the very beginning until I finally gave up, it was a pointless battle.

Five months after Adam was removed from the home and I was informed by the state social service worker that Adam had escaped from one of the shelters—I was struck with complete terror and fear for my family's safety. In my heart, I knew Adam would return to the house one day, but I thought it would be several years before that happened. I knew if Adam returned now, he would not visit to say hello—he would come to hurt and permanently silence all of us.

Adam's case had already been rescheduled four times, spanning over a five and a half month waiting period. It was infuriating to see that the agency carelessly bounced Adam around from shelter to shelter, without being in a locked facility and he had very little supervision. As he floated from shelter to shelter, he received no formal treatment and was able to enjoy recreational activities—bowling, movies, and ice cream.

When I contacted the social service agency and the court system I was told since Adam was a minor, I could not take a restraining order out against him. I was instructed to take a restraining order out against my Bob since he was Adam's father, and then the order would transfer to the minor child. The court and other social service personnel said the only person who could implement a no contact order against Adam instead of Bob, would be the state social service caseworker that was handling the case. For weeks I called the caseworker, telling him to implement a no contact or restraining order, and he never responded. Out of desperation, I had a state Congressman write a letter on my behalf to the Director of the state's social service agency. The letter clearly stated that Mrs. Silva is in fear "for her safety and that of her family" and that we wished to reach a solid court date for Adam.

About a week after the Congressman sent his letter on my behalf, I received a letter from the Regional Director of the state's social service agency. She stated, "I encourage you to participate in the treatment of your stepson. He has a long hard road ahead of him and will need the support of his family." In several documents, I had clearly indicated that I was in fear for my family's and my personal safety. Numerous times I had requested a restraining order or no contact order to be put in place. Yet this woman was still insistent that I have continued contact with the perpetrator?

I was so disgusted with the state social service department, that I actively started to fight back. I wrote a letter back to the Regional Director documenting all of the mistakes and unprofessional work the agency had done. I informed her that her letter proved she was ignoring my requests for protection, devaluing my feelings and emotions, and re-traumatizing me. In the letter I clearly asked if she would "support" someone who had raped, sexually abused, and tortured her children. As I wrote, I realized I did not have to feel like I was being abused by the system any longer. I did have power—the ability to document all of the agency's failings, hold them accountable, and then make sure my family was completely removed from their system.

I mailed a copy of the letter to the Governor, the Attorney General, and the Director of the state's social service agency. I indicated to all of the officials in the letter that I was scared for my family's safety, and that several times I had requested a no contact order, yet those requests were not respected by the social service system. I explained how the court system had failed since they rescheduled the case over four times and still had no solid date. I stated that I was appalled that a Regional Director from a social service agency could be so insensitive to a family's needs. I also enclosed a copy of the letter that I sent to the Regional Director and the letter she had sent to me. I stated that both biological parents and myself, believed Adam should be sent back to Cape Verde. I finished the letter by noting I could not understand why the State was fighting to keep such a dangerous person, who was not an American citizen in our country.

Miraculously, after waiting five and a half months for a court date to be scheduled, everything was resolved in one week. Within one week, they rushed Adam into court, and he was sentenced to a local treatment facility. If he did not follow the rules or progress in the program, he would be sent to the juvenile detention center immediately. Within that week, Adam was placed in a locked treatment facility for juvenile sexual offenders.

A few weeks later, Bob and I had to go to court. Before we entered the courtroom, our male social service caseworker mentioned that he had documentation from the probation officer stating that she made numerous attempts to contact Bob and me, and we did not respond. She noted that we were not involved parents and were not open to supporting Adam. Bob and I looked at each other and could not believe the words we were hearing. Neither one of us ever received a call from the probation officer. I knew that the social service, treatment facility and mental health workers were all able to reach me since they had my cell, work and home phone numbers. Was the probation officer lying or was our incompetent caseworker lying? I asked for a copy of the report, but the caseworker said it had to remain in the file.

A few minutes later we had to enter the court chambers. As we moved our way to the front of the courtroom, we noticed there were many people around the table on the left. We were instructed to sit at the front table on the right. As the case began to unfold, we realized there were five people representing Adam. Three of the individuals were lawyers and the other two were caseworkers. Bob and I sat quietly at the other table with no one assisting us. The judge and the team for Adam all spoke in a back and forth dialogue—in words Bob and I could not understand. No one explained the process or what our rights were. No one asked our opinion. No one cared what we thought. Why we thought we were there—to voice our opinion that Adam should be sent back to Cape Verde—was never discussed. They had their agenda.

The clan shuffled their papers, stated a few words and sat back down in their finely pressed suits. This was clearly their daily routine. They were so used to shuffling families through the system, that the people just became numbers on paper. The only words Bob and I were able to state the entire time we were there, was our names. As we were escorted out of the room, I turned to Bob and said we had to hire a lawyer as soon as possible.

Shortly after this, Bob and I received an invitation from the social service caseworker. The invitation was to participate in a meeting that would discuss the overall treatment plan for Adam. At first, I was going to attend because I wanted to share the insight I had about who Adam really was and the tactics he had used. But, as the date approached, I became overwhelmed with a sickening feeling in my stomach. I thought, "Would they possibly be stupid enough to have Adam in the room with us on that day?" I sent a fax to our male caseworker, asking if Adam was going to be present to discuss his treatment plan. The caseworker sent a fax back responding, "If it would make you feel uncomfortable having him there, I will tell the program not to send him." I had made it perfectly clear numerous times that I did not want any form of contact with Adam. I had recently written to the Regional Director, Governor, Attorney General and Director of the social service agency, stating I was afraid of Adam and wanted some form of protection from him—yet our male caseworker was inviting us to sit down and have a friendly treatment chat with Adam. I was completely sickened and realized I had been upset for months—helplessly watching the abusive and dysfunctional ways the state social service system operated. Earlier in the week I had spoken with Joey and David's counselor, who helped me realize I had the power to wash my hands of Adam. She helped me affirm that I needed to focus solely on my children and safeguard my sanity. I finally understood that the social service agency "professionals" would never understand my family's needs. I acknowledged that I needed to cut myself off from any communication with the state department. I quickly sent a response back to the caseworker stating I could no longer be involved in any portion of the programming for Adam and all contact had to be made through Bob.

As I thought about the State's plan of action, I could not believe that the "professionals" were planning to have a thirteen-year-old boy who had raped his siblings, stolen from everyone around him, lied and never showed any signs of remorse—be present to advocate for himself and participate in his own treatment plans. I thought, "Shouldn't the adults, who are supposed to be the "professionals," take control of the situation, use their own expertise, and make the treatment plans and the final decisions?" This was an enormous example to me of how the perpetrator always has more rights than any victim. The institutions and services are set up to empower perpetrators who are even given the right to set up their own treatment plans! I finally could understand that my sole focus needed to be on protecting myself and my children from such a backwards and disastrous system.

As Bob and I realized the social service system was failing, we knew a system so dysfunctional could never provide the necessary treatment to "cure" Adam. Afraid for our safety, we continued to request permission to send Adam back to Cape Verde. But our caseworker stated, "Oh, we won't allow him to go back to where he was abused." This was the same caseworker who originally sat in our kitchen and told me how disturbing it was to see such advanced perpetrator skills in Adam. Yet, in a few months, he transformed into being Adam's strongest advocate. Despite all of the requests Bob and I made in person and through documents for a restraining order and permission to send Adam back—the caseworker became the "professional" who persistently asked if Adam was going to be reunited with our family. Ironically he believed Adam should not be returned to the country where he was violated, yet he saw nothing wrong with Adam living in the same household with Joey and David. The abuse the boys had suffered from Adam was totally irrelevant to the caseworker.

About four months after Adam entered the treatment facility, the staff and caseworker began seeking a long-term placement for Adam. They suddenly realized Adam had no one else in America. They had to finalize where Adam would go and who would pay for the care he had received. According to the prosecution lawyer, the judge in the case began asking why the state was caring for a child who did not have any family in the country, and who was not himself an American citizen. She began to ask why he was not sent back to Cape Verde where he had other family members (Bob's family) who could provide a safe and caring home.

Soon after one of the court sessions, I received a frantic phone call from the prosecution lawyer. She explained that the only way to make the State pay for Adam's treatment, and not make Bob and me responsible, was for charges to be brought against Bob. She could see that we had no rights and were left blind in the situation, she said, "You guys have already been through hell. I don't want to see it get worse for you. I think it is a good idea for you to get a lawyer." She explained that in order to initiate the process of sending Adam back to Cape Verde, the judge instructed the state social service system to file "Dependency" against Bob. I was told that the five ways a state could get involved in a family were: Abuse, Neglect, Wayward, Delinquency and Dependency. By filing this charge against Bob, now the state could take total control of Adam's case. Dependency meant that Bob, "Through no fault of his own," was unable to provide the many social service needs for Adam. Thus, Bob needed support from the state to get support and resources for Adam. Also, with the Dependency charge against Bob, the State would now have to pay for Adam's treatment. It was our understanding that if we did not go along with the charge, then Bob would have to pay for Adam's treatment.

For months, Bob and I had been advocating that Adam should be sent back to Cape Verde. We had the funds ready to buy a ticket on a moments notice and Bob's family was prepared to take Adam into their home in Cape Verde. I went to Immigration for help with getting Adam deported, but they could not authorize it. All I could do was document that I was withdrawing my sponsorship of Adam and would no longer support him in this country. I contacted the deportation unit in Boston, Massachusetts for help. But they told me unfortunately Adam committed the crime when he was young, so no one would authorize him to be deported. The clerk informed me, "If he committed the crimes when he was older, maybe seventeen years old, he would have automatically been sent back." Ultimately, State did not want to send him back to Cape Verde and consequently, Adam was going to stay. The State wanted to keep Adam in therapy for as long as possible. Thus, I could not understand why there was confusion over who would pay for Adam's treatment. Clearly the State wanted to keep him, so the State should pay for the care. Why they needed to bring charges against

Bob, forcing them to pay for the treatment they wanted for Adam, was incomprehensible.

Luckily, the prosecution lawyer in the case forewarned us of this procedure so we would not have a heart attack when they served Bob with papers. She later re-explained the process and said it could hopefully work in our favor of sending Adam back to Cape Verde. But, my gut told me a something different. My fear was that the social service system would now, through the dependency charge, gain total control over Adam's case and advocate for Adam to stay in America forever. Meanwhile Bob would have a record and our family would have to live in constant fear of Adam's return.

I quickly made a few phone calls and found a lawyer that several others recommended. I understood from everyone that he was supposed to be the best in dealing with this type of situation. Bob and I were able to meet with him one evening and he stated we had nothing to worry about. He said the dependency charge was not a big deal and would allow the state to be responsible for Adam's treatment. He said we really did not need a lawyer for such a simple case. His understanding was that the State would automatically want to send Adam back immediately after treatment. I assured the lawyer that we had been ignored throughout the entire process and truly needed his services. I explained to the lawyer that the sole reason we were hiring him was to get legal permission to send Adam back to Cape Verde. I told him, "If at any time you realize this case will drag on and Adam will not be allowed to be sent back, please tell me so we can stop pursuing this legally. Our only wish is to be able to send Adam back."

For the next court appointment our lawyer could not attend, but we were instructed to let them know that we had a lawyer and needed the case to be rescheduled. Our male social service caseworker was there and the first thing he asked us was if we were considering family reunification. As we adamantly stated definitely not, I asked him if Adam was going to be there for the court session. I thought it was a ridiculous question since Adam should not be there for a charge against Bob, but things were so bizarre with the State system—I had to ask. I said a little joke that if Adam was going to be there, I could just run out and hide in the car. The caseworker was serious and responded, "Yes, he could possibly be here today. Why would there be a problem?" Luckily, Adam was not there on that day.

The next time we went to court, our lawyer was able to attend and there was an incredible transformation. Our caseworker who only a few weeks earlier said the agency would never allow Adam to be sent back to Cape Verde, now stated, "Well, you understand that Adam would only be sent back to Cape Verde once he has completed his treatment."

At first, it appeared that hiring the lawyer was a good decision. He obviously had clout, since every lawyer in the courtroom purposely went over to shake his hand. Also seeing the caseworker suddenly change his tune regarding Adam being sent back was wonderful. But as the months passed, I started realizing nothing was happening. The lawyer had shown up to court maybe once or twice but I had no idea what he was doing. He never explained what his plan of action was, yet we were paying him for showing up to court that was rescheduled several times. For each showing, his travel and time were paid at $225 an hour. He showed up to court a few times, but Bob and I could not understand what he was doing. It seemed I was doing all of the work.

Even though we had the lawyer representing us in court, I continued to pursue things, and sent all communications to the lawyer. I sent a second letter to the Governor stating we wanted to send Adam back to Cape Verde. I mentioned that I could not understand why the state was looking into other long-term placement for Adam since he had other family in Cape Verde that would take him. The same Regional Director of the social service agency then contacted me by phone. She told me the department needed to do a home visit on Bob's parents since they had agreed to take Adam into their home. I could not believe that a state agency would do a home visit to Cape Verde, but I was hopeful that he was finally going to be sent back. When I did not hear from her for several weeks, I called again. Now the story switched. She stated they needed to have a translator to speak with Bob's parents over the phone. I told her the Cape Verdean Consulate in Boston would probably be able to provide translation services. I gave her the phone number and she said she would contact them.

Several days later, I decided to call the Cape Verdean Consulate on my own to see if the Regional Director had followed through. I spoke with the woman there who was appalled at our situation and stated,

"We see that a lot. Many times the state departments do not know their place and get too involved in issues that are outside of their boundaries." She told me that she was very sorry for everything we had experienced, and was in total agreement that Adam should be sent back to Cape Verde. I waited a few more weeks with no response from the state social service department and finally contacted the Consulate again. I learned that the state had never contacted them. Bob's parents in Cape Verde were also never contacted.

As I could see that the system was failing again, I called to meet with the lawyer to understand what his game plan was. Bob and I listened as he explained how we needed to appeal to the state on a different level. We were supposed to express how happy and appreciative we were that Adam was now "cured" through his treatment at the facility. Then we needed to say that we wanted him under our care. Once he was released to our custody, we could ship him out on the next plane back to Cape Verde. When he explained this ridiculous maneuver, I did not feel comfortable at all. How could I participate in such a charade?

I was desperate and quickly met with an individual I knew from the Governor's office to plead my case. I explained our story, and that we received no assistance from the system, which was abusive and purposely kept us uninformed. I explained how dangerous Adam was, and that he should be seen as a threat to everyone in the community. I stressed that Bob and I wanted to send him back so we would not have to worry about him coming after us or hurting other American families. I explained what the lawyer had planned and he said, "Claire, no one would just release Adam to you and your husband. Your family would need to participate in months of family re-unification therapy." He thought the lawyers plan was unrealistic. He said he would look into Adam's case but could not promise anything. I could see by the end of the conversation that the severity of our situation and my family's needs fell on deaf ears.

Immediately after meeting with the Governor's staffer, I called to cancel services with the lawyer. In total we paid the lawyer fifteen hundred dollars for showing up to court three times. During each of those appearances he never "had the opportunity to bring up the conversation" of deporting Adam—even though that was the sole reason why he was hired.

Despite being reassured by the Governor's office that Adam would not get free college—several months later I was told differently by a woman who works in one of the treatment facilities. She informed me that the clients get free college, often through federal funding. They receive new brand name clothes, as Bob often indicated to me after visiting Adam. The perpetrators also get free health insurance, dental insurance and assistance with getting their own apartments at the completion of therapy. Meanwhile the personnel who work at the facilities make a few dollars more than minimum wage and will never have the same opportunities the clients have. I was also told that there were facilities housing perpetrators all over the state with most surrounding families unaware of who their neighbors are. The perpetrators are allowed to go to public school, have community jobs and go to various recreational activities without supervision.

Bob reported the same issues after his monthly visits with Adam. During each visit, Adam was dressed in new expensive clothes and sneakers—outfits Bob and I would never be able to afford for him. Adam was allowed to attend public school at the local high school and was told by treatment facility staff that he would probably get free college. The program also advocated for Adam to get a part-time job in the community. No one was alarmed about his past criminal behavior and he was allowed to be in society with everyone else.

Since he was potentially going to be working, I wanted to make sure he was listed as a sex offender on his record. But, as a juvenile, Adam's records were totally protected. Even though Adam was found guilty of second-degree sexual assault, which carries a ten year term of registering as a sex offender—no one would be able to see his record. Adam would eventually be able to obtain any job working with children.

Soon after firing the lawyer, meeting with the Governor's staff person and verifying Adam's protected record, I sobbed uncontrollably. I realized I had spent over two years trying to fight the system—and lost the battle. I tried to warn as many officials as possible, that Adam was a ticking bomb. Yet everyone saw Adam as a victim that needed help. I worried about the individuals Adam would harm in the future, and thought about the families whose loved ones would potentially be hurt or murdered by Adam. I pictured the news crews coming to our door for interviews once the bodies were discovered. I knew how dangerous

Adam was and I knew he had a dark future ahead of him—but no one listened. I had to give up fighting and trying to protect everyone else. I had to just worry about my family and make sure we were as far away from Adam as possible.

During the two years that Adam was at the treatment facility, the administration made about three attempts to involve Bob. Each time they invited Bob to participate in the treatment planning sessions, they made the appointments during the afternoon—the same time that Bob had to get to work for his second shift job. He could not miss any work because he would accumulate points for calling out and eventually lose his job. We sent a letter to the facility and the state agency to inform them that a morning meeting would fit into Bob's schedule, explaining that afternoon appointments would cause Bob to lose his job. However, both agencies continued to invite Bob during hours they knew he would be at work. During each of these "treatment-planning sessions", Adam would also be present. I could not understand how a system can have a child who has committed heinous acts against other children, participate in his own treatment planning—while ignoring any input from the parent(s)?

During the monthly visits to see Adam, neither the treatment facility nor the state agency ever offered any information to Bob. Was Adam making progress with his treatment? What were the after-care plans for him? Where would he go and when would he be released? Legally we never knew what was happening with Adam's case either. In the beginning, I registered our family for the Victim's Assistance program offered through the Attorney General's office. The mission of the program was to help the victims. By registering, we were supposed to be kept informed of the status of Adam's case. I called the program a few times and was promised return phone calls. But, no one ever returned the calls.

When Adam was first removed from our home and we began talking about sending him back to Cape Verde. As we discussed his future deportation out of America, I heard very clearly in my mind—"The system will fail, the system will fail." From within, I knew that meant people would be see Adam as a young, innocent adolescent who needed guidance and support. The system would provide services for him and he would be protected from being sent back to Cape Verde. Then,

Adam would later be free to commit crimes in America without ever being stopped—and there was nothing I could do. My gut was warning me from the beginning, but I still had to try to fight the system. I was trying and will continue to protect my children from the predator in our family—my stepson, Adam.

I have included all of this detail to give the reader a true understanding of how the systems work to empower perpetrators. It does not matter if it is a court, church, school, social service agency, town, or state—almost every system is designed to protect the perpetrator, while providing nothing to the survivor or the survivor's family—who are often left feeling defeated and alone.

If you are currently in the same type of situation, stand tall and survive with dignity. Try to find others who have been through the system to help support you and give you valuable advice. Know what you are up against. Understand the twists and loopholes, which seem to be intentionally placed to keep you down. Expose the dysfunction of each institution and agency that attempt to re-traumatize you by strengthening and protecting the perpetrator. Tell others your story. Recognize that you have to be strong for your child and your family. Challenge the dysfunction and refuse to give up. Don't lose your power along the way. Let the anger and frustration motivate you to be more determined. Advocate for change and don't accept anything less than support and respect for your child and yourself.

Each person has roles, which play an important part in society. Parents have the role of protecting and educating their children. Others who are not parents, yet have contact with children, need to recognize how powerful they are in their positions. A teacher comes across hundreds of kids daily and could potentially spot children that are showing signs of trauma or showing behaviors that the child could potentially grow into a perpetrator. He/she could intervene, and ask questions. Once a child discloses, the social service system will get involved to protect the child. A doctor or nurse plays a vital role. A child knows fully that he or she is going to the doctor for their body. So if anything ever happened to their body—they would have to report it. I had asked Joey, "If the pediatrician had asked you if anyone ever touched you in your private areas, would you have told him?" He said "Mom, of course! I would have told the truth because that is a doctor. They need to know everything that is going on with your body." Nurses and doctors during physical exams, could easily check in with children saying, "I'm sure your parents have told you, that you and everyone else has private areas on the body and those areas are not to be touched by other people. If anyone ever did touch those areas or make you touch their areas then you can tell your parents, a teacher, the school nurse or any other adult that you feel you can talk to."

Anyone who is in constant contact with children has the opportunity to observe children's behaviors, and see if any children are isolated from their peers. People, who don't have children, usually work with other adults who have children. Adults without children can encourage parents to make sure they are having regular check-in conversations with their kids ensuring that they always feel safe. Parents can support other parents and help them understand how prevalent sexual abuse really is. Judges and lawyers can study and know the effects on children that have been sexually abused, which will help them see what a horrific crime sexual abuse truly is. Consequently, they can work towards stronger sentencing of perpetrators to keep children safe. Regular citizens can work with legislators to implement stronger laws—forcing perpetrators to be held accountable for their crimes.

Police officers play a crucial role since they are often called into homes for domestic violence. They can see if the child in the home is being traumatized not only by seeing or hearing the adults fighting, but if they themselves have been violated. An officer's demeanor, professionalism, consistency and manner with which he/she handles the case, can foster a child's disclosure. The police officers in our case were the best people that initially helped us in our crisis. The lead police officer was calm, professional and sincere. He understood the gravity of the situation and knew we needed to be protected from Adam. He checked on us regularly after Adam was removed to make sure we understood what the process was. He was one of the only professionals that helped our family.

With today's crisis in the Church, clergy are in the perfect position to initiate a pattern of reform. Survivors have been so horribly violated—they question God's existence. They question their purpose in life. They question themselves inside and out. It was heart wrenching to interview survivors and find, not only were they violated physically, mentally and emotionally, but they were stripped of their spirituality. Their hopes and faith had been stolen. Their belief in God had been wiped out. The survivors who were able to hang onto their faith seemed to be in a much stronger place of self, than the survivors who yearned for comfort and tranquility. Any person holding a position within a religious institution has the obligation to validate a survivor's struggle. He or she can express that God's plan was never for a human being to attempt to destroy another through sexual abuse. It is a precious opportunity to bring a survivor who is suffering closer to self understanding, closer to patience through the struggle, and ultimately closer to the peace, love and joy of God. Everyone is in a position to listen, learn, educate, support and empower survivors.

Chapter 11
The Role of Spirituality

In a million years, Bob and I would have never believed that our children would be sexually abused. We did everything within our power to keep them safe. We carefully screened all daycare providers, vigilantly watched the boys in any public areas, and warned them of strangers whenever possible. The feelings of devastation upon learning that both Joey and David had been sexually abused by Adam were unbearable.

Previously, I never had an interest in writing or reading. But as soon as I heard of Adam's stealing behavior I was compelled to start telling our story. My nature is to share. If trauma happens in my life, I'm the first person to talk about it. I've always held the belief that if my situation can help someone, I should never hold that information secretly. My personality fit with writing the book, but between juggling raising my kids and working—writing a book was something I never intended or wanted to do.

This chapter serves two purposes—to chronologically document how our family and those around us were being guided during the traumatic period—and to reaffirm how I personally was led and strengthened through spiritual forces. I hope this chapter serves others by helping them understand that each individual has love, support, and guidance from higher level forces that are usually not detected by the human eye.

Despite my unwillingness to be a writer, my Guides made sure finishing this book became my passion. I was led from the beginning outline to the final completion. Many times I put the boys to bed and tried to work late at night. I was always exhausted and usually fell asleep at the computer sitting up. Several evenings I woke up after a few minutes of dozing off, and realized my fingers kept typing. When I read what was typed in, I had no idea where the thoughts came from. Sometimes two paragraphs would appear while I slept, with several spelling mistakes—but filled with ideas or phrases that were extremely profound.

Throughout the process of writing the book, there were several instances when I felt blowing on my head, forehead, face or shoulders—a clear sign of Spirit Guides or Loved Ones visiting. I also felt warmth around me as if someone was very close to me, ready to hug me. The last few weeks that I was writing, I had visions of words and phrases appear before me. While writing, I had many moments of clarity where I could see back in the past and realize there were so many events—telling me we were not alone in our trauma. From the beginning, until the end, I hated the process, but became obsessed with writing and finishing the book. It was as if someone grabbed me, forced me to sit down, and started dictating into my head exactly what I needed to write.

Honestly, it has not been an enjoyable experience. Writing has been a painful and time consuming process. From the beginning, I wished the ordeal of writing was over. There were many times I was typing, stopped what I was doing, called the boys into the room, hugged them tightly, and cried. It was excruciating to already know what my boys had lived through and then have to re-experience everything by writing about it. But the book served as my therapy to get my feelings, and emotions out, and I knew from a higher level, that the information had to get out to the public. I had to get the book out to families who needed to learn how to protect their children, and people who could help kids who may have already been violated—professionals who could improve their effectiveness when working with children and their families.

The only way I, as a mother of two children who were sexually abused was able to stand strong for my children, was through spirituality and a strong network of support. My personal ideas about different forms of spirituality began when I was a child. There was a story in our family that had been passed down from generation to generation about my grandmother's uncle who died in his native country, Poland. When he died, the candle blew out in the room where his wife, and niece sat praying. At the same moment, his brother who was in the United States, saw him walking towards him on a busy city street. When he passed, the brother turned around to see him and he was gone.

As a kid I was obsessed to hear that story and the whole idea of—where do we go when we die? Are we still in contact with the people we love? I often begged people to tell me ghost stories and then shook uncontrollably at night in fear. Another influence on me during my younger years was church. As a kid I had the opportunity to ride on a big bus with some friends. The bus took us to a local church where there was a lot of preaching, singing, clapping and dancing—I instantly felt at home. One evening as I started going to sleep, I had a very spiritual experience. I felt someone with me, guiding and protecting me. After that I always knew I was not alone.

Later as a young adult, I started pursuing the questions I had as a young child. After losing my grandfather, I began having intense dreams. My grandmother suffered a massive stroke soon after, and I longed to communicate with both of them. I learned how to meditate, read many life-after-death books, and began to experience different visions, auditory sensations, feelings, and times of prophetic knowing.

In 1995, I had two extremely powerful spiritual experiences which helped me form a basis for my own spiritual insights. The two events were incredibly dramatic and emotional, and made a lasting impression on me. One experience was terrifying and the other was heavenly. Both served their purpose in teaching me about my own abilities and my own purpose in life.

Shortly after I met Bob, I yearned to reconnect to my own form of spirituality. I had briefly learned how to meditate a few years earlier, but I had not practiced for a while. Early one evening, after a tiring day at work, I decided to sit by a waterfall and meditate. I went to a grassy area in the center of a small city and sat on a park bench which was next to a rolling river. The waterfall there was wide and sent great amounts of moisture into the air. I sat for a few minutes and began to center myself.

As I meditated, I began to feel a presence next to me on my left side. It was a very eerie and uncomfortable feeling. The energy was unmistakably negative. It was so strong I finally opened my eyes—expecting to see someone sitting there. As I opened my eyes, I could see there was no one next to me. I looked all around me, and found that I was totally alone. I closed my eyes again and began to go through the process. For a second time, I felt negative energy next to me. Again, I opened my eyes and checked my surroundings and found nothing. Finally I closed my eyes and said, "OK God, for whatever reason I am sensing this. I'm just going to sit here and see what You need me to experience." As I thought the words, I suddenly had a vision which became clearer as the seconds passed. There was a man sitting on the bench with me. He was on my left side and had his right arm outstretched toward my neck. In his right hand, he held a knife to my throat. He had a horribly unnerving laugh. He needed power and control over people. I understood I was nothing to him.

The image was so disturbing I had to calm myself. I said, "God, I know even if someone ran up behind me right now and stabbed me in the back, I would still be fine. Yes, my body may die, but I know I will still be alive and I will be safe with You." As I felt calmness cover me like a warm blanket, I heard something in front of me. It sounded like a tiny pebble had moved. I opened my eyes and saw a real man standing in front of me, starring at me. Since I had just been so calm, I did not flinch or startle to suddenly see this person. I calmly said hello and remained in the same spot. The man sat down next to me on my left, and started to talk to me. He said his name was Mike and he worked in the neighboring building. He didn't really like his job, "But it's a job." As he spoke I knew inside of myself that I needed to talk about my work. I needed to explain that I worked with tough, at-risk teenagers who did not have fathers and strong mother figures in their lives. I felt from within that I needed to show him that I was a person who truly cared about people. As we spoke, he rested his right hand very close to me on the back of the bench. He had a very distinctive laugh that was filled with indifference and selfishness.

After talking for a few minutes, I realized I needed to leave. I stood up, shook his hand and said, "Mike it was nice to meet you. I have to get going. Have a nice day." He responded by saying, "Well, when am I going to see you?" I said, "Oh, I don't usually come here, so I don't know." He became adamant and said, "No! What day and what time?" I quickly answered, "I told you, I usually don't come here. If you see me, you see me. If you don't, you don't. Have a nice day." I started to walk away and he jumped up to walk along side of me. As I walked down the path, with him on my side, I thought "Is this guy going to follow me to my car?" The path led to a couple of stairs and as I stepped up, I glanced down for a few seconds. When I looked up in Mike's direction—he was gone. I searched everywhere around me and saw no one. I could not understand how he had appeared and disappeared so quickly. It did not seem humanly possible. He had moved within seconds without a trace. I was truly baffled over the entire experience.

Later that night, I told Miladys about the event. I told her about seeing the negative energy which became a man and then told her about Mike who sat next to me. As we spoke, we understood that I had been warned. My body began to shake uncontrollably as I realized how close my life had just come to ending. I had never had such a strong feeling in my life. I knew from deep within my soul, that Mike was capable of kidnapping, raping, and murdering me and then walking away as if nothing ever happened. As I shook in fear, I suddenly understood that I had been warned and the only reason why Mike did not hurt me was because I had the few seconds of calmness and was not startled when he first appeared. If I had flinched and gasped in fright as he appeared in front of me—it would have excited him and he would see the situation as already winning control. For several days I walked around dazed, thinking about the event and studying every detail. I knew Mike could have easily killed me, but I was alive because God had warned me.

I had learned about the "third eye" but never believed I had one. In books that I read, the third eye was explained as the space in your forehead where people can see visions. The disturbing event helped me realize that my third eye did work, but I was terrified to ever have it work again. After such a dramatic experience, I mistakenly understood for years that meditating had brought the negative energy to me. I vowed to never meditate again since I thought it was delving into evil energies.

Luckily, in 2002, I met my teacher, Tony Santos who asked me, "If the experience was not as dramatic, would you have paid attention?" He helped me understand that it was not meditating that brought the evil energy to me. It was through meditating that I was able to calm myself, be prepared and remain protected from such a negative person.

The experience had to be that unnerving for me to pay attention. My guides were telling me in a loud and clear way that my third eye did work and I needed to trust it.

A few months after the incident with Mike, I had another profound experience. I had been dating Bob for eight months and had a history of wondering why I was in the relationship, and where was it going. From the beginning of our relationship I constantly thought about ending our ties. I had just come out of a long term relationship and could not understand why I was already entering into another one with Bob. I could see great qualities in him and really enjoyed Bob's company, but I did not want to be serious with him. Soon after Bob and I started to see each other regularly, I went away for a camping trip with Miladys. Since I was going through so much internal turmoil of wishing for higher spirituality and understanding the relationship between Bob and me—it made for a bizarre and extremely powerful weekend.

As I sat complaining in the cabin one day, Miladys got sick of hearing me moaning and said, "Claire, go for a walk and talk to your higher self!" So I organized a few things I had lying around, and then set out on my journey. As I walked, I thought to myself, "What does 'your higher self' mean?" I made my way down an isolated long dirt road, and began to slow down my racing mind. I began to enjoy the scenery around me. I was always so mentally busy, I never took the time to quiet my mind and enjoy the moment. As I walked, I talked to God. "What is my higher self?" "What does that mean?" It seemed like such a bizarre concept. But as I walked and thought about it, I began to hear a slight whisper. The whisper told me to walk further down the path and where I was to sit. I followed the directions and then quietly questioned, "Why am I still in the relationship with Bob?" The whisper said, *"Bob is not the one, but he will bring you closer."* I could not believe what I was hearing and earnestly asked, "Closer? Closer to what? Closer to getting pregnant? Closer to insanity? Closer to death—is he going to give me some disease? Closer to what?" As I pleaded for the phrase to be completed, there was no answer.

Eight months later, is when I got my answer. This was the second powerful experience which helped me shape my own sense of spirituality. One day I was visiting my parents and sat with my mother. We were talking about our relationship and how it was so great that we were both in the same choir and the same photography club. We were happy that we had many of the same interests. As we talked, the conversation turned to discussion about the relationship between Bob and me. Since Bob could not speak any English, it was difficult for my parents to get to know him. It was confusing because they and I could not understand why Bob and I were still together. As we spoke, I said to my mother, "Well, I don't really understand it, but I'm just going to enjoy the time together. We worry about making the "right" decision or the "wrong" decision. Who is to say what is right and wrong? As long as you learn something, how can it be wrong? I've found some of the most difficult times in my life have been the times where I've learned the most, and it has shaped me into who I am today."

As we spoke I sat and looked at my mother, who was sitting on my left. Her eyes were filled with love and concern for me. She then said, "Bob is not the one, but he will.." Before she could finish the sentence, I knew what she was going to say. I knew she was going to finish by saying "bring you closer to—yourself." As she started the phrase, I saw something so amazing to my right. Words are so limiting, and cannot possibly explain the event fully. I was overcome with a total feeling of love, admiration and pride. As I looked to my mother on my left, I also saw a being on my right. The entity was nodding and smiling at me. It had total love for me. The feelings of pride it had for me were unbeliev-able. It was proud of me that I was finally understanding things.

I had a mission in this life and was not supposed to be worried about my relationship with Bob. I saw Bob on a path throughout life—by my side. He was there to help me find myself and help me find my reason for coming into this life. My focus had to be on my mission. I was overcome with emotions and sobbed uncontrollably begging my mother, "Do you see it? Do you see it?" I tried to tell her what I was seeing, but words were not enough. For those few seconds, I starred at the entity and was captivated by its beauty. It was made of white light that was so white it almost had a hint of blue. There was white light all around it too. It did not have a face like a person, it was almost like looking at a skeleton head—but it was the most incredibly beautiful thing imaginable. I have never experienced love similar to that. As I cried uncontrollably, I looked at my mother and at the glorious essence. I could see their love for me in images. My mother's love for me was equal to the love the entity had for me. Then I saw my mother's love as a particle of sand on a beach. The love from the entity was mountain ranges upon mountain ranges that sprawled without limits. Despite the size difference in the visions, both were equally important.

For those few seconds I popped out of my life and saw it as a brief period of time. Everything made sense. Everything fit together perfectly. I had a mission for the years of life that I would be here, and had to hold true to it. The entity understood my entire life and loved me for living it. There were no worries, fears, or concerns in my life. Everything happened for reasons which made sense in the end.

The experience lasted for a few seconds and then faded away. I instinctively knew that the energy and event could only last for a few seconds. I knew the confines of the human body could not withstand the intensity of the entity and the surrounding energy. If people were to experience such an event for longer periods of time, their bodies would explode to free the spirit within. I understood that all human beings are given this love. The love is always with us, and always waiting to be shared with us.

Eight years later, despite such a huge family tragedy, I was able to hang onto my spirituality. Through friends' and my own personal experiences, I quickly recognized there were spiritual influences around us—helping to guide and protect us. On many levels, I learned about the depths of sexual abuse. From spiritual insight, I gained strength. I was able to look at our family's trauma on a different level and understand that my personal mission was to help society recognize sexual abuse (especially from juvenile perpetrators) and help protect children. Our family's trauma has helped me learn that everyone has guidance from Higher Forces. God, our Angels, Spirit Guides, and Loves Ones who have passed on were with us throughout our ordeal. I learned that the heart is directly connected to a Higher Power, our Spirit Guides and Loved Ones who are trying to help us. They communicate with us through our hearts. The language they speak is feelings, thoughts and emotions.

From when I was a child, I always had a hunger to learn more about God, Spirit Guides, Angels, and people who had died. As I grew older, I was afraid there were people who were very good at fooling others and could trick them into believing they had spiritual abilities. I could see how dishonest people could take advantage of people during emotional times in their lives and feed them any kind of garbage they could come up with.

During my early twenties, I went to a few "psychics" who spoke so generally, their words would apply to anyone. But, in my late twenties and early thirties, I was very fortunate to receive information from a few extremely gifted individuals. They were able to give me messages that related to my life, in great detail. I began to learn that Spirit Guides and Angels really did exist. From our horrible family tragedy I now understand we were never alone. God, our Spirit Guides, our Angels, and Loved Ones were with us from the beginning. I can attest to the fact that God has perfect timing. He places people and situations in our lives to help us.

When we first learned of the atrocious acts committed against my children, I screamed to God for help to understand why and how it happened. At the time, I thought I would never experience peace again in my life. I can now proclaim that God and all of the other Spiritual Forces have been there the whole time—helping me find each piece of the puzzle, showing me how to put the pieces together, and ultimately helping me understand what sexual abuse truly is.

I was destined to write this book from a long time ago. Back in 1995, I was leaving a long-term relationship and felt very confused about life. I went for a reading from a woman whom my boss was friendly with. From that day forward until now, that same woman has given me three readings. During each of the readings she always asked, "When are you going to start your book? Why aren't you writing?" I could never understand what she was talking about since I was not a reader and was definitely not a writer! During the last reading with her in August 2002, I questioned, "Every reading you give me, you tell me I'm supposed to write a book. I don't like writing and I have no idea what I would write about. I don't see myself writing a book in my life. Can you at least tell me what I'm supposed to write about?" She responded by saying she saw the book was going to be something "that would help children." She also said, "Claire, don't worry that you don't feel like writing now. You will come to a point in your life where all of a sudden you have to sit and write down all of your ideas because it starts coming so quickly to you."

For years, I never felt inspired to write. But four months after that last reading, we learned of Adam's stealing behavior—I was immediately compelled to start writing. At the time, I did not know how expansive the book would be. During that last reading the woman also told me that I have a mark on my hand that signified I would save someone's life. Was it Joey's life that was saved by removing Adam from the home?

When we began the process of returning all of the stolen items, I had a profound experience. Returning stolen items is an extremely serious and embarrassing situation, yet as we walked into a friend's home, I felt myself leave my body and view the scene from a different perspective. I could hear my voice narrating the scene saying, "And here she comes carrying the Box of Shame." From that point, I immediately started jotting down the chapters and ideas for each section.

As I wrote, I remembered events which helped me understand that we were being guided. Before I ever started writing and we were still innocent to the crimes Adam was committing—Bob and I were having a very difficult time in our marriage back in June 2002. I contacted a friend of mine who regularly deals with divorce cases in her law practice. One of her first questions was what I would do with Adam. She explained that since I never adopted him, legally I had no rights to him. In case we did get divorced, I did not want to separate the children from each other, so I started thinking I should adopt Adam.

I was confused and called Julia to tell her about my situation. She immediately said in a very strong voice, "Claire, whatever you do, don't ever adopt that kid!" I could not understand why she had such a strong reaction and asked why she felt that way. She explained that I should never worry about taking on an additional responsibility for another child who technically is not mine. She told me I should worry about my own children and myself. Her reaction was very puzzling to me, but the strength with which she made her statements stuck with me.

Soon after this conversation, Bob got a job and our marriage improved. Adam was able to convince us that he was able to watch the boys for the short time we needed daycare each afternoon. I again called Julia to tell her of two situations I witnessed as I came home. One day I saw the microwave almost on fire from something Joey had put inside. Another day I saw Joey laying on the floor, holding his bleeding finger—which he had accidentally cut with a knife while trying to sharpen a pencil. As I unfolded the details to Julia, she immediately and adamantly stated, "Claire, that kid can never watch your children again! You have to get daycare set up today or you don't go to work tomorrow! You are a good person and I don't know how to support you as a friend if something happens to one of your children. If you ever lost one of your children, you would never be the same person you are now. You would never recover."

I thought her reaction was beyond extreme. But, again, her words and her intensity stayed with me. That she mentioned the possible loss of one of my children got me very nervous. A few minutes later, my friend Beth called and I received a similarly intense reaction. Beth stated, "Don't leave the children with Adam. He is not old enough for that responsibility!"

At the time, I was in a total workaholic stage. Bob had been laid off for a while, and I saw myself as the only source of income. I was so worried about finances, I could not see straight. I did not realize my children were in an unsafe situation. My mind downplayed the scenes I was coming home to, and probably would have continued to allow Adam to be the "babysitter." However, after intense reactions from Julia and Beth, I started to snap out of my fog. I was able to set up daycare for the boys with my neighbor, Danene, who we had recently met. I took great care to not insult Adam. I did not want him to think that he had done a poor job watching the boys. I used the excuse that since school had started—he should be able to take advantage of any extra help offered by teachers without worrying about watching his younger brothers.

Months later, when I learned how twisted Adam was and what he was doing to the boys, I called Julia. I asked her, "How did you know? Out of all of the people around our family, you were the only one who felt something. How did you know?" She then stated, "I don't know what it was, all I know was something came over me and made me speak that forcefully to you. At the time it even scared me that I was talking to you in such a strong way—but I knew I had to. I felt I had to protect Joey. He is such a special boy and I felt if I didn't talk to you that way, Joey was going to be harmed." Then she stated, "I don't know what you and Bob are going through. I can't imagine what you guys have to go through as parents. But, the one thing to remember is—you still have your little boy you can go home to and hug every night. I think if Adam remained in your home, you would not be able to hug Joey anymore."

Julia is an amazingly intelligent, educated, humble and fun person. She is incredibly full of life and totally appreciates the special moments others take for granted. I often found myself taking mental notes as she spoke. Her words were always significant and sincere. During the time when she believed Joey to be in danger, Julia felt something intensely, and she allowed it to guide her. Her trust in a Higher Power that was coming to her—allowed her to warn me. Her strength with her words shook me. Her determination to make me understand—saved my children. I know when I look at Joey—he is alive because Julia intervened to save him!

Having a "sense" about things, which Julia had, was something I had yearned for since childhood. If Guides and Angels were real, I wished I could find someone to prove their existence, and teach me a different form of spirituality than organized religion. In October 2002, I found two people. I enrolled in a class that taught people how to develop their own personal medium abilities. A medium is someone who has the ability to communicate with people who have passed on. A good medium will relate specific details from Loved Ones to the person still living—the details should then prove to the person living of their Loved Ones continued existence. Through the class, I met my teacher, Tony Santos and a close friend, Barbara Ann Colangelo.

Unlike my usual schedule of being late for everything, I was very early the first morning of class. I patiently sat outside of the building in my car. As the rain fell down and the fog filled my windows, a car pulled in next to me. The woman in the car unrolled her window and I followed her lead. She introduced herself as Barbara Ann Colangelo and told me she was waiting for the same class.

Barbara explained that she was already pretty active with doing readings on people, and was just looking for more knowledge. To finally find someone who supposedly had the "ability" was amazing. I was intrigued to ask her about her talents see if it was real. I started asking her many questions such as, does she see things, hear things, or feel things, and does she do anything special for information to come to her. She said, "Well, for instance, right now I am seeing a woman who looks just like you and she is right next to you. She is your sister." I knew I never lost a sister so I politely said, "I never lost a sister." She was persistent and said, "I think she is your twin because she is the same height and looks just like you. I am also getting the name George. Does that mean anything?" Again I said no. Then she said, "Oh, I'm sorry, it is Georgia." A little shocked I said, "Well, I was born in Georgia". Barbara Ann then politely explained to me, "You need to call your mother tonight after the class and then call me back. I am seeing that your mother bled during the seventh month of the pregnancy with you. That is the time your sister was passed. Your sister received a soul as a fertilized egg, but she did not develop into a fetus. The cells remained as a lump of blood cells that never developed. That is what was passed when your mother bled. Also, your mother was put on bed rest for one week." Since Barbara Ann was such a gentle, kind person, I politely agreed to call my mother that night. But I could not believe I really had a sister that had died. I knew my mother never bled during the pregnancy with me because she would have told me. My mother had also never mentioned anything about being on bed rest.

In class I met several wonderful, kind, open people who were all seeking a higher understanding of spirituality. When my teacher, Tony Santos, came in, he spent a lot of time explaining history and general information about psychic versus mediumship abilities. As the morning turned to afternoon, Tony began to demonstrate how we could practice sending energy to someone and experience receiving energy from someone else. He explained it as a feeling that someone is touching us without using his or her body. We could touch and be touched by others using energy. One by one, Tony came to each of us and we had to identify when he was touching us, and where on our bodies—top of the head, forehead, throat or heart. Of course our eyes had to be closed. When it was my turn I was very skeptical that I would feel anything. As I sat there, I thought what a joke it was since all I could feel was him breathing on my face. I told him I could not feel anything. He tried again and sadly I reported to him, "Tony, I couldn't feel anything, all I could feel was you breathing on my face." I was stunned when he said, "Sweetheart, I was not blowing on your face. That was the energy touching you!" He then showed me that it was impossible for him to blow on my face since he was concentrating and continually had his face turned down towards his lap. I was stunned to realize I really did feel blowing on my forehead—it was the exact area he had been touching! For me, that moment was like a whole new world opening! I was ecstatic!

Later in the afternoon, Tony explained how a person could enter another person's energy to read them as a medium, or enter the energy to read the person psychically. This manner of reading would give personal information about the person that most people would never know. Luckily Tony chose me as the guinea pig to demonstrate how to read someone in this manner. I could always find a skeptic's explanation for everything, so I needed him to prove to me that it was real. Immediately he started saying things that hit me on such a personal level, I was almost brought to tears. He said a few things about my relationships with family and friends and then said that I had "a strong sense of abandonment which started very early in life. It has something to do with your mother." It colors your relationships with everyone. You are afraid of being abandoned." He then stated, "You often contemplate about leaving this life". This was true. I loved my children and knew I had a good life. I was a good employee, a good mother, and a good wife. I did the best job I could with raising my children and our family. But, I always felt a feeling of emptiness that I could not explain. I really did not know what my purpose in life was. I needed to feel something, and I could not find it. I was not suicidal, but the idea of God taking me because of some life threatening disease or an accident seemed like a trip back home. I would not call it suicidal—I was passively living. I did not appreciate the miracle of life and the process of personal growth and self-identification. He then told me, "You are not supposed to pass yet. Let me tell you, if you did ever kill yourself you would be stuck on the other side—trying to learn the lessons you were supposed to learn over here. You are supposed to stay here. It is easier to learn the lessons while you are here, instead of trying to learn them over there. Speaking of life's purpose, why aren't you writing your book?" I laughed and said "Ugh! Another person telling me to write a book? Can you at least tell me what this book is supposed to be about?" He then stated that he saw me journaling something in my family or the history of my family. He too felt that it was a book to help children.

I was blown away by what Tony said during the individual reading and the experience with the energy—I realized I had finally found my teacher. As he wrapped up class, I felt total devastation. I could not have that intense of an experience without any form of follow through. I asked if there was anything else I could participate in to keep learning about everything he discussed. He mentioned he had a weekly class, which he would start the next week. I had to go, but suddenly realized who would watch the boys for me? Luckily, Danene who was already babysitting the boys during the day said it was no problem for me to go the additional hours one night a week. She was so supportive and told me I had to take the class! Her support from the beginning when I started taking the class and throughout the process of writing this book has been endless. She has been an unbelievable friend who I truly appreciate and value. From the years of watching my boys, she became a loving second mother to them. She supported me throughout every detail of our trauma and felt the pain as we did. Her unconditional love and support have truly inspired and motivated me to tell our story.

That night after class, I called my mother and asked her if she had ever lost a child. She stated, "No". I asked if she ever miscarried, again the answer was "no". I then asked if she had ever bled during her pregnancy with me. Surprisingly, she stated, "Yes, when I was seven months pregnant with you I bled. The doctors put me on bed rest for a week in the hospital. We were afraid we were going to lose you." I told her what Barbara Ann had said, and her reaction was "Claire, if I had lost a baby I would have known it."

But I felt a deep clarity from within. I immediately called Barbara Ann in tears knowing she really did see my sister. I knew my mother could not understand that my sister was a lump of blood cells that never developed. My entire life of desperately yearning for a sister suddenly made complete sense. The longing to believe my life had a purpose was just beginning to become clear to me. I was starting to see the beauty in my purpose with my life. I really did lose a sister and now I finally found her. It was very comforting to have Barbara Ann then say, "Claire, she chose not to come through because she felt she could help you more with your psychic abilities from there." Barbara went on to state the month I was born in, that I had a brother and his name, that my father was having health problems that were being studied, and that

I had a grandmother who had passed and a description of her personality. Everything she said was totally true. Barbara and I then continued to be close friends, which helped give me strength during the difficult months that followed.

In November 2002, through the weekly mediumship classes with Tony, I went to a workshop involving a physical medium. During the class the man organized the room to be a dark room. All of the windows and doors were closed off and there was no light, except a small red bulb. He passed out pieces of cloth to each of the workshop participants and we were instructed to hold the cloth on a piece of paper on our laps. He opened a few bottles of ink on a desk and started giving messages to people from their Guides. As he spoke, I could feel blowing on my hands the whole time. When he finished the process, he walked around with the red light to shine it on each of our cloths. As the red light illuminated the cloth, we could see the faces of our Spirit Guides, or Loved Ones who had passed appearing. We then had to roll the cloth up and not open it for 12 hours or the images would disappear.

As I jumped into my skeptic mode, I thought, "He probably had the images already implanted on the cloth." But several people in the room started yelling out, "That is my uncle," "Wow! That is my dog". I was so curious to open my cloth at home and really study it. When I was finally able to open it, one of the first faces I noticed was a man who I instantly thought, "Why is this drug addict loser on my cloth?" Feeling guilty about my first instinct, I tried to study the face. Immediately, I knew that the image was Bob's brother, Jose, who passed about nine years earlier. I was never able to meet Jose since he died before Bob came to America. Not a single person in Cape Verde or America had a picture of Jose that I could use to verify the image—Bob's family had always been too poor to have pictures of anyone. Even though my heart knew it was Jose, I wanted Bob to verify that it was his brother. At the time, Bob was not comfortable with the medium classes and never wanted to discuss Angels or Loved Ones who had passed. It seemed to be against his culture. He even warned me not to discuss stuff like that with his family, "Because they will think you are a witch."

Bob quickly glanced at the cloth and then looked away. Again he peeked at the images and said, "I really don't believe in that stuff." The proof was when I showed the cloth to friends of ours who had grown up with Jose. I explained the workshop and that I thought Jose's image had appeared on the cloth. Nervously the two looked at the piece of material and turned pale when they saw that the impression was Jose. They knew there were no pictures of Jose and I had never met him, so they shook a little when they asked, "Clara, aren't you afraid"? They could not believe I was so calm to have a spirit, whom I never met, coming to me and appearing on my cloth. But, I was ecstatic that they could verify Jose's image.

Later, Bob explained that he was too embarrassed to tell me earlier, but Jose did have serious problems with drugs. He was brilliant, and able to fix people's watches, radios and stereos with no education. He wrote and played amazing songs that people would travel from all over to come and see him perform. But he was always mad he could not get out of Cape Verde. His father had traveled to Portugal and continued to help several of Jose's other brothers and sisters from other mothers—but never helped Jose. In his frustration, he led a very chaotic life and then died of an infection in his leg at thirty years of age—the age he had always told everyone he would pass away.

A few weeks later, in December 2002, Jose visited me. Before we knew of Adam' stealing behavior, Bob and Adam sat working together one afternoon on a joint project. I had to do some laundry so I asked Adam to bring down his clothes from his bedroom. Since Bob needed Adam's help, he told me, "We are busy. Can you just get the clothes from his room, and bring them down, because he is helping me right now." Since Adam was a thirteen-year-old teenager, I believed he should be responsible with his own belongings. I made it a personal habit to never check his or anyone's pockets when doing laundry. I believed if anyone left something in their pocket and it was broken from going in the washing machine—then the individual would learn not to do that again. With that philosophy, I would normally just grab the clothes and never check any pockets.

That afternoon when I had to get Adam's clothes, I was guided. I grabbed the first pair of jeans that was on top of the pile, and without thinking, reached into the right front pocket. I instantly felt the sinking feelings as a parent, when I realized Adam had my father's college ring. As I looked at the inscribed initials inside and the name of the college, I felt Jose on my right side. His presence was overwhelming. I told him,

"Jose, if this kid is innocent you have to tell me quickly. If this kid is guilty, you have to show me everything as soon as possible."

Within the next few days, after talking to friends and family members, I began to hear Adam's name too often. Our friend's voice recorder was missing and Joey's friend's valuable card was missing. After finding the ring and hearing about other missing items, Bob decided it was time to go through Adam's room. That is when I took Adam out of the house Christmas Eve and Bob found the other numerous stolen items.

Throughout those initial weeks of feeling overcome with embarrassment while returning each of the stolen items to the rightful owners—I always felt Jose next to me. His calming presence allowed me to separate from my emotions and look at the situation from a different perspective. Shortly after returning all of the stolen items, I felt Jose come to me one day, and tell me that he had helped us as much as he could, but now he had to leave to help a young man who had an addiction problem.

Soon after, Bob and I brought Adam for his first psychological evaluation. As we sat waiting, Bob told me that he was too embarrassed to tell me something earlier. His brother, Jose showed the same behavior as Adam. Jose used to steal things from every house he went in. He eventually was thrown in jail for many years and upon release got the infection in his leg. Upon hearing about Jose's life, I understand that Jose's personal life struggles had become strengths for him. For the short time Jose was with us in spirit—he was able to use his life experience to guide us during the difficult process of finding and returning all of the stolen items.

On Christmas Eve 2002, when we confronted Adam about all of the stolen objects I could not believe what I was seeing. Adam stood in front of us with no signs of remorse, sorrow, shame or guilt. I desperately studied his face for any glimmer of emotions and was horrified to see there was nothing. I spoke on a personal level and still there was no reaction from him. I wished I could enter his brain to see what was inside. How could someone be so cold? It was as if he was not even human. I stared intensely at him wondering if he felt anything.

We had been learning in class for weeks how to read people. But I was always very skeptical and received the nickname from my teacher—"Clairvoyant the Skeptic". I had seen a few things in class, but never believed I really had abilities. But, now as I stared at Adam, and wished I could understand him, I accidentally fell into his energy. I suddenly saw visions and understood him on a much different level. I saw, felt and knew that he was going to be a professional thief. He was never going to stop and was probably never going to be caught. The vision progressed, and I saw him raping and killing people. I saw that there was something wrong with his mind and he would be able to do unconscionable things with no remorse. I was horrified by the information I received. I knew this was who Adam really was—a true sociopath who would hurt and murder many people. I quickly had to get away from him. I was terrified!

Later that evening, I told Bob about the vision and explained that I wanted Adam out of the house immediately. But, Bob stated all we knew was that Adam had been stealing. We had no other proof of anything else. Bob added that we were Adam's parents and needed to get services set up for him since he needed help. I told Bob we could get counseling for Adam, but I was not comfortable with him still being in our home. I had seen Adam on a much different level and I knew most people would not be able to accept what I had seen. I explained to Bob that if we learned of any other crimes Adam was committing, I wanted him out of the house immediately.

I could not share my vision with most people. When I told family and friends what I had seen and that I wanted Adam out of the house immediately, they thought I was being ridiculous. Everyone tried to comfort me by telling me stories of their childhood when they or friends they knew stole things. In their eyes, I was to look at Adam's stealing as a developmental stage and he would soon learn not to do it anymore.

It was not until I showed Adam's picture to Tony, my medium class teacher, in January 2003 that my vision was confirmed. Since Tony is a professional psychic and medium, he was able to look at the picture and within seconds tune into Adam's energy. He immediately began giving me details of what he saw, but hesitated with giving such severe information. I told him, "Tony, I don't care how bad it is. You have to tell me everything." He stated, "Adam is going to be a professional thief and he won't stop. There is something wrong with part of his brain. He does not feel guilt or remorse for his actions." I asked if there was any medication or surgery that could fix that portion of his brain and he responded, "Claire, that part of his brain is fried." He went on to explain that this is a genetic condition that was passed on from Adam's biological mother and his maternal grandmother. It was true. Both Adam's mother and his grandmother seemed developmentally slow. He explained how there was no medication or surgery that would help Adam's brain—the genetic combination from his mother and father had helped his brain to be distorted. He said, "If they studied him through an x-ray, they would see that there are portions of his brain that are developmentally smaller than they are supposed to be. Those areas are responsible for emotions and his connection to his own actions. He does not feel empathy for others." He then stated "I see him with a knife. I see him with a pillow over a five-year-old boy's face and the boy's name begins with a "J". I see police at your door and trouble at school."

As he studied the picture it was painful for him to look at. After lifting the picture several times and each time putting the picture upside down to avoid looking at it—Tony painfully responded, "Claire, I have never seen negative energy like this in my life". He then asked, "How strong is your marriage? You need to tell your husband that Adam needs to get out of the house right away. Claire, you need to be very careful with this kid's anger. Do you guys fight in the kitchen a lot? I see him as a young man and he is big. He can get very angry and I see him trying to hit you. Claire, just get this kid out of your house." Now I knew I could no longer doubt my vision. Tony's reading only confirmed exactly what I saw in my vision Christmas Eve. Adam was a dangerous person and I needed to get him out of my home as soon as possible.

A few days later, I spoke with Barbara Ann who tried to get more information by zooming into Adam's energy. She said she was not getting the same information that Tony and I were getting. She believed Adam was just a little confused, but not that he was capable of such horrific crimes. She decided to do an automatic writing on me. Barbara Ann has the ability to directly communicate with her Spirit Guides and Angels. As she asks a question about someone or something, she can hear responses. She writes everything down as she hears it. The following reading was in response to her asking for more information about Adam:

Automatic writing by Barbara Ann Colangelo 1/14/2003

Stop putting thoughts into your own senses. You are on the right track but there is more to this that meets the eye. The boy has been through what we call a washing out. He has been through the ruins of a battered heart and a tainted soul. His ears are of steel where he cannot hear the loudest cries for attention and the plea for compassion toward the members of the house he is living in. The medical sense of his deformities lies way deep within his structural growth from the time of his mother's conception. She has been battered repeatedly and in the interim he was a product of a lost soul in which he became lost from a very early stage. His motor skills and his auto skills were deformed as a result of the lack of care during his mother's childbearing years. Yes, he is surrounded by evil and yes; he does not care for the human heart because he does not have the capacity to do so. However, his behavior is in part a result of a deformity in his head as to a deformity in his spirit. In mortal words, he is hopeless. There is no hope as the people around him feel. However, the only hope is that of the Higher Power to come and take care of him because the mother figure in his life right at this time is falling down herself. Her body is failing her as her mind and spirit. The two sons in which she bore are surrounded by danger, as she believes they are. But they are protected totally by the white lights that she has surrounded them with. She has stepped out of their realm only to pay attention to the evil force that is surrounding the son of her life partner. She has called upon Angel Gabriel to assist her because her powers are not enough to correct the grave situation that exists in her house. He must warn her that she must not destroy the light connection that she has made even if the situation at hand begins to turn. It will be very traumatic for the whole family but I ask her to totally trust in the Higher Powers and know that she is not going to go alone. There will be medical evaluations at hand and there will be psychological ramifications as well. However she must not feel that she is letting him down and she must not feel guilty about the "tough Love" process which two of her family members will endure. In the long run, she will finally have a sense of peace within her home but not until the stormy waters will rage through. She must trust her instincts and do what her heart says. Find a medical expert whom she can totally trust and go the motion so that her unsuspecting son will be totally unaware of the spiritual cleansing he is about to receive.

That afternoon, Adam told me he threw up a few times at school that day, starting at about the same time Barbara Ann had done the reading. He then threw up at home in the evening and showed me the color because it seemed very strange. Each time he threw up, the vomit did not reflect anything he had eaten during the day. It was a brown colored bile substance. He did not feel sick, but kept throwing up. Normally he was never sick so this was very unusual. No one else in the house got sick during this time, which ruled out a virus. Was this the son that was experiencing a "spiritual cleansing?" Or did that refer to Joey, David or my son, Paul who at the time was not yet conceived.

The reading mentioned the poor treatment Adam's mother received during her pregnancy. I didn't know what that meant so I asked my husband. He told me that the two of them dated for only about two months. Bob was seventeen at the time. Once they separated, and Bob was no longer in the picture, the men took full reign over her. It did not matter that she was pregnant—the men raped her daily. Bob explained that Adam's mother was mentally slow, not able to protect herself, and the men from the village used that to their advantage. There was a rumor amongst the men that if they grabbed her forcefully and dragged her into the woods—when they penetrated inside her body, she would grab onto them tighter. The rumor was fueled by the idea that the more forceful the men were, the more "turned on" she got.

The reading also mentioned my failing health. During those months, my body was responding to all of the stress and negative energy in the house before I knew what was really occurring. I had strep throat, bronchitis, walking pneumonia and mono. As noted in the reading, it was true that I always protected my children with white light. I never shared this with anyone before, but I routinely prayed and visualized white light all around them for protection. As the reading stated, I also had a huge sense that things were going to get very explosive within the family. I had the disturbing vision of Adam on Christmas Eve, and now was just waiting to find out what else he had done. In my mind, I just needed confirmation of any other crimes and he would be removed as soon as possible.

In January 2003, Joey and I meditated together, and he was finally able to start disclosing the scare tactics Adam had been using against him. I know the only reason why Joey was able to overcome his fear and tell me, was because of the meditation. Once the fear was removed, it was very natural and comfortable for him to start disclosing everything.

Two days after our mediation, Joey fell down the stairs, hit his head and suddenly remembered the terrifying things Adam forced on him. Adam had chased him with a knife, held his nose and mouth so he could not breathe, and made him roll down the staircase. At the time of Tony's reading, none of us knew of these incidents. Yet Tony was able to see Adam with a knife and with a pillow over Joey's face—symbolic of the suffocation attempt. Tony saw the police who were called to our home and he saw the disturbing indifference Adam had at stealing from his school.

I know Joey falling down the staircase and bumping his head—triggering his memory to recall details of what Adam had done, was intervention from Joey's Guides. He did not get seriously hurt from the fall. He was just frightened. Until then, Joey had completely forgotten and the memories were hidden deep within his conscience. The motion and the slight bang to his head was enough to force him to remember and disclose his terror. The odds of falling and remembering everything when Adam was out of the house at his first counseling session are more than coincidental. Adam was usually always with us. To have the few hours without Adam there and to begin processing his sinister hidden ways—was clearly intervention from a Higher Source.

Adam's teacher's initial reaction when I left a voicemail message that Adam had been doing some bad things to Joey was another piece that is beyond coincidence. Robert's immediate reaction of fearing that Adam had sexually abused the boys was either good instincts on Robert's part or intervention from a Higher Source. No one else around us who had been told of the physical and mental abuse ever suspected Adam would commit sexual abuse. When I asked Joey a few days later just to relieve my mind of Robert's initial reaction, I never would have believed the answer would have been yes. Robert trusting his instincts and verbalizing it to me was what helped me discuss sexual abuse with Joey and eventually get Adam out of the house. If Robert did not tell me his first reaction, Adam would have still been in the home and the sexual abuse would have continued against both boys.

On Sunday, February 2, 2003, Adam was removed from our home. I had mixed emotions of relief that he was taken out and sadness at the trauma the boys had suffered. Bob and I were devastated to know what happened to our children and that Adam was the one who committed the crimes. We did not know what to do with ourselves.

The next day I went to my weekly medium class—hoping to have some spiritual insight to help me escape from the endless pit of volatile emotions I was falling into. My classmates already knew about our increasing family saga from the reading Tony had given from looking at Adam's picture. Upon hearing the latest traumatic news of Adam sexually abusing Joey, everyone grieved with me.

My teacher comforted me by saying he used to assist in sexual abuse counseling through his work at a local hospital. Having the advanced spiritual abilities, allowed him a higher understanding of trauma and despair. He said, "Claire, you have to understand, there is nothing you could have done to prevent this. This was meant to happen. It is between your son (Joey) and his Creator. Only your son knows how this will affect his life. This will shape who he is from this point forward." Tony helped me understand some of the ways to talk to Joey without further traumatizing him. He stressed that I should not talk about Adam as a horrible person. It was up to Joey to define his views towards his perpetrator. He explained the things that Joey needed to hear in the beginning and what he would need as time went on. Tony stressed that I should follow my heart and that it would guide me on how to speak with my son now and in the future. He also explained how some of the things I was experiencing were normal for parents. Tony explained that as a mother, having carried a child in my body for so long—many times the mother relives the trauma her child has been through. He assured me that it was very normal to experience. His words helped ease a very difficult time and helped me years later.

As the weeks progressed, I was able to understand some things on a deeper level. Since birth, everyone always mentioned how special Joey was. When he was first born, he had a birthmark on his rear end. The mark was a distinct profile of a person kneeling, holding their hands together in prayer, and looking up to the sky. This birthmark was so clear, it was non mistakable. As the years flew by, and Joey grew, I completely forgot about his birthmark, until Adam was removed.

When we first bought our house we found some cheap pictures in a local store to hang on some of the walls. Joey wanted a drawn picture of Jesus, who was kneeling and praying as he looked up to the sky. From the day we purchased the picture, it was always special to him. He felt protected by having it on his wall in his bedroom. I never made the connection until one day as I sat on Joey's bed, and I looked up at the picture. I instantly remembered Joey's birthmark and realized that the kneeling Jesus in the picture was in the same position as the person kneeling and praying in Joey's birthmark. The location of the birthmark was on Joey's rear end—the part of his body that had been so horribly violated. I quickly understood and remembered what Tony had said, "It is between your son and his Creator." Only God knows why this happened to Joey. Only Joey can determine how this will affect the rest of his life. But, I do believe that while Joey endured the horrible torture, Jesus was with him the whole time—before the abuse happened, during the ordeal, and after.

As previously mentioned, when Bob and I first learned of the sexual abuse, we immediately confronted Adam. After Bob screamed at Adam that he had to be sent back to Cape Verde, and Adam stated his uncle did this to him, I immediately brought Joey and David into another room. I wanted them as far away from Adam as possible. After Bob exploded in rage, I shuffled the boys into another room. I wanted them to know that Bob and I were not upset at them and that they were safe. As we sat in the other room, Joey began to cry and said, "Mom, I don't want Adam to be sent back to Cape Verde." I assured him nothing was going to happen right away. I told him we had to talk to some professional people who would help us figure out what should be done next. Joey then quietly whispered through his tears, "Mom, I am so sad that Adam's uncle did that to him." At that point, Joey showed me the immense compassion the human spirit is capable of feeling. Joey had endured incredible torture—mentally, physically and emotionally, yet he forgot his own trauma and felt true love and sympathy for the human being who had committed the terrible crimes against him.

I, as an adult could not feel true compassion like this. I had slight feelings of sympathy for Adam, but my true concern was my children—their safety and how they were doing mentally. Once Adam was taken out of the home, I felt relief. I no longer felt the constant draining of my energy. His constant need for all of my attention had finally ended. I realized I could finally be close to my children. Adam was no longer there to separate me from them—as he did for years. His attempts to monopolize my time and energy were over. Now that he was gone, I could finally be mentally and emotionally present for Joey and David.

As I felt the energy around me lift, I realized the house energy was still not completely comfortable. As I gradually shared our family story with friends, I was shocked to learn that several people had felt bizarre energy in our home, but never wanted to tell me. Five separate friends all reported that they felt too uncomfortable to say anything since it was a new home for us—but the second they hit the top of the stairs near Adam's room, each of them felt an unexplainable urgency to run back downstairs. Each of the incidents of extreme discomfort occurred with different individuals on completely separate visits to our home. Each friend then held their uncomfortable feelings in secret.

Miladys was one of the friends who could feel the negative energy. One evening, she came over to help me clean out Adam's room. It was in the middle of the winter and it was freezing cold outside. Miladys noticed that the air in the room felt extremely thick and heavy, so she opened the windows. Both windows in the room were left wide open for two hours. But, the air was so thick in the room, no breezes ever entered inside. I had always felt a strange presence of energy on that side of the house from when Adam took the far end bedroom. But to have my uncomfortable feelings confirmed by other people and to now witness the thickness of the air in the bedroom—was very disturbing.

Almost every object in the bedroom had been destroyed or broken by Adam. As Miladys made her way through the junk, she threw out everything she could find. Before she entered, she had no problems with her health. But after spending some time in the room, she started having extreme difficulty breathing. She started having complete sinus and allergy attacks. The attacks were not from excessive dust because there was not much dust in the room. The problem was the air and energy in the room!

The air was so incredibly thick in the room—you could physically feel it. It was creepy to witness how the windows were left wide open for two hours, yet no fresh air entered. I had turned off the heat in the room days earlier, yet the room stayed hot and stuffy. The air was heavy, and served as a barrier to any new air coming in.

Throughout my entire being, I could feel evil in the room—it was indescribable. Joey and David kept coming in to see Miladys and I cleaning. They wanted to join us and play inside the room. I could feel the intensely low energy in the area, and knew something horrible would happen to the boys if they remained inside. They kept climbing on the furniture and going near the open windows almost like they were being drawn into a dangerous situation. It was as if something was pulling them in to then have them dive off of the couch and land on their heads. This force was luring them into the room to hurl them out of the open window. I could see what could happen to them but felt numb, as if it was a movie playing before me. It was the eeriest sensation. I finally banned the boys from the room completely. Despite Adam being removed, I could sense there was something still in his room. I had to protect my family from what was inside.

I spoke with several different people to find out how to properly clean out the room. I burned several herbs and powders, which I learned from class, were remedies for removing demonic energies according to Native American tradition. I put salt in all four corners of the room and Miladys dropped a ring of salt outside on the ground, around the perimeter of the house. I washed the walls with a concentration of salt and water and was horrified to witness a distinct smell of something burning. We removed everything so it remained a bare room, but it did not help. Joey and I prayed several times in the room and still the energy felt unbalanced. I knew I could have zoomed in clairvoyantly with my energy to see what was in Adam's room, but I was too afraid. I knew there was something there, but I did not want to see who or what it was—I just wanted it out.

As the weeks passed I could feel the negative energy growing and gaining more power. I was terrified and didn't know what to do. One evening, I was traveling to my medium class and felt totally overwhelmed by the energy in my home. I felt like this evil force was winning and I could not stop it. As I drove thinking about how helpless I felt, I suddenly could feel someone touching my head. I was wondering who was with me in the car then I suddenly felt a single hair from the top of my head get plucked out. I was not frightened because the energy was someone comfortable. I assumed it was my friend, Frank who was like a brother to me. He had passed seven years before and loved to play jokes on me. When I arrived for class, I did not tell anyone about the experience.

Once in class, I explained that I was still distraught about the creepy energy in my house and didn't know what else to do. I explained that I had prayed, burned, used salt and nothing helped. As the students read my energy, they noticed a ring of protection around me with blue light. They thought maybe the uncomfortable feelings in my home were my own fears, but could not explain why they were seeing protection around me. They could not understand why I would need protection if the problem was my own fears.

As I drove home I could feel someone touching my head again. I called my friend Barbara Ann. I was still so nervous with returning home to the weird energy in the house, I didn't even think to tell her about someone touching my head. We talked about different things for a few minutes and then suddenly Barbara Ann asked me, "Claire, are you driving?" I said "yes." Then she said, "Well, I am seeing a woman in a long green dress that has been draped around you hugging you this whole time. I think this is your grandmother and she told me she plucked a single hair from your head." My grandmother's favorite color was green and she always wore dresses or skirts. She had come through during other readings, so this visit made sense to me. To know my grandmother was there to protect and comfort me, instantly made me realize—I was not alone. I went home that evening feeling calmer about the scary energy. I knew eventually it would get cleaned out.

Shortly after that experience, I went to an angel reading class in mid March 2003. One of the first things the instructor passed around was an angel house prayer. The instructor told us that the people who developed the prayer used a process called dowsing, and took two years to find the right words to use. The prayer described entities that may be present in the home that are not contributing positively to the household members. In the prayer, those entities are asked to change and if not possible, they are told to leave the household.

As soon as I arrived home that evening, I read the prayer out loud several times. I sat in the living room and stated each word with strength and determination. A few days later I did notice an improvement in the house energy. As time went on the negative energy feelings were replaced with empty energy feelings. The energy was not good and it was not bad, it was just there. I realized the prayer was finally what cleaned out the imbalanced energy for good.

Shortly after using the prayer, there was one afternoon when I felt compelled to send positive energy to Adam. Despite everything he had done to my children, I still cared for him. I had raised him as my child and could not easily break the mother-child bond. I worried about him and still felt tied to him as his mother. The bond was difficult to discard—I would always be his mother in his mind, and I felt responsible for that role. However, the survival and safety of my family was most important to me. I knew it seemed cold and indifferent, but I decided my children and I would never see or speak to Adam again. For my mental well being and certainly for my children's safety I had to make that difficult decision. I knew any contact with him would further traumatize my children and could eventually mean life or death. I had to respect the severity of the situation and protect my children.

Even though I decided to cut off all forms of communication with Adam, I realized I could still send positive thoughts and prayer in his direction. That day, I prayed for Adam and started meditating. As I focused, I could see him standing alone in the middle of his room at the facility. I concentrated and spread white light all over him, covering him from head to toe. As I covered him and studied him, I envisioned him completely encapsulated with white light. But, suddenly, I noticed a small ribbon of gray light connected to him that I could not wipe clean with the imagined white light. The gray color extended from his stomach area as a small ribbon. As I studied Adam—the gray ribbon grew bigger and bigger and in a few seconds covered him and the entire room in dark light. I again mentally spread white light over Adam, covering his entire body and filling the room. Once again, I saw the ribbon of gray light, increase in size, wrap around him, and cover him completely. I finally decided to sit back and observe the situation. I said, "Okay God, let me see what this is." As I looked at Adam standing in total dark light, I saw something hovering above his head. It had wings and was about one foot long. The only way to explain what I was seeing was that it looked like a combination between a dragon and a gargoyle. I then noticed that there was another one behind it. As one stayed, hovering on top of Adam's head, the other quickly swooped down and circled around Adam's feet. Then it zoomed up and lingered above Adam's head. After waiting a few seconds, it swooped down and encircled Adam's legs and then returned above his head. As I watched as this thing encircled Adam from his feet upwards along his whole body, I knew these beings were marking Adam as their territory. I instinctively understood they were never going to leave him—he was their possession.

As I recovered from the vision, I suddenly understood it was a form of one of those beings that had stayed behind in Adam's room in our home. As I watched the demons encircling Adam, I knew there was no way for me to separate them from him. The only hope Adam had was to have God directly intervene and clean away the dark forces. I prayed and asked God to remove the things and intervene in Adam's life. At that moment, I knew if Adam never killed anyone during his lifetime, it would only be due to Divine intervention combating the evil forces surrounding him.

Now seeing what surrounded Adam, I grew more fearful of him returning to our home. I could imagine him just sneaking in the house and scaring me from behind as I washed the dishes in the kitchen. I explained to Barbara Ann that I felt I was in constant fear and could not climb out. She recognized that I needed guidance and some answers, so she did a second automatic writing on me.

Automatic writing by Barbara Ann Colangelo 2/11/2003

She (Claire) seeks the truth. She sees beyond what most mortals can see. She hears beyond what most mortals can hear. Yet she cannot seek the truth from her own spiritual realm as it is too clouded by her own insecurities of her mortal world. She fears for her two children who have been violated by the tyrant of the second world and she fears a reunion with this child. She shall not fear. He has been removed from her world, as she will keep her two children in a safe place for as long as they both shall dwell under her roof. This child of the dark can only see light when he is in the company of those who are holy and those who have the power to denounce the evil forces around him. I speak of the second world because he is a very old soul who came to pass in the first world that was created. He has chosen to be part of this world so through his actions, others shall learn and teach. He is the sacrificial lamb. Born of the seventh moon, he was conceived from the perils of a destructive mind and a destructive soul. Her body station was that of an open wall of fire. She allowed many mortals, both men and women to find pleasure from occupying her body station. She herself was vindicated. However in her world, she only knows of this behavior to be of normal behavior. Therefore, she did not understand the concept of her body being her temple. Her body was not her temple. The birthright of her son was already determined before he entered into the earth planes. She had a hereditary condition that was determined before the baby was born and nobody but the father carrying the same chromosome could have passed it on to her son. However, nothing can be determined due to the lack of technology and common knowledge by the living environment in which she habituated. The only proof that the alleged father can obtain is to go ahead and take the test of parenthood. If he is noted to be carrying the gene of this particular condition, then there is no doubt that he is the biological father.

The reading helped me relax to know that my children were safe. It also helped me understand more of what happened to Adam's biological mother. But, I did not understand anything of what was being said about Adam. Those portions of the reading seemed too far beyond my comprehension. All I knew was to stay far away from him. The last sentences that spoke of the "alleged father" made me remember what Julia had mentioned.

When Julia first learned of Joey's disclosure, she explained to me that I needed to be thankful that Joey was alive. The next comment out of her mouth was what if Bob was not Adam's biological father. I was bewildered by this comment because I had always assumed Bob was the biological father. I asked her why she mentioned it and she responded "Bob has always wondered if he was really Adam's father or not." I had never considered that, but Julia spoke almost as if she had some other wisdom. That night I went home and talked to Bob. I asked him if he ever wondered if he was really Adam's biological father. He said, "Claire, don't you remember me telling you that I never felt comfortable claiming him as mine? That is why I never registered him with my name." My recollection of our conversations was that Bob told me he was very young when Adam was born. I thought he said in order to escape from the responsibility of raising a child, he claimed that the mother had been with other men. But, my memory was from the early years when we were first together and we had massive language barriers between us. There were many times we did not understand each other. Bob could not understand how I had misunderstood him so badly in the beginning of our relationship. He reassured me that Adam's mother really had been with many men from the village (most by force and some not by force) and he really never felt comfortable saying Adam was his son.

I soon became obsessed with wondering if Bob was the true father of Adam or not. I asked him numerous times to get a blood test. I needed to know if Bob was the biological father. The idea that we had worked so hard to bring a child into this country, who committed such horrible crimes against my children—and might not be my husband's child after all, was incomprehensible. After constant pressure from me, Bob finally took the test. We were both upset to learn that Bob really was Adam's biological father.

One of the supports I clung to during the first few months was my medium class. As we progressed in our abilities, my teacher had us practice on each other. One evening I volunteered to be read, and stated the first and last name of a young man who I knew that had tragically killed himself about a year before. The students and my teacher did not know the young man at all. As they began reading me, everyone started receiving information. I quickly jotted their comments into three pages of notes.

As the students exhausted all the information they were receiving, Tony took over. He received very confusing and disturbing information. Along with the name of the young man's father, uncle, mother and sister, he saw that the young man had been routinely gang raped by his family members. The young man's spirit explained that words "family gathering" were equivalent to "gang rape" in his home. He shared many personal things about himself—that he had attempted suicide several other times in his life, and how he made those attempts. He also showed that he was gay, but was engaged to a woman who he cared for deeply. The young man explained that he wished and hoped to have the "white picket fence" life with his fiancé, but it was not possible.

The young man showed how he ultimately ended his life by shooting himself in the chest. He explained his childhood—how he had to spread his legs while laying on top of a wooden table so the family members could line up behind him and take their turn. He then showed Tony an image of Adam, and as he discussed "gang raped," he pointed to Adam and stated "same life." Again he pointed to himself and stated "gang raped" and pointed back to Adam stating "same life."

From the beginning, I knew Adam's personal boundaries had been broken sexually. Early on, I learned about Adam's experiences with his grandmother. But I did not know of any other abuse he had suffered—until Bob screamed that he was going back to Cape Verde and Adam stated that his uncle had raped him as a kid. After hearing about the young man's comparison, I understood that Adam was probably abused by most of his family members.

When Adam first told me about his maternal grandmother giving her breasts as a toy, I kept getting visions of Adam's aunt being raped by her own father—Adam's grandfather. I could see the two of them behind the house in a separate section where the family burned wood to cook their food. I could see and believed that he had a long history of sexually abusing her and other members of the family.

Bob had explained to me that in Cape Verde, no matter how poor the family is, the boys normally sleep separate from the girls. But he told me that Adam's family all slept in the same bed in a one-bedroom house on top of the mountain. After hearing what the young man said, I felt my visions were confirmed and believed that Adam's family members routinely jumped on top of each other for sex. It did not matter who was male or female and age was also of no significance.

The bizarre thing was that Adam really never mentioned his family members. The only thing Adam mentioned about his uncle was that he suspected him of eating his pet crow. Several times, Adam told me the story of his pet crow and how he kept it tied to a rock. One day when Adam returned home, he saw that his bird had disappeared. His uncle had been home the whole day. When Adam asked the uncle what happened to his bird, the uncle said it probably flew away. But, Adam always suspected his uncle of eating the crow. Each time Adam told the story, he was angry and upset that his uncle lied and killed his pet.

A few times Adam also explained how the same uncle and his aunt used to scare him. Since Adam had to go far away to fill the jugs of water, his trip home usually occurred at night in the pitch black. His aunt and uncle told him that there were witches and other things that were going to attack him and kill him on his journey. Adam said he often walked behind the donkey, holding onto its tail and closing his eyes. He thought if he closed his eyes tight, he would be safe. The fear of the supernatural taunted Adam from his childhood. As he grew, he was still afraid and told me several times he thought he could hear someone walking behind him—but would turn and see no one.

Adam also mentioned that he witnessed his other uncles doing bad things. On several occasions he saw them get completely drunk and then beat up their girlfriends. Adam often lived with those uncles on the weekends. Bob later told me that the uncles usually switched girlfriends and lived with no morals.

All of the stories Adam had recited now seemed to be pieces of a puzzle to understand who he was. One day I told a friend who works with gang members, our personal traumatic story. She asked several questions about Adam and mentioned that she had worked with a few kids who had no emotional connection to their actions. She mentioned there was research, which showed that the early bonding years for a baby are the most critical to a child's brain development. As she was explaining this, I instantly had a vision of Adam as a baby in a tiny house, up on top of a mountain. He was left completely alone, everyday for long periods of time. I saw him all day in the same cloth diaper. He was not fed, not cleaned and not held while the family members went to work. I mentioned this vision to Bob wondering why I was seeing it—knowing it could not be true since the grandmother must have carried him everywhere with her. Surprisingly, Bob told me that it was very common for people to go to work all day and leave a small baby in the house alone. He agreed with my vision saying that it was probably how Adam was raised during the first few years of his life.

As I discovered more disturbing things about Adam and what he had done to Joey and David, I balanced my disgust by appreciating my children and fulfilling my own spiritual needs. Through the mediumship classes, I learned to develop my own abilities. I could see how God, my Angels, Spirit Guides and Loved Ones were helping our family, and I wanted to help connect other people to their higher guidance. It was enjoyable for me to watch people's reactions as I shared personal messages from Loved Ones or Guides regarding their current life situations. But, as my abilities increased, I found myself worrying if I would become arrogant in the process. I was afraid that eventually my skills would be stripped from me because I had grown into a conceited know-it-all. At the other extreme, I worried if it was all my imagination, and I really had no abilities at all.

But, after receiving a few phone calls from Adam, I forgot about doing readings completely. I was pulled down to a level of basic survival skills and again became paralyzed with fear of Adam's return. Terror and anxiety dominated every thought. I quickly saw my reading abilities fading away and briefly shared my sentiments with Barbara Ann. She encouraged me to keep practicing and not give up. She quickly did a third automatic writing on me, which had a clear message.

Automatic writing by Barbara Ann Colangelo 5/30/2003

Your eyes are sore today because of all the energy that over powered your thought process (third eye). You have tremendous capabilities and you will soon learn how far you can go with them. Take time to sit and meditate without boundaries. Leave the presence and the energy of daily routines to a stand still. Don't focus too much on to what is at hand. Your third eye has been turned to another dimension only to keep it safe for the right time. Your fading powers as you see it are only your self ego biting you back. You must stop getting carried away with trying to prove yourself to those who rely on you for messages from beyond. They have no grounds for judgment. Nobody has. Your soul is yours as is your gift of oral and spiritual communication. Everyone has problems. Everyone has stress but not everyone has the gift of enhanced spirituality. Don't feel worried that your gift is fading. Be worried about the things that are most important to you. Stay close to your children but stay close to your spirit also. Trust in our words and trust yourself. Stop allowing your ego to overpower what they say on the mortal world known as egomania. Unknowing to you, you have developed a "Claire's world" of spiritual mediumship yet you worry if the people who are receiving your information do not approve and that is what brings your mediumship process to a screeching halt. Find your path but do it slowly and pick up those along the way who wish to stand by you. You are burning your heart and your energy just to prove yourself. God shall be your judge and nobody else.

My spiritual abilities were not fading. I realize now, my focus had to shift from pursuing medium abilities to being a mom to my children and completing this book. Exactly one year from the day Adam was removed, I came home with our newborn son Paul. God helped us to focus on our family and experience peace. God had given us a new member of the family to care for and protect.

When I was closer to finishing the book, I pursued having an agent represent the work. I wondered if that was the right path, or if I should publish the book myself. Several times I had strong instincts pulling me away from pursuing the regular path authors take—looking for an agent and a publishing company. Around that time, Barbara Ann received a clear message for me. *"Cross the bridge when you get to it—then you better think fast because you are there. Be brave and trust yourself. The bridge will be strong enough to carry you, and then follow your steps to wherever they may lead you."* After realizing most agents would have trouble representing this work since it carries so many messages, I soon realized I needed to publish the book myself. I did not want anyone who was removed from my family, editing and changing what had been given to me.

For two years and eight months, I have been compelled and driven to get our story out to others. I did not write this book alone. I have been guided, led, and embraced throughout the entire process. Higher Sources want the truth of sexual abuse to be exposed. They need to see children being protected through more effective systems. I pieced this book together by connecting sentences and paragraphs and using edits from many helpful wonderful supporters—but I did not write this book. Through my children's insight, God, my Angels, my Spirit Guides, and my Loved Ones have used my fingers to put the words on paper.

My conclusion is, even if you can't feel, hear or see them—God, Angels, Spirit Guides, and Loved Ones are there, through every calm and every storm.

Chapter 12
The Healing Path

I believe there is no right or wrong way to heal from sexual abuse. Survivors, family members and others who are affected—all need to find their individual coping skills and ultimate path to healing.

The first few months after Adam was removed from the home, was a difficult time for Joey and David. Both boys had behavior and thought processing problems. Joey had severe trouble differentiating between reality and fantasy. He was often confused if things really happened or if it was his imagination. He had trouble remembering if things happened to him or to another person. David continued to be afraid of monsters and often hit other children out of frustration. His verbal skill development was delayed after experiencing the disturbing horror and trauma.

As the years passed, the boys became children again. They enjoyed laughing and playing. They no longer felt constant fear or monitored everything they said. They spoke freely about their emotions and spoke openly about things they could remember. The insight they had about who Adam was, and how he was able to manipulate everyone around him—was invaluable to the process of writing this book. Their ideas and feedback fueled every chapter. They now understand that they have more knowledge about perpetrators than other children. When our family goes to the park or the boys are in school, they have both shared their concern for other children and immediately reported anything they noticed with potentially unsafe people. Joey and David visit with two counselors who they are excited to see. They are not preoccupied with what has happened to them and see their trauma as a source of strength and knowledge.

Soon after disclosing the sexual abuse, Joey told me, "Mom, I think this is going to help me be a better cop." For a while, Joey fluctuated between wanting to be a police officer or an international agent who could help countries develop laws that protect children. Now he says he would like to build houses. David has stated he wants to drive an ice cream truck and be a doctor. Who knows what they will do later in life and how surviving such trauma will influence their decisions and affect who they become as adults. For now, the biggest concern in their lives is catching toads, riding their bikes and going places as a family. They are finally living the safe, happy and free-from-fear childhood they were denied.

Children are resilient—they can bounce back from extreme trauma and, if given tools, can learn and become stronger people. Young children who are immediately believed and protected may bounce back quickly. But adults who have been traumatized by the knowledge that their child was sexually abused may not gain mental peace for a while. As a parent, guardian or other loved one of a child who has been horribly violated, the first step in healing—is to allow yourself time to experience and express every stage, every emotion and every feeling. You will progress through your own shock, denial, anger, self-judgment, guilt, depression, awareness, understanding, and acceptance in your own time. Healing is an individual process. Similar to a survivor, no one can tell you as an individual, when your timer has gone off and you should be "all done" in the process.

Throughout our experience, I was compelled to speak to friends and family. I was driven to communicate with professionals, other survivors, and other families that experienced similar tragedy. However, my husband felt comfortable speaking to a few select people and withdrawing into himself. He believed no one was capable of helping him and that he had to deal with the trauma on his own. I had to go through my experience in my way and he had travel down his path of healing in his way.

For me to survive, I had to have answers. When I screamed to God begging for answers, He needed to make me understand why this had happened. I knew I would not be able to continue in life if God did not give me some way to understand everything. I could not have such a tragedy happen in my family without a higher purpose or higher understanding. There had to be a higher reason for my children to suffer so horribly and I begged God to tell me. Eventually God did tell me how it happened and He told me what I was supposed to do with all of the information. God answered my pleas and helped me understand sexual abuse, perpetrators and survivors, and why it happened in our family.

I know all the people who have been part of our lives, and who became close to us during this time—served a purpose. They shared their personal insight through things they learned or observed. The instincts and dreams and spiritual experiences that I had, combined with the information from friends and family members—were all little pieces. When I mentally grabbed each piece and fit them all together, I could see the entire picture. I learned and understood that we were warned, prepared and guided throughout the whole process on several levels. I knew I had to take each memory, feeling and instinct that I or others had, and clear it out of my head by putting it on paper. I needed to record everything so if I ever needed to remember, I could go back and re-experience everything through the pages. I needed to write down each memory to clear out space in my mind and create room for new positive memories.

I learned there really was nothing more I could have done to prevent the trauma my children suffered. There were so many signs indicating that this was going to happen. Yet, my children and I have learned we were never alone. We were being guided the whole time. I believe my family had to suffer through this experience to produce this book. Our story will educate and help others. Through this experience, Joey now has a strong understanding that his Angels and Guides were with him and they were protecting him—keeping him alive. When the attempts on Joey's life became too severe, the Spiritual Forces stepped in. Without God, those Angels, Guides, and Loved Ones—I am sure I would not have Joey with me today.

When I told my friend Leigh Ann everything that had happened and that I was writing a book, she was not surprised. She said "Claire don't you remember in high school, you told me you were going to write a book. You turned to me in math class and you were very intense. You said 'Leigh Ann, I know part of my life is that I'm supposed to write a book. I don't know what it is supposed to be about, but I know I'm going to write a book.'" I found this very strange, since I did not have any recollection of that moment, yet Leigh Ann can remember it clearly. How did I already have that clarity eighteen years earlier?

Writing the book helped me document all of my feelings and everything I was learning. For me to progress in my own healing, I instinctively knew I had to get past blaming myself. I knew blame could not be part of the equation if I was ever going to get through the pain, and be strong for my children.

Sexual abuse against your child or a child you love is devastating. It is common to blame yourself and to feel like a failure. It is especially difficult as you retrace things in the past, and can suddenly see the signs that something was wrong. Many times I thought, "I should have known. Why didn't I protect my child? Why didn't I ask my child back then?" But I realized self-blame is an endless pit that will never end. The more blame you pile onto yourself, it will not magically erase what has happened. Re-traumatizing yourself by reliving all possibilities and desperately searching for what you could have done to prevent it—is only hurting yourself and your child. Blame is an interesting phenomenon that parents/guardians/care-takers use to keep ourselves in the trauma for longer periods of time. It also falsely helps a parent believe that he or she is powerless and cannot help the child. Self blame ensures that the parent does not become a strong adult in his/her child's life. It is never too late to be the caring, understanding and powerful person your child needs you to be.

Not only could I potentially blame myself for being a bad parent and not recognizing that my children were being sexually abused, but I could also potentially blame myself that Adam was so mentally and emotionally destroyed. Adam lived with us for three and a half years. Maybe his psychosis was a reflection on Bob and me as bad parents. But I quickly realized Adam was lost well before we ever took him into our home. I assured myself that we had given him the best family and best situation we could offer. No matter what we did differently or how many loving, supportive, and nurturing adults we surrounded him with, Adam would have gone down the same path.

We are not taught to recognize signs of perpetrators and the effects on the children who are violated. We are not taught to watch for people that are able to commit such heinous acts. We are not taught to suspect people close to us who we care about. It is important to always remember, the perpetrator did this against the child. You as the parent or the guardian did not commit the crime.

Blame always lies with the perpetrator. Many times the perpetrator can be seen as a victim who has probably also suffered from sexual abuse as a child. But do not be fooled! A perpetrator consciously plans his/her crimes. There are many survivors who never become perpetrators. A perpetrator consciously develops each step in his or her criminal strategies. He or she plans how to gain access to the child, and how to silence the victim. The planning is part of the thrill for the perpetrator, who fantasizes about each step. Ultimately, the perpetrator follows through on the planned crime and then actively begins planning again.

The important thing to remember about sexual abuse is that you are battling something you have no knowledge of. It is almost like an invisible force. You cannot see it, smell it or feel it. But it can come close to people you love so quickly and happen right under your nose. We are not born or raised with an understanding that people intend to do others harm. Most people are raised thinking everyone is born as "good" and everyone ideally wants to do "good" to other people. However, perpetrators have no intention of doing "good." They purposely intend to manipulate and use any person they deem accessible. The blame needs to always be on the perpetrator.

If a person intentionally ran through a red light to purposely smash into a passing car—what would you think? If that person killed three passengers in the other car, would you blame yourself? Of course you would not blame yourself for that person's insane actions. You would not blame yourself for those three people who were intentionally murdered. It is the same thing with trying to blame ourselves for a sexual predator's actions. We can try to keep our children safe, just like the laws try to protect motor vehicle passengers. We can try to educate our children, just as the law dictates to use highway safety measures. But, we cannot always ensure that our children will be safe. A sexual abuse predator is the person in the car purposely running red lights. He or she does not feel sympathy, or guilt for his or her actions. He or she is the crazy motorist who is looking for the next car to smash into.

A perpetrator will assess all children on their level of accessibility, vulnerability and passivity. He or she is the person who enjoys the game and hunt to intentionally hurt people. Therefore, he or she needs to always be given one hundred percent of the blame.

Don't allow sexual abuse to become an item in your Box of Shame—through your own guilt, blame or depression. Sexual abuse is a crime that needs to be looked at as an epidemic in our society. Get sexual abuse out of your conscience— discuss it, educate others, make strides to prevent it and empower families to raise children who know how to stay safe.

As your mind goes in the past and finds those clues, use them constructively. Instead of now seeing each warning sign and blaming yourself for missing every clue, store each sign in your mind with the intention that you will use those signals to help educate others. Get active in your community and educate people on prevention.

God gives us challenges so we can experience the growth of pain, struggle and triumph. God wants us to experience how strong and wonderful each human being can be. No life struggle is boring or point-less. If you have experienced sexual abuse trauma through a loved one, or yourself, you have a calling. Find your highest potential by using God's intentions.

Our country needs your experience to learn, and keep children safe. You have the knowledge—use it to help other families. Use your experi-ence to help others in your community learn about perpetrators, about survivors and about sexual abuse. Teach others what you will struggle to learn. Form support groups and help other families heal. Break the chains of sexual abuse silence that so tightly grip our society and our lives. Open your mind, clean out anything inside that makes you blame yourself, and feel the peace and strength of a free human spirit.

Two factors that truly helped our family were spirituality and mar-tial arts. As we made the spiritual connections, we understood we had been warned, guided and ultimately protected. Martial arts was what saved Joey from completely turning lost within himself. He regained his mental strength by understanding he would never be a "victim" again and had no reason to be filled with fear. He learned he was in charge of his body and would never be violated by another predator.

For myself, early in the process—I believed I had failed to protect my children. I was afraid of Adam returning to our home and lived in constant terror. I imagined Adam in the home or knocking on the front door. Each time when I saw a different situation, I became paralyzed with fear. I did not know what I should do if my worries ever became reality. I didn't know if I would be able to protect my children or would I freeze as we all would suffer his deadly blows.

Luckily, friends referred me to *Kenneth Melbourne*, an instructor in martial arts, who lived close by, and had been teaching for many years. I was not concerned with getting different color belts or being involved in a local karate demonstration. I wanted to learn how to protect myself and protect my children. Ken is the founder of Kempo-Jitsu Pre 1900 Martial Art. His style of self-defense was exactly what I needed to feel calm again. After learning of our situation and my realistic fear of Adam returning to hurt us, Ken said, "Don't be afraid—be ready." He taught me different moves to deal with any attack. Learning how to protect myself and my children, saved me mentally. Instead of feeling frozen with terror, I was now able to work through my anxieties, picture different mental scenarios, and practice how I would handle the situation if it was real. I no longer came home late at night with the boys feeling terrified that someone had snuck into the house during the day. I entered my home ready.

Along with martial arts, a true understanding of what the evil potential of sexual abuse is—helped me. The most sincere message I have for any parents who are struggling with the realization that a child has been sexually abused—remember the most important thing—your child is alive! Yes, you are traumatized and your child is traumatized. But, if your child survived, you have a chance to work through the psychological issues for the rest of your lives. Your child, yourself, your family can consider yourselves lucky! There are many families that are not as lucky. Many children are raped, mutilated and killed. As my friend Julia said, "Claire, you still have your son to hug each night!" Those words ring so true to me. I know, if we did not have so many Sources and people intervening, that would not have been our family's reality.

My highest intention for this book is to help families protect their children, and prevent them from being sexually abused. I want people to understand sexual abuse is a common crime that happens daily.

Readers will hopefully now know some of the signs to look for. As parents, guardians and care takers, I hope people will pay closer attention to the individuals nearest their children and consider who could be a potential perpetrator. I wish that families will take time to study their children. Are the children isolating, or showing any other signs? I hope this book helps shed light on the topic so people feel more equipped to discuss sexual abuse openly—and understand how deeply it affects a child for years to come.

When my family became aware of what was happening, my first need was to find a support group of other parents. I needed to hear what emotions other parents had and what they did to cope. I was shocked to find that there was nothing throughout the state. There were no programs I could go to. The state social service system referred me to a Non-Offending Parenting group, which was strictly an education group on perpetrators. There was no support. I never heard the other people's names in the room. The program was designed so we would not talk to each other—it was strictly designed to be a session with an instructor lecturing to us. I was upset to think that if I was an alcoholic, or a gambling addict, or had family members who were alcoholics or had mental health issues—I would be able to find support groups everywhere. There are support groups everywhere for every type of problem. Yet there was nothing for sexual abuse.

I remember when I was a kid, if someone had cancer it was something that people would whisper. That was a word you would never say out loud. Now there are breast cancer support groups, prostate cancer support groups—any kind of cancer support groups. Now cancer is out in the open, and you can say the word with a normal tone. My hope is that this is what will happen with sexual abuse. I wish it will not be the last issue that our society is able to discuss and deal with properly. My dream is that there will be support groups for sexual abuse survivors and families, just like Alcoholics Anonymous—everywhere in the world. To get to that vision, it takes many people willing to become involved and willing to discuss such a difficult and hidden topic.

Another desire I have as an outcome for this book is for institutions to be truly examined. They need to be transformed from the perpetrator empowering forces they represent, to organizations that assist survivors and their families. We need to honestly address the institutions (legal, mental health, educational, religious and social service), which bind us in chains of denial and blindness. We need to shed these shackles and clearly see who operates these systems and allows this silence to keep sexual abuse a shameful common event. These systems and their leaders have to be exposed in order to develop new networks, which serve with honesty, the higher good, and an elevated conscience.

I call out to professionals within these institutions to speak to officials and demand internal changes. Institutions cannot solve all past problems immediately, but they can focus on stopping further re-victimization of survivors and their families. If an institution has not performed adequately—apologize to the survivors, and acknowledge that the system has failed. Develop new initiatives that stop protecting perpetrators. The longer the institutions wait to deal with their internal dysfunction, the more time perpetrators have to keep finding new victims!

As human beings, our goal should be to create a world of harmony and peace, where all souls are respected and valued. Children should never experience the evils of sexual abuse. They need to be protected and this must be the top priority for the cycle of evil to end.

To all individuals who have had to endure sexual abuse during their childhood, God has given you a strong spirit. If you have lived through your experience, you are a survivor! Don't allow sexual abuse to be the monster you hide deep within your conscience. Release it from your soul. Tell your story. Don Asbee, summarized it clearly, "I can say this ruined me or shaped me to be the person I am today. For all I've been through—I like me a lot. It may be the reason why I've come to be in this life—to see to it that it never happens again. The only way to stop this is for parents to reassure their kids that it is not their fault. People have actually come to me and said, 'It's in the past. Just let it go'. Well, if I believe that it is just in the past—I ensure that it remains in the future for generations. It has to stop now. We have to tell our story."

Your voice and your story need to be heard—be strong, and teach the world.

Printed in the United States
114778LV00004B/94/P